THE INTERVENTION GUIDEBOOK

Tiered Support for Secondary Students in

College & Career Readiness

CHRISTY W. BRYCE

Solution Tree | Press

555 North Morton Street
Bloomington, IN 47404
800.733.6786 (toll free) / 812.336.7700
FAX: 812.336.7790

email: info@SolutionTree.com
SolutionTree.com

Visit **go.SolutionTree.com/RTI** to download the free reproducibles in this book.

Printed in the United States of America

Library of Congress Control Number: 2025052466
ISBN: 979-8-89374-059-2

Solution Tree
Cameron L. Rains, CEO
Edmund M. Ackerman, President

Solution Tree Press
Publisher: Kendra Slayton
Associate Publisher: Todd Brakke
Acquisitions Director: Hilary Goff
Editorial Director: Laurel Hecker
Art Director: Rian Anderson
Managing Editor: Sarah Ludwig
Copy Chief: Jessi Finn
Senior Production Editor: Christine Hood
Proofreader: Elijah Oates
Text and Cover Designer: Laura Cox
Content Development Specialist: Amy Rubenstein
Associate Editor: Elijah Oates
Editorial Assistant: Madison Chartier

Acknowledgments

Turns out that writing a book is no small feat. Five years of dreaming, conceptualizing, researching, organizing, drafting, doubting, and revising—and it wouldn't have happened without my people. First and foremost, I must express my deepest gratitude for my husband, Chris, and my children, Berkley and Harrison, who entertain me, exhaust me, and surround me with more love than words could ever capture. Having you in my life will always be my greatest accomplishment. To Mom and Mindy, my constant and fiercest cheerleaders, and to the many strong women in my family, including those whose presence I still feel though they are gone—you taught me to believe that a little girl from Kentucky could do big things.

Reaching my goals wouldn't have been possible without the love and encouragement of my family and friends, including Dad, Sharon, Stew and Spence, the "Brussel Sprouts," Papa, the BCBs, and the many others who make up my village.

My heartfelt thanks go to my colleagues Kara Allen, Erin Mack Trapanese, Kelly Davis, and Winnie Cohran, whose positivity, determination, and professional drive inspire me to reach higher than I sometimes think possible. I will always be grateful to the educators, past and present, with whom I have had the privilege to work in Warren County Public Schools and through KY-ABRI. They motivate me to raise the bar for myself because our students depend on it.

Sarah Gentry, Stacy Lindsey, Sheri Brittenham, Hilary Goff, and the Solution Tree family have been a true gift, providing the feedback and encouragement I needed throughout the writing journey.

And finally, to my little guy "Floyd," whom I taught so many years ago—I wish I had known more and had been a stronger advocate for you back then. You are a constant reminder for me to push myself—and those around me—to do better for the children in our community.

Solution Tree Press would like to thank the following reviewers:

Chris L. Bennett
Executive Director of Middle Schools and Accountability
Cleveland County Schools
Shelby, North Carolina

Isabel Herrera
Middle School Math Interventionist
Dr. Josefina Villamil Tinajero PK–8 School
El Paso, Texas

Daniel J. Laverty
Principal
Hubert H. Humphrey Middle School
Bolingbrook, Illinois

Shanna Martin
Middle School Teacher and Instructional Coach
Lomira School District
Lomira, Wisconsin

Lindsey Matkin
Principal
Kinard Core Knowledge Middle School
Fort Collins, Colorado

Brad Neuendorf
Principal
Lander Valley High School
Lander, Wyoming

Janet Nuzzie
Intervention Specialist, K–12 Mathematics
Pasadena Independent School District
Pasadena, Texas

Rosalind Poon
Acting Principal
Hugh Boyd Secondary School
Richmond, British Columbia, Canada

Kim Timmerman
Principal
Adel-De Soto-Minburn Middle School
Adel, Iowa

Steven Weber
Assistant Principal
Rogers Heritage High School
Rogers, Arkansas

Visit **go.SolutionTree.com/RTI** to download the free reproducibles in this book.

Table of Contents

About the Author

Christy W. Bryce, EdD, serves as the director of Kentucky Academic and Behavior Response to Intervention (KY-ABRI), a project through the University of Louisville. In her former role as the director of intervention in a culturally, linguistically, and socioeconomically diverse district, she championed the use of inclusive instructional design and executed programs to promote positive behaviors, support mental health, and bring family educators into the homes of young children in the community.

As a former special education teacher and school psychologist, Dr. Bryce brings a rich blend of practical experience and systems-level leadership to her work. She coaches school and district leaders across contexts, from large urban systems to small rural communities, to ensure all students have access to high-quality instruction and meaningful support. With a passion for reaching every student, Dr. Bryce provides professional learning opportunities across the United States on using trauma-informed practices, scaffolding instruction, and supporting students with academic and behavioral challenges.

Dr. Bryce holds an educational specialist degree in school psychology and a bachelor of science in elementary education and learning and behavioral disorders from Western Kentucky University. She earned her doctor of education in educational leadership and policy from Peabody College at Vanderbilt University, where she deepened her commitment to bridging research and practice.

To learn more about Christy W. Bryce's work, follow her on LinkedIn (https://linkedin.com/in/christybryce).

To book Christy W. Bryce for professional development, contact pd@SolutionTree.com.

Introduction

In 2015, I sat down with my secondary school leadership team and broached the subject of a multitiered system of supports, or MTSS. They looked at me with confused expressions that suggested there must be some mistake and this did not apply to them. As a district-level director, I had been tasked with helping our middle and high schools address their stagnant assessment scores and increased behavior issues. Yet it was clear these leaders were doubtful that MTSS would help.

In elementary schools across the district, systems of intervention were rolling. Screening? Check! Progress monitoring? You bet! Multilevel prevention system? It wasn't perfect, but yes! Data-based decision making? Absolutely! Yet here I sat with middle and high school leaders. What did I have to offer them? Perhaps we should attempt to replicate our elementary model in the middle and high school context. But what about college and career readiness? What about credits and diplomas? Their schedules were complex mammoths that could not easily be manipulated, so how would this even work?

We found books on MTSS, but they focused primarily on the elementary level. We found resources on high school MTSS or systems of data collection and analysis, yet they never provided clear guidance on *what* interventions to implement. These books recommended that we delve into massive (though fabulous) databases from the What Works Clearinghouse and Regional Educational Laboratories to find the actual interventions. That would be perfect, but who has that kind of time when you are busy running a school full of students? This was what brought me to write this book—I am writing the book I wish someone had given me!

I am writing the book I wish someone had given me!

It is my intention to create a succinct, practitioner-friendly resource that distills the research on secondary-level interventions into bite-size, solution-focused chunks to assist overloaded secondary school leaders and educators. In this book, you will discover *what* interventions to actually implement. But first, we'll explore the *why* of secondary interventions and the challenges that secondary schools face in implementing MTSS successfully.

The *Why* of MTSS at the Secondary Level

Why are we even discussing MTSS for secondary schools? Secondary classrooms across the United States are *filled* with students who struggle academically and behaviorally and are not on track to reach college and career readiness. How should schools respond? Do schools have a structured plan for supporting teachers to address these needs?

With the passing of the Every Student Succeeds Act (2015), MTSS was explicitly endorsed as a promising educational model. *MTSS* is defined as "a proactive and preventative framework that integrates data and instruction to maximize student success" and support students' academic, social-emotional, and behavioral needs "from a strengths-based perspective" (Center on Multi-Tiered System of Supports, n.d.a). Evidence suggests that MTSS at the secondary level can improve student outcomes, including grades, course completion, attendance, test scores, graduation rates, and mental well-being, and reduce referrals for special education (Balfanz & Byrnes, 2025; Duffy & Scala, 2012; DuFour et al., 2024; Epler, 2015; Fisher & Frey, 2013; Koselak, 2011; Rumberger et al., 2017). Recognizing these opportunities, secondary schools across the United States have adopted MTSS as a system for strategically triaging support to maximize the impact of limited resources.

The Center on Multi-Tiered System of Supports (n.d.a) states that effective MTSS includes the following components.

- **Universal screening:** The purpose of a *universal screener* is to identify students who need additional support to reach positive learning outcomes. It is "universal" because it is utilized for the entire student body. Screening all students ensures the school is aware of each student's current functioning so the school can proactively provide the support they need. This often includes a literacy and mathematics assessment administered to every student and a social-emotional screener where teachers rate students' behavior three times per year. In chapter 1, we will examine how this might look at the secondary level.
- **Multilevel prevention system:** A *multilevel prevention system* refers to the structured, tiered supports a school has in place that increase in intensity based on each student's needs. By nature, students come to school with varying strengths and unique academic, behavioral, and social-emotional skill levels. To successfully support students' diverse needs, schools can utilize a multilevel prevention system to efficiently and proactively implement interventions. The structures and strategies throughout this book are designed to help your school build a context-specific version of a multilevel prevention system.

- **Progress monitoring:** For students needing additional support, educators must closely monitor their progress in case they require instructional adjustments. *Progress monitoring* refers to brief, frequent, reliable measures of a student's responsiveness to instruction. Examples include curriculum-based measures and behavior ratings. Secondary examples of progress-monitoring tools are shared throughout this book.
- **Data-based decision making:** Effective *data-based decision making* in an MTSS framework involves having a team of educators follow a clear, systematized process for quickly analyzing valid, reliable, actionable data from universal screening and progress-monitoring tools. Teaming may look different in each school, but effective problem solving happens when skilled educators have strategic action-planning conversations driven by data. I explore a structured process for data-based decision making at the secondary level in chapter 1.

Though none of these components is antithetical to the secondary context, some of them feel a bit challenging to reconcile with the hot topics and prevailing discourse that exist in most secondary schools (for example, graduation rates and postsecondary planning). This leaves secondary educators with three big questions about MTSS implementation.

1. **Isn't this an elementary thing?** Many secondary educators express the concern that advocates of MTSS attempt to apply an elementary-level model to the secondary context. Although MTSS at the secondary level maintains the essential components utilized at the elementary level, it can look very different in middle and high schools (Daye, 2019; Duffy & Scala, 2012; Flannery, Hershfeldt, & Freeman, 2018; Fuchs, Fuchs, & Compton, 2010; Jerald, 2006; Johnson, Smith, & Harris, 2009; Koselak, 2011; Marken, Scala, Husby-Slater, & Davis, 2020; Muoneke & Shankland, 2009). For example, due to the comprehensive history of data that has already been collected on most secondary students, "it no longer makes sense to allocate scarce resources to screening for the purpose of identifying students at risk for academic failure" (Fuchs et al., 2010, p. 24). While it may feel counterintuitive to many MTSS advocates not to administer formal universal screeners, this dramatic reframing of the core components of MTSS can limit the disconnect that secondary educators experience.

   Concerns may also arise due to the commonly recommended entry point for secondary MTSS implementation to allocate time in the schedule toward a new intervention class, time, or block. The master schedule is an integral, complex driver of a middle or high school—one that is not easily modified. Therefore, from the very beginning, this work can feel overwhelming and frustrating for teachers and school leaders. It doesn't seem to acknowledge the copious expectations and pressures that secondary educators face from existing demands, nor does it validate these educators' hard work, history, and expertise and their efforts to serve many masters.

2. **How is it supposed to look?** Literature and resources on secondary-level MTSS are significantly more limited than the research available to guide implementation at the elementary level (Clark & Dockweiler, 2019; Duffy, 2007; Durrance, 2023; Prewett et al., 2012; Shinn, Windram, & Bollman, 2016). Secondary school leaders have difficulty finding model programs to learn from their peers how to navigate barriers that exist in their context. In *The Handbook of Response to Intervention*, Mark R. Shinn, Holly S. Windram, and Kerry A. Bollman (2016) write that with limited research supporting or refuting specific models, schools are implementing tiered systems at the secondary level to the best of their ability to fit within the realities they face.
3. **What do we focus on?** One final challenge lies in the competing priorities that exist at the secondary level. As in all levels of schooling, discipline, safety, attendance, engagement, rigor, grading, climate, and culture are important, sustained priorities that require significant time and energy (Caballero, 2023). However, middle and high schools must also contend with the additional demands of college and career readiness, dropout prevention and graduation rates, and the constant pressure of credit requirements—factors that rarely drive decision making at the elementary level (Flannery et al., 2018; Johnson et al., 2009; Muoneke & Shankland, 2009; National High School Center, National Center on Response to Intervention, & Center on Instruction, 2010; Pyle & Vaughn, 2012).

Too often, secondary teachers and administrators feel as if a new system is being forced onto their existing demands and already-packed schedule. Questions prevail, and the primary purpose of MTSS in the secondary context remains nebulous. Ambiguity can lead to paralysis (Bolman & Deal, 2021; Pfeffer & Sutton, 2000), so it is unsurprising that MTSS has gained little traction in middle and high schools. Is the purpose of MTSS to accelerate basic mathematics and literacy skills, as is often the case at the elementary level, and when determining whether a student has a disability (Individuals With Disabilities Education Act, 2004)? Should MTSS prioritize intervention for students who do not meet college readiness benchmarks (for example, ACT or SAT scores), as many states require by regulation? Is MTSS going to ensure students are successful in their core classes so they can earn the necessary credits to graduate?

One can easily see how quickly the priorities for MTSS at the secondary level become perplexing and even incompatible. These questions must be answered and priorities must be defined before a context-specific plan of action develops. Shinn, Windram, and Bollman (2016) conclude, "The biggest single barrier to secondary MTSS implementation is a confused or unclear purpose" (p. 564).

The great news is that even though numerous challenges exist, secondary schools are not as far behind in MTSS implementation as you might think! Most secondary schools have pieces already in place, including data collection methods, teaming, and possibly even some evidence-based interventions, yet they struggle to overcome contextual barriers and make the connection between their existing programs and strategies and an MTSS framework.

Secondary schools are not as far behind in MTSS implementation as you might think!

Challenges of MTSS in Secondary Schools

Considering the requirements for building an effective MTSS, secondary schools must approach this work strategically. Researchers K. Brigid Flannery and Mimi McGrath Kato (2017) identify three specific contextual characteristics of high schools to consider when implementing a schoolwide system of supports: (1) size, (2) culture, and (3) developmental level of students. Notably, these same characteristics of size, culture, and developmental level (with the burgeoning adolescence of students) are also salient features of middle schools. These features can be challenging for secondary schools to navigate (Flannery et al., 2018; Flannery & Sugai, 2009; Sansosti, Telzrow, & Noltemeyer, 2010; Swain-Bradway, Pinkney, & Flannery, 2015). Let's unpack each of these contextual variables to acknowledge the challenges that secondary schools must overcome when building an MTSS plan of action.

1. **Size:** Secondary schools typically have more administrators, more departments, more students, and a larger campus than elementary schools do. To improve efficiency and reduce the duplication of efforts, administrators are often assigned dedicated roles and areas of focus (for example, freshman academy, attendance, instruction, and discipline). In large organizations, such role definition can unintentionally result in siloed efforts with minimal coordination across initiatives, whereas this is less of an issue in smaller schools with only one or two administrators.

   A departmental structure is common in high schools because it creates collaborative teams that specialize in particular content areas, which can be instructionally beneficial. However, this structure can pose significant challenges in maintaining communication between departments and communication between departments and school leadership—both of which are necessary for an effective MTSS.

   Additionally, having more students in a building increases logistic challenges, such as scheduling, and makes meeting the needs of all learners a complex endeavor. More students also increases the workload and complexity of data collection and management, which can include many data sources (for example, college readiness exams, formative and summative in-class assessments, credit obtainment, tardiness, attendance histories, and office referrals).

2. **Organizational culture:** The second consequential consideration of secondary schools identified by Flannery and Kato (2017) and Flannery, Hershfeldt, and Freeman (2018) is organizational culture. With the current design of the U.S. educational system, teachers at the secondary level are typically content experts with a passion for and proficiency in their area of study. Secondary students benefit from teachers who specialize in their content area rather than teaching multiple subjects, which teachers often do at the elementary level.

   The potential drawback to this structure is that a content teacher who teaches in a traditional seven-period schedule may serve nearly two hundred different students each day! This naturally impacts the relationship a teacher can build with each student and makes it very difficult for the teacher to identify and address each learner's unique needs. Plus, a teacher's expertise in their content area likely does not include training in teaching foundational academic skills, which some of their students may need.

   To compound this issue, some schools continue to operate with "get tough" or zero-tolerance policies, fueling a general belief that students *should already know* how to succeed academically and behaviorally by the time they get to middle and high school. These factors can make it challenging for a school to institute processes that support the "whole child."

   Plus, the size and organizational culture of secondary schools can lead to logistic barriers, such as establishing a time to provide intervention, dedicating the staff to implement intervention, and finding a physical space for students to receive intervention (Durrance, 2023).

3. **Developmental levels:** The third noteworthy characteristic of secondary schools is the developmental level of middle and high school students. During adolescence, students are increasingly driven by peer-to-peer interactions and a desire for more independence. The structure of many secondary schools provides some opportunities for student input in decision making (for example, student councils and student membership in schoolwide committees). However, these opportunities typically involve limited numbers of students, and often, these students are not representative of the entire student population.

   Student voice is essential at the secondary level to build connectedness and ensure the school is aware of the particular interests and needs of the population it serves (Flannery et al., 2018; Mager & Nowak, 2012; Martinez et al., 2019; Scales, Roehlkepartain, & Houltberg, 2022). This is especially important for schools where staff are dissimilar from students in socioeconomic status, race, religion, native language, and so on. Staff's life experiences may differ greatly from students', increasing their disconnect and impacting their ability to relate to one another.

Furthermore, resistance related to a system of supports may be driven by the developmental notion that "it's too late" or "we can't change who that student is now." However, researchers have debunked this belief by demonstrating the malleability of the adolescent brain, which continues to be under construction and benefits from instruction and support beyond academics in areas such as conflict resolution, self-monitoring, and stress management. Secondary educators can play a big role in this development (Murray & Rosanbalm, 2017; Young, Caldarella, Richardson, & Young, 2012).

About This Book

As you can see, the implementation of any interdisciplinary schoolwide framework at the secondary level is not for the faint of heart. This book is devoted to helping secondary schools maneuver obstacles and consider best practices in MTSS to create a practical action plan for implementation. In this book, I offer digestible summaries of up-to-date, secondary-specific, evidence-based practices to help middle and high schools expand and improve their current system for tiered supports in the following areas.

- Academics
- Behavioral and social-emotional skills
- College and career readiness

Throughout this text, I provide scaffolds for the reader, such as vocabulary supports, graphic organizers, and models, to help secondary educators understand that the MTSS framework is within their grasp. Secondary educators and leaders are busy people who struggle to find time to dig into resources, such as the What Works Clearinghouse or the Institute of Education Science's guides, to help provide instruction and intervention for their students. Therefore, this book's summaries define the critical kernels of each program or practice and serve as quick reference tools to immediately implement it and then continue to dig deeper, learn more about the strategies, and improve through an iterative process.

It is important to note that there is a large body of work on aspects of quality instruction and schooling (such as culture, climate, and engagement) and content pedagogy (such as alignment, rigor, mathematics, and literacy); these are necessary underpinnings of successful MTSS implementation but not the focal point of this book. Students with disabilities or those identified as gifted will likely require support beyond what is presented. Additionally, I mention but don't expand on some necessary components of building a comprehensive MTSS, including data-based decision making and teaming. I encourage schools and teams to seek out more in-depth reading, training, and coaching on these topics as they grow and solidify their system. The scope of this resource remains defining the essential components of evidence-based tiered interventions for secondary students and guiding schools to effectively launch their context-specific model of MTSS.

The following is an overview of the chapters in this book.

Chapter 1 introduces MTSS through the secondary lens. It outlines the basic components of MTSS, defines MTSS terminology (*screening*, *progress monitoring*, and so on) for a secondary audience, and gives concrete examples. It discusses barriers to implementation, such as competing priorities and siloed departments, and explores how to reimagine the components of MTSS for a middle and high school setting. Chapter 1 also covers the importance of systems and offers a streamlined model (the Early Warning Intervention and Monitoring System) for systematizing MTSS at the secondary level.

Chapters 2, 3, and 4 present secondary-specific tiered interventions. Chapter 2 focuses on academics by first reviewing the current challenges that educators and students face due to the high numbers of students whose academic skills are below grade level. It briefly discusses Tier 1 and the importance of scaffolding instruction so students who struggle academically can access rigorous content. It then explores the essential components of three Tier 2 academic group interventions for secondary students and methods for intensifying these interventions. Embedded templates offer user-friendly options for progress monitoring and fidelity checks.

Chapter 3 delves into behavioral and social-emotional tiered interventions. After examining the increased mental health needs of adolescents and the urgency around this topic, it reviews the fundamental elements of an effective Tier 1 schoolwide positive behavioral and social-emotional support system. It offers the essential components of five Tier 2 group interventions to support the behavioral and social-emotional needs of secondary students. For students with more significant needs, this chapter unpacks methods for intensifying the interventions. You will find templates for monitoring student progress as well as implementation fidelity.

Finally, chapter 4 examines the importance of college and career readiness by offering tiered interventions to ensure students are on track for future success. Educators and leaders in middle and high school know that the primary focus at this level is to help students be successful after graduation. Chapter 4 reviews the current state of college and career readiness across the United States, along with the fundamental qualities of an effective Tier 1 schoolwide college-and-career-readiness system. For students who need additional support, the chapter offers the essential components of three Tier 2 college-and-career-readiness group interventions, plus methods for intensifying these interventions, monitoring progress, and checking for implementation fidelity.

Additionally, pause points are provided in each chapter as step-by-step guidance for teams to reflect on their current processes and begin implementation.

Conclusion

This book is designed with the secondary educator in mind. You do not have to read it from beginning to end. Instead, I encourage you to review chapter 1 to gain a foundational understanding of MTSS through the secondary lens. Then, you may approach the other three chapters based on the area or areas your school decides to prioritize. MTSS is a complex framework that takes time to implement, but rather than giving up on it or avoiding it altogether, it would best suit secondary schools to find their context-specific entry point and then reflect, iterate, and improve over time.

1 MTSS and Secondary Schools

LEARNING OBJECTIVES

- Examine the components of MTSS through a secondary lens.
- Review how a structured system can strengthen and sustain the implementation of any initiative.
- Explore the Early Warning Intervention and Monitoring System as a secondary MTSS model.

Travel back in time with me a few years, when my job was to visit the homes of incoming preschoolers with developmental delays to learn about their needs and help the school build a supportive plan. I recall entering Amir's home, and his mother said to me, "I don't know what you all are going to do because we had to nail the windows shut in our home to keep Amir from escaping." I took careful notes and hesitantly approached the awaiting preschool teacher to share information on Amir, collaborate, and develop classroom supports for him.

Amir struggled greatly in preschool. When the time came to shift to kindergarten, the kindergarten teacher and I brainstormed again about how to set Amir up for success. But it was another really tough year. This continued into elementary and middle school. Eventually, Amir entered high school. Each year, teachers and staff worked hard to provide him with the support he needed. And each year, they felt as if nothing they did worked because Amir continued to struggle.

I recall walking into the high school and seeing Amir, with his backpack geared up, moving from class to class. His behavioral and social-emotional skills weren't perfect. He still struggled academically. But I saw how far he had come since he first started school so many years ago. And it struck me: His preschool teacher would never get to see this. His kindergarten teacher would never get to see this. And his high school teachers had no understanding of how far Amir had come since he started preschool as a developmentally delayed three-year-old.

It became apparent to me that we may not be able to "fix" students, and we may not always see immediate changes, but in time, we shape them. We shape their behavior. We shape their academic skills. We shape their lives and their futures. So, as educators, we must all hold hands and believe that in time, we do make an impact!

This chapter provides an overarching exploration of MTSS at the secondary level. To build a shared understanding of MTSS, I provide a snapshot of the big ideas and how these could look at the secondary level. I then share the importance of systems and dive into the Early Warning Intervention and Monitoring System, a national model for structuring MTSS at the middle and high school levels. This chapter is rich in content, with each section covering complex topics, so you may find it helpful to refer back to as your MTSS process grows over time.

MTSS Through a Secondary Lens

Secondary educators new to MTSS can better understand this process by considering how it is similar to a doctor's visit. The medical model typically involves collecting data, providing triaged support, monitoring progress, and adapting interventions based on an individual's response. Let's say you have a concern about your heart. You go to your doctor and describe your symptoms. Imagine if the doctor responded, "We better head straight to open-heart surgery!" You may feel surprised or even frightened by this immediate jump to a very intensive procedure. You may wonder why they didn't instead start with a few diagnostic assessments, such as taking your blood pressure, or a milder intervention, like practicing meditation for stress reduction or taking a low dose of medication. Perhaps it would help if a team reviewed how you respond to these interventions to decide how best to proceed. These less intensive interventions require fewer resources and possibly would be all the support you need.

Now, let's consider this scenario as a metaphor for a student in your school experiencing behavioral or literacy difficulties. Rather than jumping to an alternative school or a referral to special education, your team would first review any information you have available and determine whether you need more data. Then, you would consider an initial level of support, collect data along the way, use this data to make decisions, and then intensify the support as needed. This approach helps you selectively use your limited resources in the most strategic way. This is MTSS in action!

MTSS establishes a structured path for a team to review data and discuss how to assist students who are struggling, rather than leaving each teacher to figure it out on their own. Teaming is a crucial part of this work, and later in this chapter, I'll review ways you can organize your team. Using MTSS allows educators to create tiered levels of support so they don't jump to the most individualized, intensive interventions for every student who demonstrates some kind of difficulty.

We will use the example in figure 1.1 to launch this discussion and visualize how the MTSS framework might look at the secondary level. While the contents of each box will differ based on your school and available resources, these examples illustrate how this might take shape in a real-world setting. I examine all the figure's components throughout the book.

SECONDARY MULTITIERED SYSTEM OF SUPPORTS

	 ACADEMIC TIERED INTERVENTIONS	 BEHAVIORAL AND SOCIAL-EMOTIONAL TIERED INTERVENTIONS	 COLLEGE-AND-CAREER-READINESS TIERED INTERVENTIONS
 TIER 3 3–5 percent Individualized interventions”	Conduct diagnostic assessments. Intensify intervention using data-based individualization.	Conduct functional behavior assessment. Intensify intervention using data-based individualization.	Investigate areas of need and assign an advocate. Intensify intervention using data-based individualization.
 TIER 2 10–15 percent Group interventions”	Strategy instruction High-impact tutoring Literacy or mathematics intervention period	Check & Connect® Class Pass Behavior contracts	Nudging Career academy with targeted supports Dual enrollment with targeted supports
 TIER I >80 percent All students	High-quality curriculum aligned with state standards Effective teaching practices that promote opportunities to respond and student engagement	Schoolwide expectations Reinforcement system Classroom practices (for example, active supervision)	Career interest inventories College visits, career fairs Internships, job shadowing, apprenticeships

Figure 1.1: Simplified secondary MTSS framework example.

Visit ***go.SolutionTree.com/RTI*** *for a free blank reproducible version of this figure.*

You might think of the purpose of each tier in the following way.

- **Tier 1:** Universal support for all students (schoolwide interventions)
- **Tier 2:** Targeted support for approximately 10–15 percent of students (small-group interventions)
- **Tier 3:** Intensive support for approximately 3–5 percent of students (intensive, individualized interventions)

What do we mean when we say *intervention*? The idea of intervention can easily be misunderstood. It is not just doing something extra for a student. An important characteristic to keep in mind is that intervention must always involve instruction. Non-examples of intervention include the following.

- Providing a student with a study hall period
- Allowing a student to retake a test
- Moving a student to the front of the classroom
- Assigning a student lunch detention to address their behavior
- Placing an instructional assistant with a student
- Giving a student a point sheet for their behavior

Though each of those strategies may be helpful in certain situations, they do not include instruction in the area of need (for example, social skills, literacy, self-regulation, or study skills); therefore, we would not consider them formal interventions.

Tier 1 schoolwide supports are what we, as educators, proactively do to set all students up for success. For example, we teach behavioral procedures for arrival and dismissal to ensure safety, predictability, and consistency. We adopt academic standards and utilize engagement strategies as the core instruction for all students. We create a diverse set of career pathways to allow students with varying interests and skill levels to select a path that meets their needs. Tier 1 includes the structures, strategies, and data collection that allow secondary schools to meet the needs of most students.

The literature suggests that there will be a subset of students—typically between 10 and 15 percent—for whom Tier 1 is insufficient (Bailey, 2020; Center on Positive Behavioral Interventions and Supports, 2025; Fuchs et al., 2010; IRIS Center, 2026; Johnson et al., 2009; Lewis & Sugai, 1999; VanDerHeyden & Allsopp, 2014). However, the percentage of students needing additional support may be significantly higher for schools that are beginning MTSS or schools that have high numbers of under-resourced students and communities. These schools may have to set context-specific criteria for identifying who to prioritize for support. Regardless of your school's student population, it's important to reserve limited resources of time, funding, and staff by building a system that considers those students who, like in the earlier heart metaphor, may need only *mild* interventions. Tier 2 is the way to do this.

I have found it helpful to refer to Tier 2 interventions as *group interventions*, as this highlights the fact that they must be streamlined, efficient, practical, and *implemented in a similar way* for targeted students. This differs from a Tier 3 level of intervention, which typically is *individualized*. These group interventions may involve small groups (two to five students) or large ones (twelve to fifteen students), depending on the particular intervention being implemented. When you attempt to individualize Tier 2 interventions for each student, the system becomes too cumbersome and impractical to sustain for 10–15 percent of students. Ideally, select a small number of Tier 2 group interventions to utilize at your school and then stick with those and do them well. Don't let your team be easily distracted by a cool new resource you run across on Pinterest or at a conference. Instead, focus on the most evidence-based interventions and implement them with fidelity. You don't have to figure this out alone—this book equips you with the tools and guidance to make this happen!

When student data indicates that a student is not making sufficient progress and needs more than a Tier 2 group intervention, your team may determine that a Tier 3 level of support is required. Tier 3 becomes more intensive and individualized; therefore, this must be reserved for a very small number of students in the school, typically less than 5 percent of the student population (Bailey, 2020; Fuchs et al., 2010; IRIS Center, 2026; VanDerHeyden & Allsopp, 2014).

A Tier 3 level of support involves digging deeper and collecting additional information to identify how to build an intervention plan that is more student specific. Notice the language here: The *support* is tiered, not the student. You might indicate that a student needs a Tier 3 level of intervention but not that they are a "Tier 3 student." This book will help your team explore methods for intensifying and individualizing intervention for these students.

Well-Established Systems

As James Clear (2018) notes in *Atomic Habits*, his book on how to implement change, "You do not rise to the level of your goals. You fall to the level of your systems" (p. 27). The most effectively led secondary schools create and commit to defined systems. Well-established systems allow stressed, overworked educators and administrators to shift into a proactive mode, lean on shared leadership, and not feel constantly overwhelmed. Without strategic definitions of your systems, unexpected systems will inadvertently form on their own; therefore, be intentional about defining *what you do* and *how you do it*. Once intentionally designed systems become entrenched in the school culture, educators have a chance to get their heads above water!

To explore the power of systems, let's take a hypothetical systems journey. In your home, you like to be proactive, intentional, and efficient. You probably love it when a full toilet paper roll awaits you in the bathroom. To this end, you purchase mega-size packs of toilet paper when they are on sale. Yet, you do not have the space in your bathroom to store all these backup rolls, so you place only a single pack in the bathroom cabinet and keep the remaining backups in your basement closet. When the time comes, and you see an almost-empty toilet paper roll before you, you must respond.

Not wanting to have to run downstairs at an inopportune time, you immediately set an action trigger (because you know these are key to a well-established system; Heath & Heath, 2010). Once you pull the last roll from the smaller pack in the bathroom, you don't just throw away the wrapper. Instead, you place the empty wrapper on the basement stairs as a cue.

The next time someone heads downstairs, the wrapper prompts them to grab a new pack of toilet paper to restock the bathroom cabinet. This ensures a fresh roll awaits you whenever it's needed. But in an unwieldy, systemless world, you may or may not have the necessary toiletries in place. When a well-defined process is established, all relevant humans know the expectations, and the system takes care of itself.

Unfortunately, too often, we see systemless schools struggle to implement programs or initiatives. Due to numerous constraints, schools and districts tend to lean too heavily on professional learning as the lever to effect change. However, implementation is an art in itself. Research on system implementation highlights the importance of having a team of stakeholders who identify priorities, design the system, consider the context and available resources, implement the system, reflect, and adapt (Bohanon, Love, & Morrissey, 2021; Fixsen, Naoom, Blase, Friedman, & Wallace, 2005; Metz, Burke, Albers, Louison, & Bartley, 2020). Schools are complex organizations, especially at the secondary level. No leader can do it all. One day of professional learning cannot make it happen. Instead, you must identify priorities and work as a team to develop the system needed to clarify to all what you do and how you do it.

As a young educator, I did not realize the absolute necessity of being strategic and intentional in the implementation of new initiatives. Many educators have been raised on the idea of top-down, mandated initiatives that often start at the district office and then trickle down to the school leaders and teachers. However, implementation research demonstrates these most effective strategies: Tap into the local expertise, adapt based on the contextual fit, and create feedback loops between leadership and those doing the frontline service (Fixsen et al., 2005; Metz et al., 2020). Implementation research bridged with MTSS literature provides the underpinnings of the strategies throughout this guide. MTSS can be your school's system for strategically providing the support students need.

MTSS can be your school's system for strategically providing the support students need.

To effectively implement MTSS, consider the following school infrastructure and support mechanisms (Center on Multi-Tiered System of Supports, 2025c).

- A focus on prevention, meaning that everyone understands that the purpose of MTSS is to provide all students with the level of support they need
- Leadership personnel who are actively involved in MTSS implementation
- School-based professional learning for teachers on data-based decision making and effective instructional practices
- Cultural and linguistically responsive assessments and instructional practices
- Available resources, such as staffing, curricula, and community partners, to effectively implement MTSS

- Schedules that strategically support MTSS implementation
- Communication with families about MTSS, their children's progress, and their input throughout the data-based decision-making process
- Communication with all staff about MTSS implementation, their involvement in that implementation, and ongoing opportunities for teacher teams to collaborate
- MTSS teaming that includes relevant stakeholders (students, teachers, and families) and has set procedures for meeting, collecting data, analyzing data, and making decisions
- Measures of fidelity and evaluation used to monitor the implementation of instruction, assessment, intervention, and other MTSS processes

Numerous resources exist to assist leadership teams with each listed aspect. It is beyond the scope of this book to explore each of these infrastructure and support mechanisms, but I will briefly review one secondary-specific and somewhat simplified model of MTSS that can help a school address many of these important features of MTSS implementation. It is called the Early Warning Intervention and Monitoring System.

Early Warning Intervention and Monitoring System

In all areas of MTSS, data drives the work. The Early Warning Intervention and Monitoring System (EWIMS) provides an evidence-based, systematic approach for structuring a data-based decision-making process in middle and high schools (Balfanz & Byrnes, 2025; Marken et al., 2020; Scala, Husby-Slater, Chamberlain, & McPhee, 2023a, 2023b). EWIMS takes many key components of MTSS and streamlines them into a secondary-friendly model.

For example, conducting a schoolwide universal screener three times a year is often one of the first steps of implementing MTSS at the elementary level. This can be very costly and time consuming, but most agree that the benefits outweigh the costs in the early grades (Fuchs et al., 2010). Rather than conducting a traditional academic universal screener (for example, STAR, i-Ready, or MAP) or initiating a social-emotional or behavioral universal screener (for example, SAEBRS or SRSS), EWIMS restructures data collection and analysis at the secondary level. As stated in the introduction, leaders in the field of tiered supports recognize that with the comprehensive history of data already collected on most secondary students, "it no longer makes sense to allocate scarce resources to screening for the purpose of identifying students at risk for academic failure" (Fuchs et al., 2010, p. 24). Therefore, by utilizing early warning indicators as part of EWIMS, the MTSS team may decide to review college-and-career-readiness data, grades, failure reports, the rate of course completion, office referrals, or other existing measures of schoolwide academic and behavioral data.

This does not mean that a middle or high school should never use a formalized universal screener; however, to determine screeners' value, schools should reflect on their current practices, the instructional time lost for assessments, and how impactful these assessments are in changing the instruction and support that students receive.

As part of EWIMS, secondary schools contemplate their unique goals and contexts to identify students who are not meeting educational milestones; then the schools provide interventions, monitor students' progress, and adjust interventions as needed (Balfanz & Byrnes, 2019; Faria et al., 2017; Scala et al., 2023a, 2023b; Seeskin, Massion, & Usher, 2022). EWIMS considers the limited resources and numerous barriers at the secondary level, the competing priorities of college and career readiness and graduation, and the rich repository of historical data to emphasize a focus on attendance, behavior, and course performance rather than traditional approaches to screening (Marken et al., 2020). By monitoring factors such as attendance, course performance, and behavior, schools can identify which students are more likely to drop out of school, connect students with appropriate interventions to reduce chronic absenteeism and course failures, and increase their likelihood of graduating (Faria et al., 2017).

EWIMS consists of seven steps (Scala et al., 2023a, 2023b), as shown in figure 1.2. In the following sections, I briefly unpack each step of the EWIMS process.

Develop Your Team

There are endless models for teaming, many of which create effective systems (DuFour, DuFour, Eaker, & Karhanek, 2010; DuFour et al., 2024; Hannigan, Djabrayan Hannigan, Mattos, & Buffum, 2021; Koselak, 2011; Mattos et al., 2025; McIntosh & Goodman, 2016; Scala et al., 2023a, 2023b). The team designed to focus on all students at the Tier 1 schoolwide level may be referred to as the *MTSS team*, *EWIMS team*, *Tier 1 team*, *Positive Behavioral Interventions and Supports (PBIS) team*, *response to intervention (RTI) team*, *student support team*, or *school leadership team*. In some secondary schools, this team may be responsible for each level of the MTSS process, not just Tier 1 core instruction. Alternatively, some schools have found that Tier 2 collaborative teacher teams—small groups that analyze and make decisions using classwide or small-group data—may be better suited to coordinate Tier 2. Finally, the team that designs a Tier 3 plan may be a uniquely built, student-specific team that focuses on intensifying and individualizing intervention just for that one student. Importantly, successful teaming is determined not by the specific model but by the fidelity and the effectiveness of the processes implemented, such as analyzing data, identifying trends, and adapting interventions based on student responsiveness.

For the purposes of this book, the team that focuses on Tier 1 core instruction is called the *MTSS team*, and those that make decisions about Tiers 2 and 3 are called the *Tier 2 team* and *Tier 3 team*, respectively. The Tier 2 team is responsible for group interventions (small or large) at the Tier 2 level, and the Tier 3 team is responsible for individualized, intensive interventions for students who need additional support.

1. Develop your team: Establish roles and responsibilities, set team meetings for the year, clarify the purpose, and establish communication methods, routines, and expectations.

2. Select a data integration tool: This tool should be designed to quickly pull, organize, and present student data. These data integration and visualization tools are typically online platforms that pull data from the student information system and any academic or behavioral data systems to provide easy-to-read graphs for the team to easily analyze large amounts of data.

3. Review early warning indicators: This review should identify students demonstrating risk factors and pinpoint patterns at the school, group, and individual levels. Early warning indicators at the secondary level include data such as attendance, behavior, student engagement, and course performance.

4. Interpret data: Determine what additional information is needed for students identified as demonstrating risk (for example, student, teacher, or family input, progress monitoring, in-class assessments) to hypothesize root causes and determine how best to intervene.

5. Select and implement interventions: Identify the intervention that will best fit the needs of the student(s). Communicate this plan with all relevant stakeholders (students, families, teachers).

6. Set goals and monitor student progress: Goals and monitoring include ensuring fidelity of implementation and making adaptations based on student data.

7. Review your EWIMS process: During your review, identify what's working and what's not and determine how best to improve.

Source: Adapted from Scala et al., 2023a, 2023b.

Figure 1.2: The seven steps of EWIMS.

However, your school should determine how best to structure teams based on current staffing, availability, and priorities. Figure 1.3 presents an example of this teaming model for MTSS implementation, but it certainly is not the "right" way or only way to structure teams at the secondary level.

Select a Data Integration Tool

EWIMS will be most effective if you utilize a user-friendly data tool. There are numerous platforms available that connect with existing student information systems along with any academic data systems (for example, STAR, i-Ready, or MAP) or behavior data systems (for example, SAEBRS or SRSS). Panorama, Branching Minds, and eduCLIMBER are just a few such platforms. Some states have developed a state-specific tool to organize this data. Whatever data tool you select, it must be automated, provide data visualizations, and deliver customizable reports to streamline the process and reduce logistic barriers for teams.

Review Early Warning Indicators and Interpret Data

Your school MTSS team has multiple data-based decision-making tasks. Before the team can identify students who need additional support, they must reflect on universal, schoolwide data to determine whether most students' needs are being met by initial core instruction. At the secondary level, this data typically includes three areas: (1) academics, (2) behavioral or social-emotional competencies, and (3) college and career readiness.

If many students (typically more than 15 percent of the total school population) are not having success in initial core instruction, as measured by academic assessments and course performance data, there is likely a "core issue." Improvement may be needed in instructional practices such as modeling, explicit instruction, feedback, engagement, opportunities to respond, and scaffolding. This issue is also true for behavioral or social-emotional supports. Your team may determine, based on office referral data or climate surveys, that additional Tier 1 behavioral supports are needed; for example, you may need to establish schoolwide expectations, clarify common-area procedures, or determine methods for reinforcing appropriate behaviors.

In secondary schools, ensuring students are college and career ready is a fundamental priority.

Importantly, effective Tier 2 intervention cannot solve a core issue, as it is impossible to efficiently provide this additional support to large numbers of students. If a large percentage of students require Tier 2 interventions, the school must investigate the quality of classroom instruction and schoolwide behavioral supports to address these foundational practices first (Center on Multi-Tiered System of Supports, 2020; Clark & Dockweiler, 2019; DuFour et al., 2024; IRIS Center, 2022c; Mattos et al., 2025; National Student Support Accelerator, 2023; Scala et al., 2023a, 2023b).

In secondary schools, ensuring students are college and career ready is a fundamental priority. Most educators are familiar with the measures of academic, behavioral, and social-emotional skills mentioned previously, but readily available measures of college

Team	Member(s)	Meeting Frequency	System Level of Focus	Purpose
TIER I	• Principal • Assistant principal • Counselor(s) • Department lead(s) • Grade-level representative(s) • Special education representative(s) • Family representative(s) • Student representative(s) • Community representative(s) • Specialists (for example school psychologist, literacy consultant, and behavior coach)	Monthly	Tier 1, all students May also examine an overview of Tier 2 and Tier 3	• Monitor the fidelity of MTSS implementation. • Review schoolwide data, including academic, behavior, course performance, attendance, and college-and-career-readiness data. • Determine the effectiveness of Tier 1 schoolwide supports. • Analyze disaggregated data to identify specific groups of students whom Tier 1 may not be serving well (for example, freshmen, female students, students of a particular racial or ethnic group, or students with disabilities). • Explore options for improving Tier 1 (for example, scheduling adaptations, grading practices, and teaching of schoolwide expectations). • Identify professional learning needs to address any schoolwide trends of concern.
TIER 2	• Each teacher in a department or other established grouping of teachers in the school • Special education teacher assigned to that department or group • Administrator or curriculum leader (as needed) • Paraprofessionals (as needed) • Specialists (as needed)	Weekly	Tier 1 and Tier 2 May also examine an overview of Tier 3	• Analyze classwide or grade-level data, including academic, behavior, course performance, attendance, and college-and-career-readiness data. • Explore options for improving classroom instruction (adjust instructional strategies using Universal Design for Learning, provide just-in-time interventions for small student groups, and so on). • Identify students who need Tier 2 support and select an appropriate Tier 2 group intervention to implement. • Review progress-monitoring data (more frequent student-specific data) for students receiving Tier 2 group interventions, and adjust interventions as needed.
TIER 3	• Student • Family members of the student • Teachers of the student • Administrator (as needed) • Specialists (as needed) • Other student support person (for example, outside mental health provider)	Yearly or as needed	Tier 3	• Analyze student-level data, including academic, behavior, course performance, attendance, and college-and-career-readiness data. • Determine whether additional data is needed. • Set goals for identified areas of concern. • Identify Tier 3 intensive and individualized interventions based on student data. • Review progress-monitoring data and adjust interventions as needed.

Figure 1.3: School teaming system example.

*Visit **go.SolutionTree.com/RTI** for a free blank reproducible version of this figure.*

and career readiness may be a bit less familiar. To assess the effectiveness of current Tier 1 college-and-career-readiness practices, secondary schools may choose to review data points such as the percentages of students who are doing the following.

- Earning all necessary credits to be awarded a high school diploma
- Meeting benchmarks on college readiness exams (for example, the ACT and SAT)
- Applying to college and completing the Free Application for Federal Student Aid (FAFSA) form
- Completing college-level coursework and earning college credit before high school graduation
- Completing career pathway coursework and passing associated assessments
- Earning a recognized industry certificate
- Demonstrating employability skills (for example, timeliness and organization) as measured by rubrics or other assessments

Data points like these, along with attendance, graduation rates, and validated surveys of student perceptions of college-and-career-readiness-related programming, can help paint a comprehensive picture of the college-and-career-readiness landscape in your building. As part of a review of Tier 1 schoolwide practices, an MTSS team can consider this data to determine what is working and not working, what professional learning may be beneficial, and if any staffing, programmatic, or scheduling changes are needed.

After considering the effectiveness of Tier 1, the MTSS team identifies students who need additional Tier 2 support. Your school will need to establish clear criteria for determining a student's risk level based on early warning indicators such as attendance, behavior, engagement, and course performance data. This will, in essence, be your universal screener. It is as if you are quickly taking the temperature of all students in your building and identifying which ones are of most concern.

Schools may set their own criteria for these early warning indicators using locally validated thresholds—the levels at which early warning indicators signify elevated signs of risk in your context. Your school could also consider the specific criteria identified by research to reliably predict students who are most likely to experience academic failure at the secondary level. These early warning indicator thresholds include the following.

- Student attendance
    - Exceeding nine absences per quarter or thirty-six absences per year in grades 6–9 (excused or unexcused)
    - Missing over 10 percent of instructional time in grades 9–12 (excused or unexcused)
- Student behavior
    - Exceeding two office referrals per quarter or six per year in grades 6–9

    - Exceeding one suspension per quarter or two suspensions per year in grades 6–9
- Student course performance
    - Missing the credits needed to move from ninth to tenth grade *and* receiving at least one failure in a core course
    - Having a grade point average below 2.0 on a 4.0 scale in grades 9–12
    - Failing one or more courses in grades 9–12 (Allensworth & Easton, 2007; Allensworth, Gwynne, Moore, & de la Torre, 2014; Balfanz, 2009; Davis, 2012; Marken et al., 2020; Therriault, O'Cummings, Heppen, Yerhot, & Scala, 2017/2023)

With clear criteria in place, the MTSS team will be better equipped to identify students who are demonstrating risk and to determine whether additional data is needed to guide intervention selection and implementation.

Select and Implement Interventions

Does your MTSS team have a plan for this step? Perhaps this is why you are reading this book! This section supports you to make informed decisions and dig deeper into the interventions that your team decides to implement based on the needs of your student population, current initiatives, and available resources.

Once your school has established a few optional Tier 2 group interventions in its makeup, assigning a student to a group should be a relatively straightforward process. It may involve notifying the coordinator of that particular intervention to add the student to their list or possibly changing the schedule for that student for one period. However, determining interventions at the Tier 3 level can be a bit more complex. When progress-monitoring data (discussed in the next step) indicates you need to move to Tier 3 supports, you can utilize the Taxonomy of Intervention Intensity (Fuchs, Fuchs, & Malone, 2017; National Center on Intensive Intervention, 2019) to develop a student-specific intervention plan. The Taxonomy of Intervention Intensity provides guidance on using validated methods to develop a more intensive, individualized Tier 3 plan (Fuchs et al., 2017; St. Martin, Vaughn, Troia, Fien, & Coyne, 2020).

Contemplate the specific dimensions listed in figure 1.4 (page 24) and how you could adapt them to intensify intervention for a middle or high school student.

Considering these dimensions, a Tier 3 team could come together and use the "Strategies for Intensifying Interventions Template" to create a Tier 3 plan. (Visit **go.SolutionTree.com/RTI** for a free reproducible of this template.) By collecting additional diagnostic data (for example, functional behavioral assessments or diagnostic literacy or mathematics assessments) to pinpoint specific learning needs, this team could consider the student's current instructional day and determine how best to intensify interventions in strength, dosage, alignment, attention to transfer, comprehensiveness, or other behavioral or academic support. Specific examples of how you could complete the "Strategies for

When data reveals that your Tier 1 schoolwide supports, plus added Tier 2 group interventions, are insufficient for a student to be successful, you can intensify interventions by changing the following.

STRENGTH

Determine whether the intervention has strength. In other words, does research indicate that the intervention can be effective, or do you need to consider a different intervention?

- Is there high-quality evidence of the intervention's effectiveness, and is the student similar to those involved in the research studies?
- The What Works Clearinghouse and the National Center on Intensive Intervention are reputable organizations that provide summaries of research on numerous interventions on their websites.

DOSAGE

Consider expanding the student's opportunities to respond and receive feedback through actions such as:

- Increasing the number or length of intervention sessions
- Having smaller group sizes, reducing distractions, or making the intervention groups more homogeneous

ALIGNMENT

Consider how well the intervention matches the student's academic or behavioral needs and the student's grade-level expectations. Improve alignment by:

- Increasing instruction on the targeted skill
- Breaking down the skill into smaller, more discrete steps to be explicitly taught

ATTENTION TO TRANSFER

Increase the likelihood that the student can transfer the newly taught skill to their other classes or environments by:

- Aligning the skill with the language of core instruction and instructional routines
- Preteaching content rather than reteaching or repeating content
- Embedding just-in-time interventions such as guided practice at times throughout the day
- Explicitly teaching the skill in multiple settings
- Explaining how intervention instruction connects to other situations in the student's life

COMPREHENSIVENESS

The comprehensiveness of an intervention considers how well the intervention incorporates best-practice instructional principles of explicit instruction, such as:

- Using precise language to teach key concepts
- Providing models and think-alouds for new concepts
- Presenting concrete examples and explaining the steps of a process
- Practicing a gradual release approach
- Having students explain concepts in their own words
- Providing ongoing practice in new skills
- Chunking tasks
- Providing immediate and explicit error correction

OTHER BEHAVIORAL OR ACADEMIC SUPPORT

Consider that a student requiring academic support may also need behavioral support and a student requiring behavioral support may also need academic support. Ideas for adding other support include:

- Creating a motivational plan with the student
- Adding small-group instruction in the needed skill areas
- Combining or aligning academic and behavioral strategies
- Increasing peer support to model and promote positive behaviors

Source: National Center on Intensive Intervention, 2019. Adapted with permission.

Figure 1.4: Strategies for intensifying interventions.

*Visit **go.SolutionTree.com/RTI** for a free reproducible version of this figure.*

Intensifying Interventions Template" are incorporated into the Tier 3 sections of chapters 2, 3, and 4 to demonstrate how it can be used for secondary students in the areas of academics, behavioral and social-emotional skills, and college and career readiness.

Set Goals and Monitor Student Progress

Intervention is strongest when instructional changes are based on student-specific data (Dennis & Gratton-Fisher, 2020; The Reading League, 2024). Once students begin receiving intervention at the Tier 2 or Tier 3 level, progress monitoring is the optimum method for data collection. Progress-monitoring tools are research-validated methods for measuring student progress and showing growth over time (Bailey, Colpo, & Foley, 2020; Gersten et al., 2009; Hougen, 2015); these tools are an integral part of intensifying and individualizing intervention through the tiers. Depending on your school's teaming structure, a Tier 2 team or Tier 3 team may be charged with analyzing these student-specific, frequent measures of progress to determine how to proceed. Based on the rate of progress, the team may decide to continue the intervention if the student is responding adequately, intensify the intervention due to a lack of sufficient progress, or (hopefully) reduce the level of intensity and eventually exit the student from tiered support. Setting goals and determining exit criteria can help the team make these decisions.

Progress-monitoring tools at the secondary level may include algebra curriculum-based measures, cloze and maze curriculum-based measures, oral reading fluency and writing fluency curriculum-based measures, and direct behavior ratings (Chafouleas et al., 2013; Deno, 1985; Fuchs, Deno, & Mirkin, 1984; Hosp, Hosp, Howell, & Allison, 2014; Johnson, Galow, & Allenger, 2012; Matta, Volpe, Briesch, & Owens, 2020; Miller, Crovello, & Swenson, 2017; Miller, Patwa, & Chafouleas, 2014; Sims et al., 2023; Stecker, Fuchs, & Fuchs, 2005; Truckenmiller, McKindles, Petscher, Eckert, & Tock, 2020). Progress monitoring involves the following.

- Goal setting
- Data graphing
- A series of six to nine data points
- Validated measures (Curriculum-based measures and direct behavior ratings are two of the most common; Bailey et al., 2020; Christ & Silberglitt, 2007.)

Digging into the intricacies of administering these tools, graphing data, and conducting an error analysis of these tools is beyond the scope of this book. I encourage you to partner with specialists in your building or district (for example, school psychologists and special education teachers) or refer to the National Center on Intensive Intervention's (2021) Academic Progress Monitoring Tools Chart for specific guidance on how best to utilize such tools to monitor progress and ensure a student's intervention is meeting their needs.

Review Your EWIMS Process

The implementation of any school-improvement initiative is optimized through ongoing reflection. Your MTSS team can utilize existing instruments, composed of the most crucial MTSS components identified by research, to guide this reflection practice. Conducting a formalized self-reflection on your school's implementation of the MTSS process will help your team determine actionable steps for improvement. The Center on Multi-Tiered System of Supports (2025b) provides one example of an MTSS fidelity rubric, and numerous others are available, such as the Self-Assessment of MTSS Implementation (Stockslager, Castillo, Brundage, Childs, & Romer, 2022), the Self-Study Guide for Implementing High School Academic Interventions (Smith et al., 2016), and the PBIS Tiered Fidelity Inventory (Center on Positive Behavioral Interventions and Supports, 2025). These tools can assist the MTSS team in monitoring the fidelity of implementation, identifying professional learning needs, and determining the necessary actions for improving and sustaining the work.

Considering this bird's-eye overview of MTSS, figure 1.5 summarizes the essential components of MTSS and how these can look at the secondary level. The statements in the figure are not hard rules; instead, they are examples that demonstrate how these components could look in a middle or high school.

Conclusion

This chapter was designed to succinctly translate many years of MTSS research and guidance for secondary-level educators. I challenge you to consider these practices and explore the critical elements of the specific evidence-based interventions provided in the next three chapters to launch MTSS in your school or district.

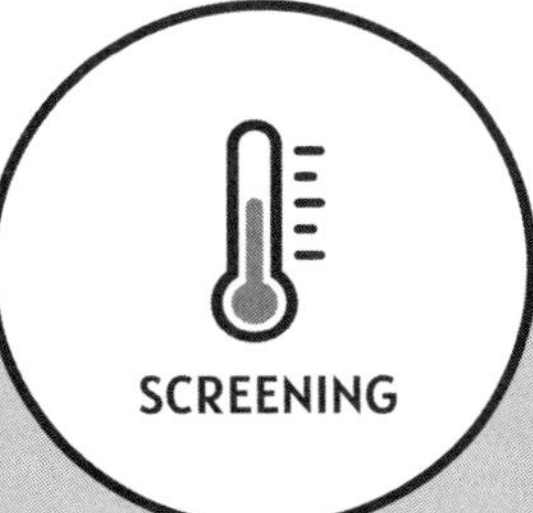

A systematic process to:

- Evaluate the overall effectiveness of Tier 1 (core instruction).
- Identify students who need additional support.

EXAMPLES IN PRACTICE

How could this look in a middle or high school?

A school MTSS team meets monthly to review existing data sources to determine the effectiveness of core instruction and identify students who need additional support. The following are potential sample screening data sources and criteria.

Early Warning Indicators (as part of an EWIMS)

- Attendance—Students who miss more than 10 percent of instructional days, regardless of reason (excused or unexcused)
- Behavior—Students with over two office referrals per quarter
- Course performance—Students with grades below 2.0 on a 4.0 scale, one or more course failures, or are not on track to be promoted from ninth to tenth grade

Academic Screening Data Sources

- Students scoring in a "below basic" range in reading or mathematics on the state accountability assessment
- Students scoring "below basic" on standardized measures of reading or mathematics assessments (for example, STAR Reading, STAR Math)
- Students scoring below peers on grade-level common formative assessments
- Students scoring below grade level on curriculum-based measures (CBMS; for example, fluency CBMs, comprehension CBMs)
- Multilingual students scoring below expected levels in listening, speaking, reading, and writing on assessments such as the ACCESS

Social-Emotional Data Sources

- Students scoring in the "high risk" range on a social-emotional screener such as the Student Risk Screening Scale-Internalizing and Externalizing Overview (SRSS)
- Students with significant personal challenges such as those experiencing homelessness or those in foster care

College and Career Readiness

- College readiness assessments—Students not on track for meeting college readiness benchmarks on ACT, SAT, and so on
- Career readiness assessments—Students not on track for passing end-of-course assessments, ASVAB, ACT Workkeys, Pre-PAC, industry-based credentials, and so on
- Grades and course completion—Students with no well-defined pathway, failing one or more pathway courses or insufficient credits for graduation
- Measures of employability skills—Students with ratings below expected levels on surveys or rubric-based assessments

Source: Allensworth & Easton, 2007; Allensworth et al., 2014; Bailey et al., 2020; Balfanz, 2009; Bresina, Baker, Donegan, & Whaley, 2018; Center on Multi-Tiered System of Supports, n.d.b, 2025a, 2025b, 2025d; Center on Behavioral Interventions and Supports, n.d.a, 2024; DuFour et al., 2024; Faria et al., 2017; Flannery et al., 2018; Gersten et al., 2009; Hougen, 2015; Hughes & Petscher, 2016; IRIS Center, n.d.; Kamil et al., 2008; Marken et al., 2020; Marzano & Pickering, 2005; McIntosh & Goodman, 2016; MTSS Center American Institutes for Research, 2016; Muoneke & Shankland, 2009; National Association of School Psychologists, 2016; National Center on Intensive Intervention, n.d.a; National High School Center, National Center on Response to Intervention, & Center on Instruction, 2010; Pyle & Vaughn, 2012; Scala et al., 2023a, 2023b; Smith et al., 2016; Therriault et al., 2017/2023; Vaughn & Fletcher, 2010.

Figure 1.5: Essential components of MTSS through a secondary lens. continued ▶

Formal data collection used to:

- Assess student progress.
- Examine the effectiveness of an intervention.
- Determine adaptations needed in the intervention.

Secondary-level progress monitoring may not need to be administered as frequently as at the elementary level.

EXAMPLES IN PRACTICE

How could this look in a middle or high school?

The team will regularly review data sources such as:

Early Warning Indicators (as part of an EWIMS)

- Attendance—Changes in attendance since the intervention was implemented
- Behavior—Changes in behavior since the intervention was implemented
- Course performance—Changes in grades since the intervention was implemented

Academic Data Sources

- Performance on grade-level common formative assessments
- Curriculum-based measures (for example, fluency CBMs, comprehension CBMs)
- Performance on assessments built into a structured intervention program, like Read 180

Social-Emotional Data Sources

- Direct behavior ratings (formalized monitoring of a targeted behavior)
- Conversations with the student and the student's family to collect anecdotal data on the effectiveness of the intervention
- Conversations with teachers to collect anecdotal data on the effectiveness of the intervention

College and Career Readiness

- Formative or shortened assessment measures of college or career readiness

A structured process of analyzing data to:

- Evaluate the overall effectiveness of Tier 1 (core instruction).
- Identify students who need additional support.
- Assess a student's progress and responsiveness to an intervention.
- Guide adaptations to be made to an intervention.

EXAMPLES IN PRACTICE

How could this look in a middle or high school?

The school develops a structured process, including:

- A data system used to easily track and review early warning indicators along with other data (for example, college and career readiness data)
- A teaming plan that clarifies the purpose, membership, expected frequency of meeting, and tier level of focus for each team
- Teams with assigned roles in which different people are responsible for scheduling team meetings, compiling relevant data, typing up notes, keeping time, and so on
- Time built into the school day to allow for teaming
- A clear method for analyzing and interpreting data and planning tiered supports based on data

MULTI-LEVEL PREVENTION SYSTEM

Tier 1 Schoolwide Interventions

- Alignment with state standards
- High-quality, culturally responsive, evidence-based, and differentiated curriculum and instruction designed to meet the needs of all students
- Vertical and horizontal curriculum alignment
- Effective teaching practices that promote opportunities to respond and student engagement
- Expected student behaviors are taught, prompted, and reinforced

Tier 2 Group Interventions

- Targeting approximately 10–15 percent of the student population
- Evidence-based intervention aligned with core curriculum
- Increased opportunities to generalize skills

Tier 3 Intensive Interventions

- Targeting approximately 3-5 percent of the student population
- Evidence-based intervention that is intensified and individualized based on student needs
- Goals that are set and monitored and adjustments made based on data

Secondary Considerations

- The focus of MTSS shifts to treatment (teaching needed skills) rather than prevention or identification.
- Due to the long history of data, it may be appropriate to move secondary students directly to a particular level of tiered support rather than progressively moving them through each tier.
- Intervention may need to continue for longer periods of time.

EXAMPLES IN PRACTICE

How could this look in a middle or high school?

Tier 1 Schoolwide Interventions

- The school develops a student-created video to clarify schoolwide expectations such as being on time to class or how to go through lunch lines.
- A teacher leads a classroom circle at the beginning of the school year to collaboratively define classroom expectations and identify methods for communicating with students when they are not meeting these expectations.
- A teacher creates groups of students within the classroom to provide just-in-time interventions based on formative assessment data and departmental or collaborative teacher team input.
- The school integrates ongoing college and career activities to prepare and coach students and their families through the postsecondary transition.
- The leadership team uses fifteen minutes of each faculty meeting to share schoolwide data and briefly brainstorm strategies for improvement.

Tier 2 Group Interventions

- The school builds time into the master schedule to allow identified students to participate in high-impact tutoring sessions. Teachers collaborate with tutors by sharing the upcoming content and the specific needs of these students to connect the tutoring to core instruction.
- A teacher works with the MTSS team to utilize the Class Pass intervention with a student in their class to reduce disruptive behavior.
- The MTSS team identifies a small group of students who barely missed the cut score for participating in dual credit but demonstrate motivation and strong grades in their courses. These students are allowed to participate in select dual-credit opportunities and are monitored closely by a staff member, providing check-ins and additional support (for example, tips in organization and planning) as needed.

Tier 3 Intensive, Individualized Interventions

- A student with significant literacy needs is reviewed by a Tier 3 team to develop a plan. The plan includes a literacy intervention period with a specially trained teacher utilizing evidence-based literacy strategies in addition to scaffolding to support their literacy needs in core classes.
- A student with significant behavior challenges meets with a Tier 3 team to develop a comprehensive behavior contract considering what is driving the student's behavior (for example, peer attention). The school includes the student's family and outside therapist in planning and requests for the therapist to support the student's social skills. The behavior contract includes reinforcements such as setting a time each Friday when the student can choose a peer to join them to be excused from class and assist the library media specialist.
- An advocate is assigned to a student to meet with them and their family to establish goals for completing school and determine postsecondary plans. The advocate identifies barriers and assists the student in accessing needed support (for example, offering transportation options, providing an alarm clock, obtaining a computer to take home for homework).

LEARNING OBJECTIVES

- Review the power of scaffolding to ensure Tier 1 core instruction is accessible to all students.
- Explore the essential components of three Tier 2 academic group interventions for secondary students.
- Consider methods for intensifying academic interventions for secondary students.

"I graduate next year. I gotta learn to read!" These words, spoken to me by a six-foot-two, seventeen-year-old high school student, will haunt me forever. In secondary schools, we often feel overwhelmed by pressures for all students to earn credits, score well on high-stakes testing, and complete career pathways. These things are important! Yet we can't lose sight of the accumulated, foundational academic struggles that so many students experience and the impact that these will forever have on their beliefs in themselves and their future opportunities to live and function independently in society.

This chapter explores trends in middle and high school students' academic skills, along with best practices for scaffolding Tier 1 core instruction, to help struggling students access rigorous academic standards. I provide summaries of three Tier 2 academic interventions for secondary students and strategies for intensifying interventions for students who need support at a Tier 3 level.

The Academic Needs of Secondary Students

Secondary educators are under immense pressure to effectively teach, monitor, and support all learners toward the goal of college and career readiness. Standards are rigorous, and the target is high. However, teachers often find themselves in a predicament, having to make difficult decisions about their instruction because many of the students sitting before them have not mastered previous years' content or even foundational skills such as reading, writing, and basic mathematics.

The 2024 National Assessment of Educational Progress (NAEP) in reading comprehension found that only 30 percent of eighth graders in the United States performed at or above proficiency in literacy, which is lower than the pre-pandemic scores of 2019 for this same age group (NAEP, n.d.d). Let's imagine how this would play out in an average middle school classroom of twenty-five students—approximately seventeen of the twenty-five students would struggle with reading, and only eight of the twenty-five students would perform at or above a proficient level (see figure 2.1, page 32).

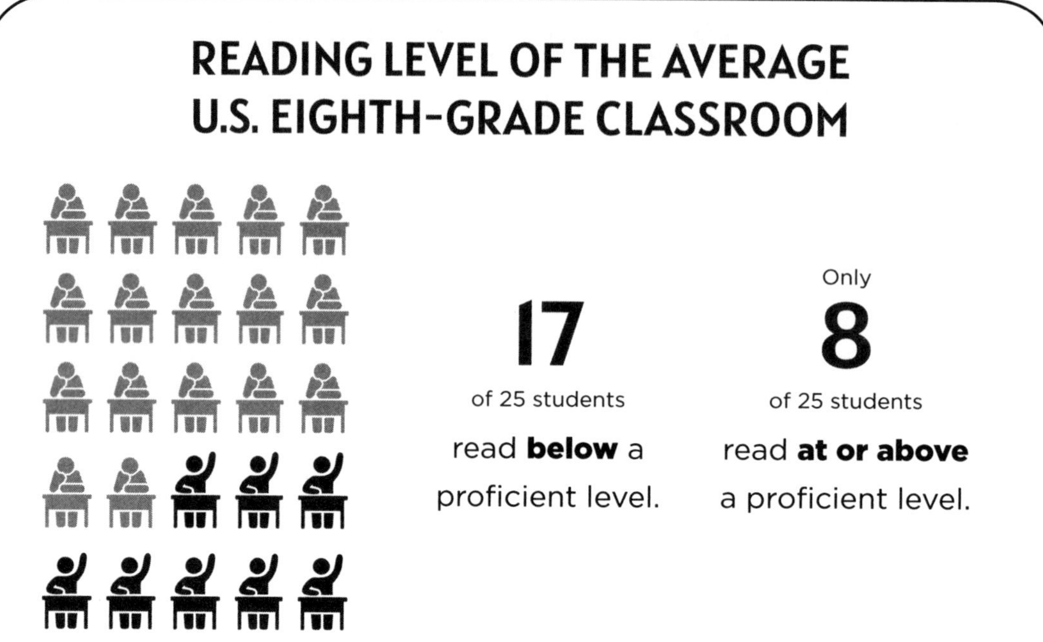

Source: NAEP, n.d.d.

Figure 2.1: Reading level of the average U.S. eighth-grade classroom.

Proficiency in literacy impacts all areas of a school, causing ripple effects in student engagement, course completion, college and career readiness, and even graduation. Numerous hardships await adolescents who struggle with reading. Years of frustration can lead to feelings of inadequacy and a belief that they cannot succeed academically, and students with reading difficulties recognize the lifelong significance of these challenges (Moats, 2014; National Research Council, 1998; Novosel, 2015). Secondary educators are presented with the task of supporting these students' reading skill development, as well as the incredibly difficult job of adjusting their content instruction so students with reading challenges can access grade-level standards.

These same trends are evident in mathematics. The 2024 NAEP mathematics assessment indicates that only 28 percent of eighth graders performed at or above proficiency (NAEP, n.d.c), which is lower than the pre-pandemic scores from 2019. This suggests that in the average secondary mathematics classroom, eighteen of the twenty-five students would function below a proficient level in mathematics, and only seven of the twenty-five students would perform at or above proficiency (see figure 2.2).

According to the 2024 national graduating class profile report from ACT, students' average composite scores dropped (from 19.5 in 2022–2023 to 19.4 in 2023–2024),

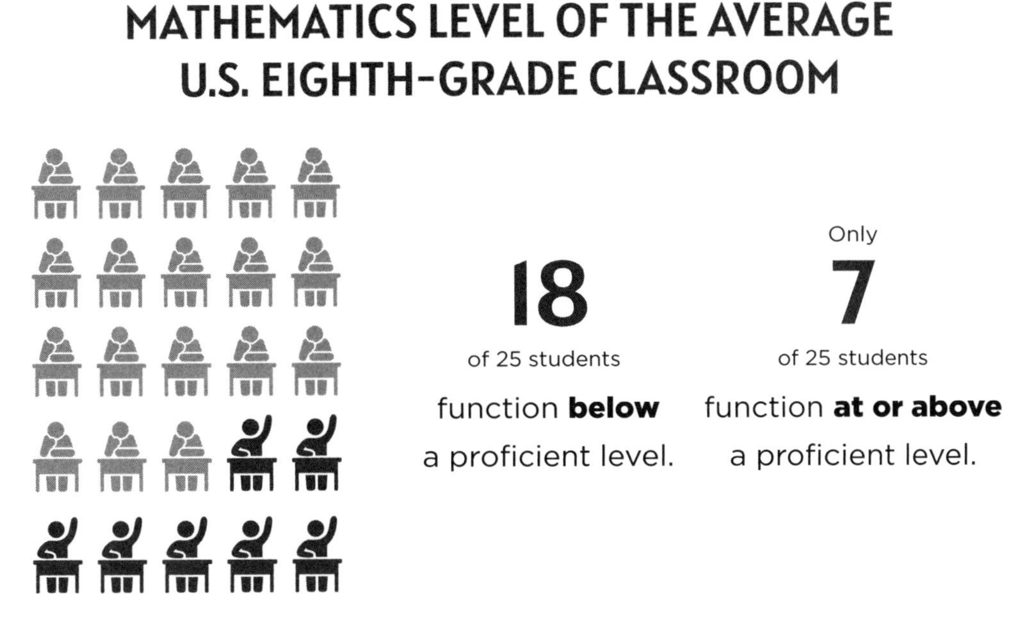

Source: NAEP, n.d.d.

Figure 2.2: Mathematics level of the average U.S. eighth-grade classroom.

as did the percentage of students meeting three or four benchmarks (from 31 percent in 2022–2023 to 30 percent in 2023–2024; ACT, 2024). These changes may feel insignificant, yet they are part of larger trends in which average composite scores and percentages of students have continuously been dropping (from an average composite score of 20.6 in 2019–2020 and 37 percent of students meeting three or four benchmarks in 2019–2020).

These numbers are alarming, but the data trends are exacerbated for students living in poverty, students with disabilities, students of color, and multilingual students. Each of these groups performs significantly below their peers academically (Burchinal et al., 2011; NAEP, n.d.c, n.d.d; National Center for Education Statistics, 2025; Paschall, Gershoff, & Kuhfeld, 2018; Shores, Kim, & Still, 2020; Skiba et al., 2011). This is a widespread and enduring issue. Culturally responsive practices must be foundational in all we do. It is outside the scope of this book to fully explore this issue, but I encourage schools to disaggregate data by student subgroups (students who are experiencing housing insecurity or living in poverty, students of different races and ethnicities, multilingual learners, and so on) to reflect on their practices and seek professional learning that addresses identified needs.

As discussed in the MTSS Through a Secondary Lens section in chapter 1 (page 12), there could be many drivers of the high rates of students needing additional academic support across the United States. What makes these issues even more complex is that students who struggle academically may also demonstrate challenging behavior in class, whether it's due to frustration, embarrassment, or efforts to avoid academic tasks. Conversely, students who struggle with behavioral or social-emotional skills early on may develop academic weaknesses, often related to being removed from class and missing instruction or having difficulty maintaining attention to tasks for various reasons (for example, ADHD or trauma exposure). By the time students are in middle and high school, these overlapping challenges can make learning feel overwhelming to the students and insurmountable to the teacher (see figure 2.3).

Figure 2.3: Overlapping challenges faced by secondary students and teachers.

With such variation in the skills of secondary learners, a classroom teacher is left in a very difficult position. The pressure is on to ensure all students reach college and career readiness, yet many teachers are unsure how best to meet the existing demands of the diverse needs of their students.

Tier 1 Instruction and Scaffolding

Here's the good news: With proper support, students struggling in literacy and mathematics can access high-level learning (Baker et al., 2014; CAST, 2024; DuFour et al., 2024; Fisher & Frey, 2014; Mattos et al., 2025; Regional Educational Laboratory Southeast at Florida State University, n.d.a)! Let's discuss how to make this happen.

As educators, we set the stage for effective instruction by developing a rich understanding of the state standards and high-quality instructional materials in place. With this foundation, Universal Design for Learning offers guidance for giving all students access to rigorous instruction based on the fact that learners are highly variable. Universal Design for Learning acknowledges that, as educators, we must design multiple means of engagement, representation, action, and expression in the classroom, regardless of our content (CAST, 2024). When we approach instructional design with an intentional focus on removing barriers to learning, students with wide-ranging skills and abilities can reach high levels. I encourage you to explore the Universal Design for Learning framework more deeply. For the purposes of this book, I will focus on the concept of scaffolding, which is part of this framework.

With proper support, students struggling in literacy and mathematics can access high-level learning.

Imagine a very tall building that all students need to climb. Some will take off and reach the top without us. Many will need proper supports to be successful, and a few will need significantly more scaffolding. But with that, they can reach incredible heights!

When you work in schools, you quickly get a sense of the culture of a building. Some schools operate with very high *expectations*, having celebrations for high test scores, recognition of students based on academics, and clear standards for ensuring rigorous instruction. However, these schools may not provide the high *supports* necessary for some students to reach these levels. By contrast, some schools provide excellent supports, such as high-quality tutoring, explicit embedded vocabulary instruction, and homework and organizational support. Yet they may unintentionally lower expectations for students, which can ultimately do its own damage. Our job as educators is to lean on the most effective pedagogical strategies and keep the building tall—keep expectations high but also ensure supports are in place for those who need them.

High expectations with high supports! Figure 2.4 (page 36) provides a visual introduction to the power of scaffolding.

Imagine going to a beginners' class at the gym and hearing the instructor say, "Today, everyone will be bench-pressing two hundred pounds." I don't know about you, but this would terrify me! Instead, I need to start by bench-pressing just the bar (ha!) and increase the weight a little at a time with support and guidance. An effective trainer considers the individual's unique functioning level and maximizes their growth by differentiating and seeking ways to accelerate their progress. Middle and high school athletic coaches do this every day. During practice, players perform different drills, depending on their unique strengths and needs. Effective coaches know this is key to optimum improvement.

Wheelchair ramps are a real-life example of scaffolding as part of Universal Design for Learning. Although wheelchair ramps are designed to give people with mobility challenges access to buildings, ask yourself who else might benefit from this adaptation, such as families with strollers, individuals who depend on walkers for stability and balance, and delivery drivers whose dollies are loaded with packages. Installing the wheelchair ramp prior to the need does not lower expectations for the person entering

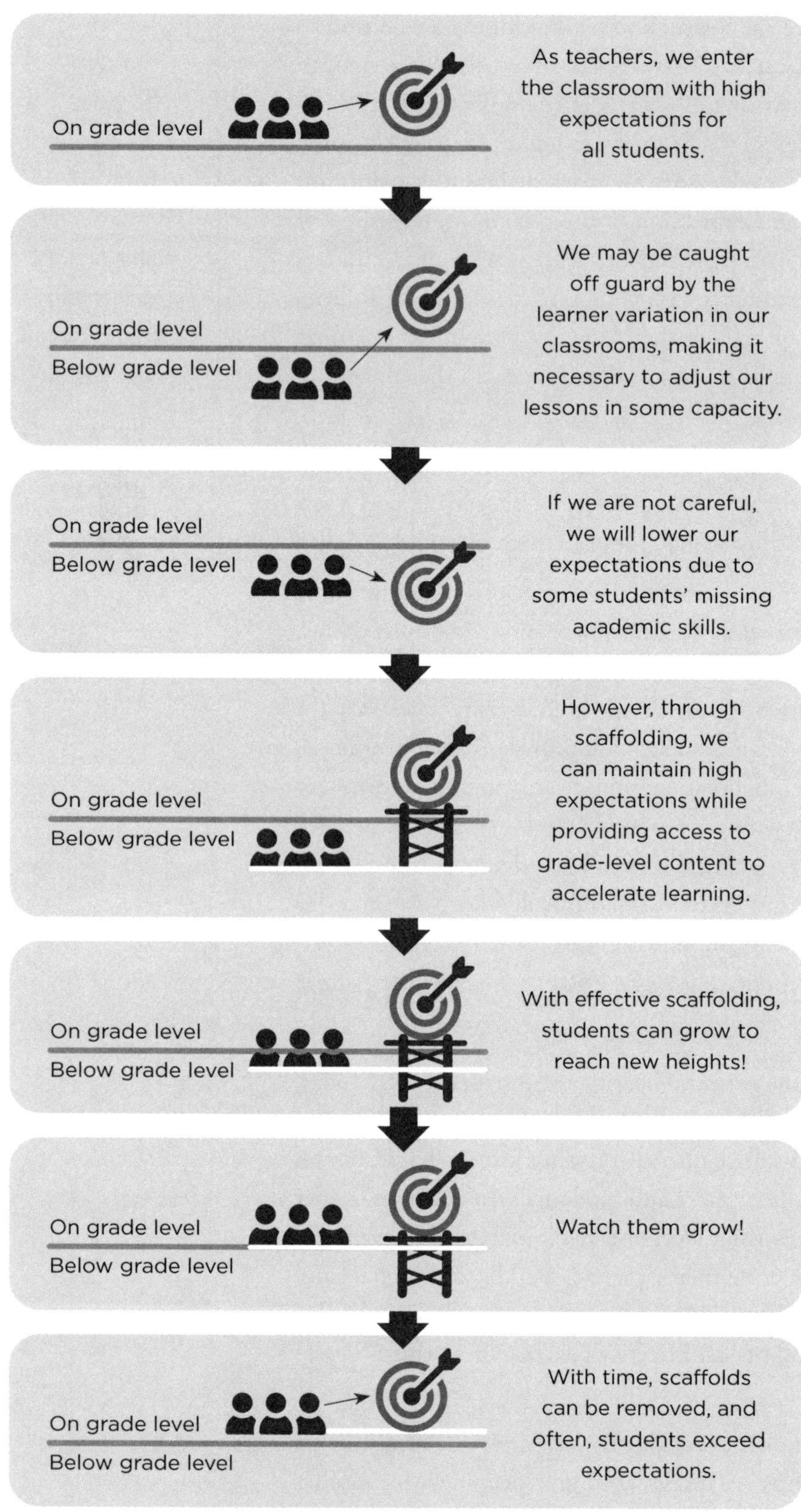

Figure 2.4: High expectations with high supports.

Source: Gaddie & Bryce, 2021. Adapted with permission.

the building. Instead, it provides access to numerous individuals in a nonjudgmental, proactive, purposeful way.

Instructional scaffolding is a process by which a teacher systematically builds new learning with consideration of students' existing knowledge, skills, and experiences (Baker et al., 2014; CAST, 2024; Darling-Hammond, Alexander, & Hernández, 2024; Regional Educational Laboratory Southeast at Florida State University, n.d.a; TNTP, 2021). Scaffolding can serve as a more accessible entry point to the broader Universal Design for Learning framework. It involves the use of structures to access rigorous learning goals. Activating prior knowledge, incorporating graphic organizers, preteaching vocabulary, and providing corrective feedback are all examples of scaffolds. Scaffolds are designed as temporary, just-in-time interventions. They are tools, like training wheels, for student learning. Scaffolding happens at *all levels* of a tiered system of supports.

Have you noticed the scaffolds embedded throughout this book? My learning target is to increase secondary educators' understanding of MTSS—a concept to which they may have had little exposure. Therefore, I have integrated tools that allow readers with varying experiences and preexisting knowledge to access this learning. The following are just a few of the scaffolds included throughout this book.

- **Visuals:** Simple visuals and graphics are scattered throughout the text to boost engagement and make complex topics easier to understand.
- **Preteaching of vocabulary:** People learn new vocabulary by connecting words to existing schemas—the mental frameworks they already possess. Figure 1.5 (page 27), which describes the essential components of MTSS through a secondary lens, is one example of vocabulary preteaching. This figure introduces language that may be new to you by connecting it to familiar concepts.
- **Graphic organizers:** I place graphic organizers throughout the book to provide you with visual structures to connect content in a meaningful way. Graphic organizers help you see relationships and patterns that exist between concepts.
- **Models:** Throughout the book, I summarize specific interventions in a snapshot format that lists key considerations, and I share sample fidelity and progress-monitoring forms. These tips and documents model what the approaches could look like in the secondary context. If I summarized an intervention with an abstract narrative only, you would have to imagine what it would look like, and the idea you developed in your mind may or may not be accurate.
- **Reflection opportunities:** You need time to process new information. The pause points provided throughout this text call your attention to intentionally chunked segments of content. They slow you down so you can check yourself and solidify a connection between what you already know and new information.

Challenges to Scaffolding for All Students

Is it OK for me to make these adjustments for any student?

You may be wondering, "Is it OK for me to make these adjustments for any student?" Some educators may think that it is inappropriate or even unethical to provide scaffolds or utilize Universal Design for Learning techniques for general education students who do not have an Individualized Education Program (IEP), a multilingual learner plan, or a 504 plan. This is a mistaken belief! Instead, it is critical to acknowledge that students vary greatly, and the strategic use of instructional tools ensures *all students* can have access to and engage in critical, rigorous learning opportunities (CAST, 2024).

Consider this: In education, the following statements are *all true.*

- Specific modifications and accommodations listed on a student's IEP, 504 plan, or multilingual learner plan are legally required to be implemented

(Americans With Disabilities Act, 1990; Civil Rights Act, 1964; Every Student Succeeds Act, 2015; Individuals With Disabilities Education Act, 1997; No Child Left Behind Act, 2001; Section 504 of the Rehabilitation Act, 1973).

- Modifications and accommodations for high-stakes testing (for example, state accountability systems or formal college readiness exams such as the SAT and ACT) are typically not allowed for students without an IEP, 504 plan, or multilingual learner plan (ACT, n.d.a, n.d.b; Americans With Disabilities Act, 1990; Civil Rights Act, 1964; College Board, n.d.; Every Student Succeeds Act, 2015; Individuals With Disabilities Education Act, 1997; No Child Left Behind Act, 2001; Section 504 of the Rehabilitation Act, 1973).
- It is appropriate for educators and their collaborative teams to make instructional decisions about specific classroom practices for all students.

These statements may all seem obvious, but sometimes, educators operate under the belief that they cannot change or adapt their instructional practices for students without an IEP, 504 plan, or multilingual learner plan. In fact, in some circumstances, educators must make difficult decisions about which essential standards to prioritize or select, or how to teach or assess content (DuFour et al., 2024; Mattos et al., 2025; Student Achievement Partners, 2021).

For example, a formative assessment analysis within your Tier 2 team may indicate that instructional adjustments are necessary during a particularly challenging unit for which numerous students lack the prerequisite skills. Or you may have a tough unit that you still need to cover during the last month of school. When you are down to the last few weeks of the school year, the school's or district's pacing guide or curriculum map may indicate that a lot more content needs to be taught than time will allow. Therefore, you may have to prioritize standards and adjust your plans for the remaining instruction. Such situations are undeniable parts of teaching.

Adjusting instruction and integrating scaffolds are what we do as effective teachers. Ideally, we determine instructional adjustments as part of a collaborative teacher team to ensure educators rely on colleagues' expertise and existing student data to guide these decisions. The goal of scaffolding is to maintain high expectations while also providing the necessary temporary supports to *remove barriers* to learning. For example, some students in a ninth-grade biology class will likely read significantly below grade level. Without literacy supports, these students will be severely limited in learning the content. With literacy supports such as vocabulary preteaching, graphic organizers, guidance for close reading of stretch text, increased wait time, or videos or technology supports, these students will have the opportunity to access high-level content (Baker et al., 2014; Fisher & Frey, 2014; Johnson et al., 2009; The Reading League, 2024; Swanson & Deshler, 2003). This could even ignite students' passion for the content!

Even though students without an IEP, 504 plan, or multilingual learner plan do not typically receive accommodations or modifications on high-stakes standardized assessments, there are times when these students would benefit from deliberate lesson scaffolding throughout the school year. Scaffolding is not against the rules or unethical; it is best practice.

Scaffolding Models and Strategies

With the understanding that scaffolding is a necessary part of instruction, let's explore *how* to implement it. Secondary educators often are unsure exactly what scaffolding entails. Let's unpack how to scaffold one specific literacy component: vocabulary instruction. No matter the content area, grade level, or student achievement level, all students benefit from direct vocabulary instruction (Archer, 2015; Baker et al., 2014; Fisher & Frey, 2014; Hougen, 2015; Marzano, 2004). This involves gradually shaping understanding of a new word through multiple exposures and gradual release of responsibility. Vocabulary instruction becomes even more powerful when teachers consistently use and model a vocabulary strategy with students, practice it, and integrate this same scaffold into multiple units to ensure students understand the strategy and can use it independently.

Before I share a few specific evidence-based vocabulary strategies, let's consider some commonly used non-examples. Having students copy vocabulary from a dictionary at the beginning of a unit, presenting vocabulary in isolation, and focusing on rote memorization do not lead to meaningful retention. These passive learning activities do not engage the learner or ultimately help them use the word in their own writing or speaking.

Figure 2.5 (page 40) summarizes four powerful scaffolding strategies for explicitly teaching vocabulary.

The needs are great, but the opportunities are endless. Maintaining high expectations for students will be more successful when teachers are empowered to provide the support students need to make them attainable. To this end, in the next section, I explore three structured Tier 2 academic interventions to strengthen your school's tiered system of supports.

MORPHOLOGY INSTRUCTION

Morphology instruction involves studying the smallest units of language that have meaning (morphemes). You can scaffold content instruction by engaging students in the study of roots, prefixes, and suffixes of key vocabulary. This allows students' vocabulary to grow exponentially as they gain understanding of numerous word families.

This is an excellent opportunity to integrate *cognates* (words that share an origin and a similar sound, such as *microscopio* in Spanish and *microscope* in English) for multilingual students.

CONCEPT MAPS

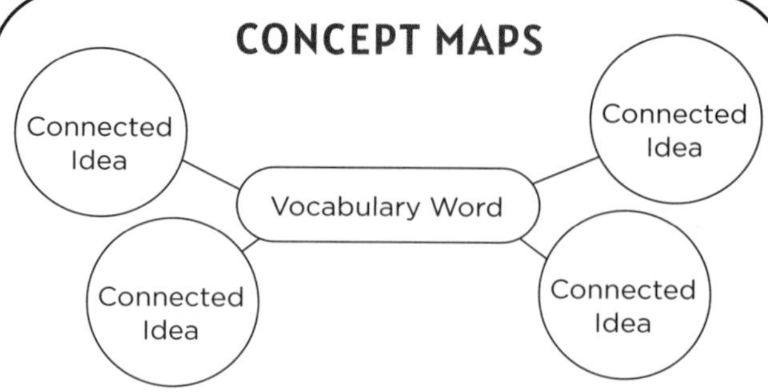

Concept maps or *semantic maps* activate prior knowledge by connecting new vocabulary words to other words that students know. This activation may include using graphic organizers or visual or verbal word associations or having students brainstorm concrete examples and non-examples from relevant text. You could create vocabulary maps before an activity and add to them throughout the lesson to solidify learning.

These tools help make abstract concepts more understandable and create deeper learning of the concepts, especially when they are student driven.

VOCABULARY FRAMES

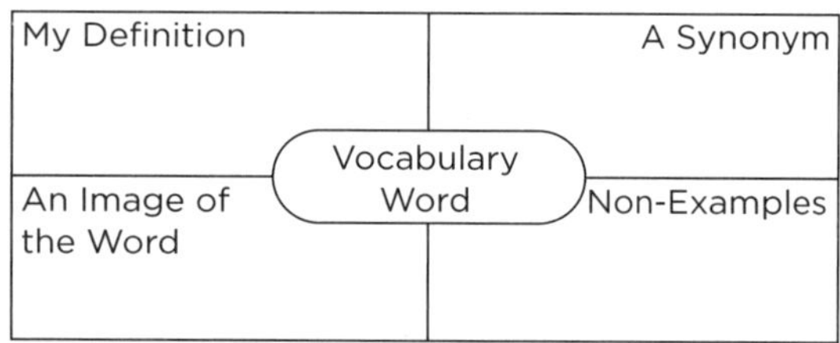

Vocabulary frames are a strategy for structuring the learning of a new word. The key vocabulary word typically appears in the center of the frame or index card. In each corner, students may record a definition in their own words, a nonlinguistic representation such as a picture or drawing of the word, examples and non-examples of the word, a synonym or antonym of the word, a sentence that includes the word, and so on.

SENTENCE STARTERS

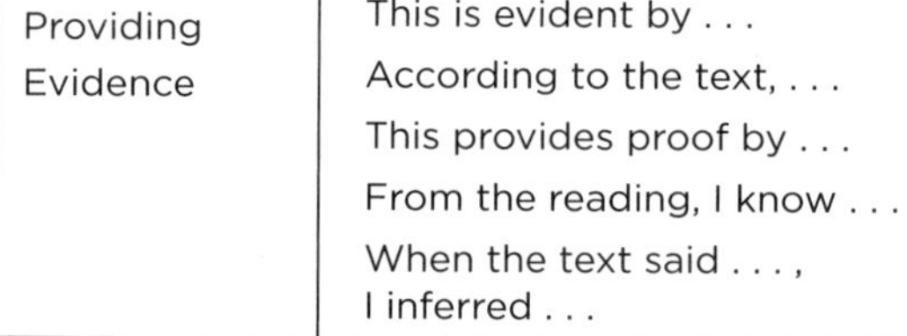

Providing Evidence	This is evident by . . . According to the text, . . . This provides proof by . . . From the reading, I know . . . When the text said . . . , I inferred . . .

Sentence starters or *sentence frames* can help students communicate with others to build their understanding of new vocabulary. This approach works best when it is explicitly taught and when teachers incorporate disciplinary language and structure. For example, when focusing on activating prior knowledge, sentence starters could include "This reminds me of . . ." or "This makes me think of . . ." If focusing on comparing and contrasting, a sentence starter could include "This term means . . . , but it doesn't mean . . ."

To emphasize the importance of reflecting on learning, a sentence starter might include "The big idea of this concept is . . ." Sites such as ColorinColorado.org offer excellent examples and guidance on this tool.

Figure 2.5: Four scaffolding strategies for explicitly teaching vocabulary.

LONG-TERM GOAL FOR TIER I: Our school will have a functioning MTSS team that analyzes schoolwide academic data at least quarterly to determine how best to structure classes, pathways, teams, departments, and intervention and extension classes. Our team will determine professional learning needs and maintain ongoing communication with school staff to ensure effective instructional practices are in place.

TIER I QUICK-START STEPS

1. Solidify a teaming model and clarify which team is responsible for reviewing Tier 1 schoolwide data and ensuring rigorous, supportive instruction is in place for students in your school (for example, instruction is engaging, tied to the standards, and effectively scaffolded).
2. As a team, discuss the academic goals for your school or district and how these intersect with other mission statements, goals, or initiatives. Determine methods for seeking input from the larger faculty, families, students, and the community. Brainstorm how best to share these proposed goals with these stakeholders and establish the vision to guide your work.
3. As a team, work through the MTSS fidelity rubric (Center on Multi-Tiered System of Supports, 2025b) or some other such validated self-assessment to prioritize action steps for Tier 1 academic supports.
4. Determine what data the MTSS team will review (for example, college-and-career-readiness data, quarterly or midterm grades or failure reports, and rates of course completion). Utilize a data-based decision-making process to ensure the students' academic needs are systematically supported.
5. Set MTSS team meetings for the school year and determine how best to assign roles and organize data, agendas, and notes. Identify methods for monitoring implementation.

NOTES

Tier 2 Academic Group Interventions

At the secondary level, the purpose of Tier 2 shifts to both assisting students who need additional support in core instruction and meeting the long-term goals of graduation and positive postsecondary outcomes (Daye, 2019; Fuchs et al., 2010; Stoiber & Gettinger, 2016). This can make it difficult to determine what to prioritize for academic intervention. As described in chapter 1, tackling these competing priorities is a common barrier to secondary MTSS implementation. Your school may be unsure whether to build academic interventions that will address foundational weaknesses in literacy or mathematics, to provide real-time support for core classes, or to boost students' executive functioning skills like organization and information processing.

Analyzing schoolwide data and considering your school's available resources will guide your MTSS team to identify the best focus for your unique student population. Ask yourselves, "What is the underlying cause of our students' academic challenges—ineffective study skills, the need for more explicit instruction on grade-level concepts, or missing foundational skills?" Multiple data sources, including formative and summative assessments, standardized schoolwide assessments, college-and-career-readiness assessments, failure reports and the associated need for credit recovery, and teacher observations, can help teams determine the areas to prioritize (Bailey et al., 2020). You can then use these same assessments to monitor the effectiveness of interventions and determine when you can fade support or a student can exit an intervention.

I have a note of caution about brainstorming your school's Tier 2 plan: I often see teams of skilled teachers spend a significant amount of time, energy, and resources on creating a strong student intervention plan for their maybe thirty- to forty-five-minute block of intervention time. Effective intervention matters, but too often, we overlook the other six and a half hours of a student's day! Does the student receive support in their classes so they can read the material? Is instruction scaffolded so they can access rigorous grade-level learning across content and elective classes? Intervention is strongest when you tie it to core instruction by planning collaboratively, aligning intervention with core materials, and increasing students' preparedness (Sarlo, 2013; Smith et al., 2016; TNTP, 2024a). Communication between intervention and core teachers empowers core teachers to utilize needed scaffolds within the classroom. Plus, this allows students to see that the strategies they learn during an intervention block can be applied in multiple settings. These are important discussions to have during the Tier 2 planning process.

This section provides succinct summaries of the research-based core components of secondary academic interventions. Secondary educators and leaders often have little time and opportunity to seek out and read all the most up-to-date research on best practices in tiered supports. Plus, studies show that when humans have too many options, they may struggle to make a selection (Heath & Heath, 2010; Schwartz, 2009). Therefore, this chapter simplifies this experience by outlining the essential components of three evidence-based secondary interventions as starting points. Though these intervention summaries are written in brief lists, the bullet points feature important tips for implementation identified through research. *These tips are not to be overlooked as insignificant or optional.*

The specific tools, programs, and strategies listed in this chapter may take place in varying settings, with varying staff, and during varying times, given your circumstances. Scheduling will play a role in the effectiveness of implementation. Seek out tips from educators who have already explored and identified unique scheduling models to implement tiered supports in their middle or high school (Durrance, 2023, 2025; Hanover Research, 2014; Massachusetts Department of Elementary and Secondary Education, Rodriguez Educational Consulting Agency, & Novak Educational Consulting, 2020; National Center on Response to Intervention, 2011; Weingarten, Bailey, & Peterson, 2019). Each school and district must reflect on its particular student population, along with available school resources, to determine the best fit for its context.

I selected the following three academics-focused interventions because they address different student needs and are designed to get Tier 2 group interventions up and running in your school.

1. High-impact tutoring
2. Strategy instruction
3. Literacy or mathematics intervention period

High-Impact Tutoring

Promising research demonstrates the power of integrating high-impact tutoring models into a school's MTSS (Allensworth & Schwartz, 2020; Ander, Guryan, & Ludwig, 2016; Baker et al., 2014; Cook, Dodge, et al., 2014; Dobbie & Fryer, 2011; Fryer, 2016; Kraft, 2013; National Student Support Accelerator, 2023; Nickow, Oreopoulos, & Quan, 2024; Robinson, Kraft, Loeb, & Schueler, 2024). When high-impact tutoring is built into the larger MTSS framework, there is a clear delivery structure, interventions have more instructional coherence, and staffing and professional learning are streamlined (National Student Support Accelerator, 2023). Research on the effectiveness of tutoring is conflicting, but this appears to be due to the wide range of implementation variables involved (Carbonari et al., 2024; Kraft, 2013; Nickow et al., 2024).

Here lies the key: Schools must be intentional to ensure that their tutoring model follows what they know as best practices of high-impact tutoring. Plus, schools must consider potential barriers to successful implementation, such as staffing shortages, poor tutor quality, student absenteeism, lack of space and time for tutoring, tutoring costs, outdated data systems, and limited capacity of school or district leadership (Carbonari et al., 2024; Makori, Burch, & Loeb, 2024; Robinson et al., 2024), to strategically plan and execute their model. We are all too familiar with barriers that affect much of the work we do in schools. Yet, we know there are work-arounds and solutions for when an initiative is prioritized. Figure 2.6 (page 44) outlines the essential components of high-impact tutoring.

ESSENTIAL COMPONENTS OF HIGH-IMPACT TUTORING

GOAL OF THE INTERVENTION

To accelerate student learning and reduce course failures with supplemental, high-quality instruction tied to core instruction

TARGET STUDENT GROUP

Identify students based on school-specific academic criteria (for example, students who have not fully mastered certain standards or units; students earning low grades and needing support on grade-level concepts; students with missing assignments; students who score below the 30th percentile on a district, state, or standardized assessment; "bubble" students on the cusp of proficiency).

ESSENTIAL COMPONENTS

- ☐ Identify a high-impact tutoring coordinator and establish time during their workday for activities.
- ☐ Review data to identify students who would benefit from the intervention.
- ☐ Discuss the intervention with relevant stakeholders, including family, students, and teachers.
- ☐ Clarify the priorities for tutoring (for example, content areas, grade levels).
- ☐ Identify tutors.
- ☐ Select locations within the school with few distractions for tutoring to occur (for example, empty classroom, library, cafeteria during off times).
- ☐ Determine when the tutoring will take place.
  - Hosted during the school day (for example, during an advisory period, freshman seminar, junior or senior transition course, or as an elective course)
  - Provided at least three times per week
  - Lasts at least thirty minutes per session
  - Lasts at a minimum of ten weeks, but providing at least thirty hours during the school year for each targeted student is ideal
- ☐ Assign four or fewer students to each tutor.
  - Larger groups of students require the tutor to have a higher degree of skills to implement effectively.
- ☐ Provide high-quality instructional materials aligned with core instruction.
- ☐ Identify a method for data collection for each of the following.
  - **Fidelity of implementation:** Are the tutoring sessions occurring with expected frequency? Was the student present for each tutoring session? Does the tutor work to build rapport with the student? Do the core teacher and tutor have opportunities to communicate to align instruction?
  - **Evidence of student progress:** Course performance data (for example, grades, missing assignments), formative and summative assessments, classroom observations, anecdotal teacher reports, interviews with students and families
- ☐ Explicitly teach appropriate steps for high-impact tutoring.
  - **For the student:** Identify the specific time of day and location for attending tutoring sessions and clarify expectations for engagement.

Figure 2.6: Essential components of high-impact tutoring.

- **For core teachers:** Identify students to participate in tutoring sessions, when sessions will occur to prevent students from missing critical instruction and assignments, and how to communicate with the tutor to ensure there is alignment with core instruction.
- **For the tutor:** Identify when and where tutoring sessions will occur, how a typical session should function, what materials to use, how and when to communicate with core teachers, expectations for relationship building, and how to request assistance from the coordinator.

☐ Develop a plan for fading the intervention.

- How often will the data be reviewed and by whom?
- What are the criteria to exit a student from the high-impact tutoring intervention?

TIPS FOR IMPLEMENTATION

☐ Designate one coordinator who assigns tutors to teachers and students, provides instructional coaching and guidance to tutors as needed, and champions the tutoring initiative within the school.

☐ Provide high-impact tutoring during the school day to avoid a student's work or home responsibilities or transportation barriers.

☐ Keep the focus of tutoring on students' courses, not remediation that is separate from their regular curriculum.

☐ Focus on students' individual strengths and needs.

☐ Ensure students receiving tutoring are not pulled from core classes.

☐ Partner with organizations, such as local university graduate programs, AmeriCorps, and former school district teachers, to fill the role of tutor. Tutoring is more likely to be high impact when utilizing individuals with training and skills in teaching and relationship-building as opposed to parents or volunteers.

☐ Maintain consistency in tutors as much as possible; avoid rotating or switching tutors.

☐ Provide opportunities for tutors to connect with core teachers.

☐ Prioritize relationships between tutors and students and their families.

☐ When tutoring is also made available to higher performing students, stigma around receiving tutoring can be reduced; though, this can be challenging due to the number of resources necessary for scaling up.

☐ Avoid "opt-in" tutoring programs that require a student to initiate support.

☐ Avoid minimally structured tutoring such as an open, drop-in tutoring space without materials or a clear plan or focus.

☐ An alternative model may include week-long "vacation academies" during the summer or holiday breaks in which intensive, targeted sessions are led by high-quality instructors assigned to small groups (ten or less) of students.

Source: Carbonari et al., 2024; Makori et al., 2024; National Student Support Accelerator, 2023; Nickow et al., 2024; Robinson et al., 2024; Schueler, 2020.

Let's imagine how high-impact tutoring could look in your school. Once the schoolwide MTSS team reviews available data, as described earlier in this chapter, and identifies high-impact tutoring as a needed Tier 2 intervention, move forward with the following steps.

1. **Select a coordinator:** This coordinator is responsible for overseeing the intervention, communicating with stakeholders (families, students, teachers, and tutors), and monitoring implementation.
2. **Select tutors:** High-impact tutoring works best when schools bring in tutors from partner organizations such as local university graduate programs or AmeriCorps, or identify retired school district teachers who might be interested in working part-time. Unlike parents or volunteers, these individuals arrive with training and skills in teaching and relationship building. This elevates the instruction that occurs during the intervention. Depending on the nature of the partnership, these services could be provided free to the school by the organization, or they may require payment for the tutors. Such costs could possibly be covered by Title I or Title III funding, school-improvement grants, or other school or district budgets.
3. **Determine when and where tutoring will take place:** Research confirms that tutoring is strongest when provided during the school day as opposed to before or after school (Makori et al., 2024; National Student Support Accelerator, 2023; Robinson et al., 2024). This limits the likelihood that a student's work or home responsibilities or transportation difficulties will prevent them from fully participating. Ensure the tutoring session takes place in an area with few distractions, such as in an empty classroom, a corner of the library, or the cafeteria during off times, as opposed to at a back table of the classroom while other instruction is taking place.
4. **Determine the duration of tutoring:** Tutoring is most impactful when it happens at least three times per week in sessions of at least thirty minutes and it lasts a minimum of ten weeks, but providing at least thirty hours of tutoring during a school year is ideal.
5. **Decide on the size of tutoring groups:** If possible, keep tutoring group sizes small (fewer than four students per tutor). This creates tutoring sessions that are student centered and impactful enough to justify this as a Tier 2 intervention. Most importantly, these tutoring sessions should not remove students from core instruction.

Considering all these recommendations, you can see how crucial it is to engage those responsible for building the master schedule from the beginning. Being intentional with logistic structures, such as the group size, days, and times allotted for sessions, is what makes interventions like high-impact tutoring possible.

Once high-impact tutoring is in place, people will quickly question and seek to clarify the priority for instruction and the instructional materials to use. Tutoring is most effective when it focuses on the course content a student is struggling with, not remedial skills that are separate from instruction in core classes (Robinson et al., 2024). This means you must find opportunities for tutors to connect with core teachers through a common planning time or structured conversations.

If a group of students have been identified as needing support in algebra, the tutor should partner with the algebra teacher to determine the specific content to prioritize and high-quality materials to use. As one student stated before he first started high-impact tutoring after barely passing the first quarter of Algebra 2, "I am better than this!" When this student received this structured intervention tied to core instruction, his algebra knowledge grew, and he went from failing to earning strong passing grades.

Because it is imperative to implement high-impact tutoring with fidelity, I have provided a form to monitor the critical features of the intervention. Figure 2.7 shows an example.

Date: *March 15*	Grade: *Ninth*	
Have tutors been selected by hiring retired teachers or partnering with organizations such as higher education institutions or other agencies?	(Yes) No	*Ms. Johnson is a retired teacher hired part-time for this role as the high-impact tutoring instructor.*
Is there a coordinator who matches tutors to students, communicates with stakeholders, and provides guidance to tutors as needed?	(Yes) No	*Mr. Spaulding coordinates high-impact tutoring during a protected time in seventh period.*
Was the tutor intentionally selected, and are they a good match for the student?	(Yes) No	*Ms. Johnson was selected for this role due to her experience teaching high school mathematics and her strengths in connecting with students. She communicates weekly with each student's family.*
Is there a plan in place to ensure the student consistently receives tutoring for an appropriate amount of time? For example: The tutoring is hosted during the school day, at least three times per week, for at least thirty minutes per session, and for a minimum of ten weeks or thirty hours during the school year.	(Yes) No	*High-impact tutoring sessions are scheduled three days a week during a thirty-minute flex period. Student progress is monitored closely to determine when students may be ready to exit this intervention.*
Is the student in a group of four or fewer students?	(Yes) No	*Ms. Johnson serves four students during this tutoring session.*

Figure 2.7: High-impact tutoring fidelity form example.

continued ▶

Does the student receive high-quality tutoring aligned with core instruction?	(Yes) No	*The focus of the current high-impact tutoring sessions is on Algebra I. Ms. Johnson utilizes materials matched with core instruction and provide concrete representations of challenging concepts.*
Do the teacher and tutor have opportunities to communicate and align instruction?	(Yes) No	*Ms. Johnson meets weekly with the mathematics teaching team to align tutoring with core instruction and communicate student progress.*

*Visit **go.SolutionTree.com/RTI** for a free blank reproducible version of this figure.*

Figure 2.8 shows one method for monitoring a student's progress.

Name: *Kyle M.*

Date:	*March 15*	*March 17*	*March 19*	*March 22*	*March 24*
Course performance notes (grades, formative and summative assessment data):	*After an error analysis, I provided explicit instruction to address Kyle's most common errors.*	*Kyle continued his exponent practice.*	*Kyle earned an 85 on his exponent test today.*		*Kyle shared his pre-test for unit 7 to identify content to focus on during tutoring sessions.*
Course performance notes (number of missing assignments):	*Kyle was missing one homework assignment on exponents. We discussed the importance of completing this assignment.*	*Kyle turned in his missing homework assignment.*			
Other notes:			*Called Kyle's mom and celebrated his test performance.*	*Kyle was absent today.*	

Figure 2.8: High-impact tutoring progress-monitoring form example.

*Visit **go.SolutionTree.com/RTI** for a free blank reproducible version of this figure.*

Strategy Instruction

Strategy instruction is another Tier 2 academic intervention option to implement in a middle or high school; it is an evidence-based model for explicitly teaching executive functioning skills (Deshler & Schumaker, 2006; Didion, Toste, Benz, & Shogren, 2021; Dignath & Veenman, 2021; Flores & Milton, 2020; Graham & Harris, 2005; IRIS Center, 2022a; Scruggs, Mastropieri, Berkeley, & Graetz, 2010; What Works Clearinghouse, 2017b). Your MTSS team may review student learning data and determine that knowing *how to learn* (also called *study skills* or *executive functioning skills*) is a bigger priority for students than supplemental, high-quality tutoring tied to core instruction. This suggests that strategy instruction could be the best intervention. However, before we delve into strategy instruction, let me clarify what I mean by executive functioning skills.

As adolescents transition into middle and high school, they experience increased pressure to operate with adult-level executive functioning (for example, time management, organization, memory, and information processing), and many have not yet mastered such skills. Secondary students are expected to navigate and independently manage high-level, wide-ranging content; challenging reading assignments; and instruction that includes complex vocabulary and concepts. You may find that some students appear not to be working hard or appear not to care about their assignments when the underlying cause may be related to their need to build executive functioning skills (Center on the Developing Child, 2014; Crone, 2009; IRIS Center, 2022a).

Students with strong executive functioning skills can process information, recall and retrieve information, manage their time and remain organized, study independently, monitor themselves, and generalize strategies across contexts. You will know a student has weaknesses in executive functioning if they demonstrate characteristics such as the following (IRIS Center, 2022a).

- They take inadequate or incomplete notes or copy everything the teacher says.
- They struggle to remember important information.
- They are often off task in class.
- They have difficulty keeping materials organized.
- They often forget or lose materials.
- They take more time than others to complete tasks.
- They use ineffective learning or studying strategies.
- They have difficulty transferring learning strategies to different situations.

You may be wondering, Are teachers able to *teach* executive functioning skills? Are middle and high school students *too old* to still build these skills? A rich body of research demonstrates that strategy instruction is one of the most effective approaches for supporting adolescents with executive functioning needs (Deshler & Schumaker, 2006; Didion et al., 2021; Dignath & Veenman, 2021; Flores & Milton, 2020; Graham & Harris, 2005; IRIS Center, 2022a; Scruggs et al., 2010; What Works Clearinghouse, 2017b). Plus, strategy instruction can also improve students' literacy and mathematics skills (Ennis, 2016; Ennis & Losinski, 2019; Flores & Milton, 2020; Graves, Flynn, & Ringstaff, 2021; Harris, Schumaker, & Deshler, 2011; Johnson et al., 2009; Lane et al., 2011; Losinski, Ennis, Sanders, & Wiseman, 2019; Schumaker & Deshler, 2009; Schumaker, Fisher, & Walsh, 2019; Swanson & Deshler, 2003; Therrien, Hughes, Kapelski, & Mokhtari, 2009).

Strategy instruction is a method, not a product, so let me unpack it a bit. This term may feel vague or unclear to some educators. What exactly does it mean? What would we be *teaching* during a strategy instruction lesson? Think of *strategy instruction* as an all-encompassing term for the *process of learning*. Rather than just focusing on the content, strategy instruction explicitly teaches how to understand, remember, and apply information. The specific topic for strategy instruction is determined based on the needs of the students.

For students who struggle with listening and note taking, strategy instruction might include explicitly teaching them how to capture key points of a lecture, sort through information, and determine how best to study from their notes. For students who struggle with writing, strategy instruction might include explicitly teaching a specific paragraph-writing strategy in which students organize their ideas, make a plan for writing, and then write various types of sentences to include in the paragraph. Strategy instruction in reading might include explicitly teaching the steps for paraphrasing while reading by having students read brief passages, identify the main points, and then rephrase the passages in their own words. Strategy instruction in mathematics might include explicit instruction in place value or problem solving.

Many times, this type of instruction includes the use of a mnemonic to prompt and guide students through several steps with lots of modeling, feedback, and practice. Teachers may develop their own lessons to explicitly teach strategies, but numerous curricular resources also exist to provide strategy instruction on a variety of topics. See Self-Regulated Strategy Development (https://thinksrsd.com) and Strategic Instruction Model (https://sim.ku.edu/sim-learning-strategies) for premade, evidence-based strategy instruction lessons.

Just as with other interventions, you must designate a specific time for implementation. Strategy instruction is most effective when it occurs at least three times per week, during twenty- to sixty-minute blocks of time, and in small groups of eight or fewer students. Some schools set this up as a junior or senior transition course, a freshman seminar, an elective, or a "skinny period" built into their larger block schedule. Strategy instruction can be taught by a variety of personnel based on each school's available resources. With proper training and support, teachers of any background and paraprofessionals can effectively teach strategy instruction (Keller, Bucholz, & Brady, 2007; Lushen, Kim, & Reid, 2012).

An instructional model that involves explicit instruction, practice, and feedback is critical to providing strategy instruction. Plus, teachers can level up this instruction by giving students opportunities to generalize and practice the same strategy on an ongoing basis, rather than teaching it once and then moving on. The method in which you deliver strategy instruction matters almost as much as the strategy being taught. Figure 2.9 documents the critical components of successful strategy instruction.

ESSENTIAL COMPONENTS OF STRATEGY INSTRUCTION

GOAL OF THE INTERVENTION

To accelerate student learning and increase executive functioning skills by providing explicit instruction in study skills or executive functioning strategies (for example, comprehension strategies and note taking) through an evidence-based model

TARGET STUDENT GROUP

Identify students based on school-specific academic criteria (for example, students earning low grades in class, students with missing assignments, and bubble students on the cusp of proficiency) and the current executive functioning skills of the selected students (for example, having difficulty remembering important information, taking incomplete or inadequate notes, and taking more time than others to complete tasks).

ESSENTIAL COMPONENTS

- ☐ Review data to identify students who would benefit from the intervention.
- ☐ Discuss the intervention with relevant stakeholders, including families, students, and teachers.
- ☐ Identify the prioritized strategies to teach (for example, essay writing, mathematics problem completion, goal setting, note taking, and test taking) and the associated resources.
- ☐ Select the teacher and location for this instruction.
- ☐ Determine when the strategy instruction will take place.
  - Three to five times a week.
  - Twenty- to sixty-minute sessions.
  - In small groups (preferably eight or fewer students).

Figure 2.9: Essential components of strategy instruction.

continued ▶

ESSENTIAL COMPONENTS OF STRATEGY INSTRUCTION

☐ Utilize a research-validated strategy instruction model for teaching.

- Provide explicit instruction. Teach the steps to the strategy and when, how, and why to use the strategy.
- Model the strategy. Illustrate step by step how to implement the strategy.
- Provide guided practice. Work with students to practice the strategy, giving them prompts and corrective feedback.
- Assign independent practice. Have students practice the strategy independently, and provide feedback.
- Encourage the use of executive functioning strategies such as goal setting and self-monitoring for understanding.
- Guide maintenance and generalization of the skill. Provide ongoing, varying assignments that give students the chance to implement the strategy in a new context.

☐ Determine a method for collecting data on each of the following.

- **Fidelity of implementation:** Is the strategy instruction occurring with expected frequency? Is the student present for each session? Is the teacher implementing the strategy instruction as designed? Is the student given opportunities to implement the strategy across content areas or classes?
- **Evidence of student progress:** This evidence includes formative assessment data on the student's use and generalization of the strategy, assessments tied to core instruction, course performance data (for example, grades and missing assignments), academic skill levels (for example, reading proficiency), classroom observations, interviews with students and family members, and anecdotal teacher input.

☐ Explicitly teach appropriate steps for strategy instruction.

- **For the student:** Identify the specific time of day and location for attending strategy instruction sessions and clarify expectations for engagement.
- **For the teacher:** Identify the targeted area for strategy instruction, materials to use, when and where sessions will occur, and how to utilize evidence-based approaches for implementation.

☐ Develop a plan for fading the intervention.

- How often will the data be reviewed and by whom?
- What are the criteria to exit a student from the strategy instruction intervention?

TIPS FOR IMPLEMENTATION

☐ Two specific programs already include the critical components of strategy instruction.

a. Self-Regulated Strategy Development

b. Strategic Instruction Model

☐ Ensure students who are receiving strategy instruction are not pulled from core classes.

Source: Deshler & Schumaker, 2006; Flores & Milton, 2020; Graham et al., 2016; IRIS Center, 2022a; What Works Clearinghouse, 2017b.

Effective strategy instruction demands attention to the method of instruction. For this reason, ensuring fidelity of implementation and consistent evaluation of student progress is key. Figure 2.10 provides an example form to monitor fidelity.

Date: *April 24* Grade: *Tenth*

Has an area of strategy instruction (for example, essay writing, mathematics problem completion, goal setting, note taking, or test taking) been selected based on student data?	(Yes) No	*Based on formative and summative data, the MTSS team determined that essay writing is an area of need for intervention for a group of students.*
Have a specific time and a specific place been selected for the strategy instruction, which occurs three to five times a week, in twenty- to sixty-minute sessions, and in a small group of eight or fewer students?	(Yes) No	*School leadership established a twenty-five-minute "skinny period" to allow students to receive acceleration or intervention based on identified needs.*
Have the materials and the instructional approach (Strategic Instruction Model, Self-Regulated Strategy Development, or other) been selected or designed?	(Yes) No	*Mr. Williams received specialized training in self-regulated strategy development, and a consultant from the district's local technical assistance partner will provide coaching during this first round of implementation. Mr. Williams will meet every other week with core ELA teachers to align instruction and share student progress.*

Figure 2.10: Strategy instruction fidelity form example.

Visit ***go.SolutionTree.com/RTI*** *for a free blank reproducible version of this figure.*

Figure 2.11 (page 54) offers an example of a progress-monitoring form.

Literacy or Mathematics Intervention Period

Remember, it's not too late to address substantial gaps in literacy and mathematics skills in middle and high school (Edmonds et al., 2009; Gersten et al., 2009; Guryan et al., 2023; Pyle & Vaughn, 2012; Scammacca et al., 2007; Smith et al., 2016; Wanzek et al., 2013). A specialized literacy or mathematics intervention period is a Tier 2 option to ensure an intentional focus on essential prerequisite literacy or mathematics skills.

Students who have significant weaknesses in literacy or mathematics may be better served by such an intervention period than by strategy instruction, which focuses on executive functioning skills, or high-impact tutoring, which stays closely tied to current grade-level content and course performance. A literacy or mathematics intervention period typically relies on a prescribed curriculum that targets missing literacy or mathematics skills. This intervention should align with core instruction but provide more specialized, targeted, and even foundational instruction.

Name: Nash M.					
Date:	April 21	April 22	April 23	April 24	April 25
Is the student regularly attending and engaged in the sessions?	(Yes) No	(Yes) No	(Yes) No	(Yes) No	(Yes) No
Course performance notes (grades, formative and summative assessment data):		Nash brought in his rubric from yesterday's formative writing assessment in English II. We will connect strategies taught in this intervention class to help Nash generalize to his core classes.			
Course performance notes (number of missing assignments):	0 missing assignments	0 missing assignments	0 missing assignments	0 missing assignments	0 missing assignments
Other notes:		Nash was very frustrated with this formative assessment. We discussed strategies that we would cover to address these areas.			I spoke with Nash's mom to share motivation ideas, such as how to chunk writing assignments into smaller tasks and celebrate small wins.

Figure 2.11: Strategy instruction progress monitoring form example.

Visit ***go.SolutionTree.com/RTI*** *for a free blank reproducible version of this figure.*

This type of intervention is most effective when taught by a teacher with technical expertise; however, middle and high schools often face numerous barriers to making this a reality (for example, existing staffing and scheduling conflicts). School leaders may find that purchased curricula can be helpful for teachers, especially those with minimal specialized training in literacy or mathematics interventions; though, these teachers will need ongoing training and coaching to continue growing their skills. Teacher-created materials can be used as long as they are designed by a highly skilled educator in collaboration with other educators. Many schools find that an evidence-based curriculum can minimize the "extra prep" that teachers often feel is a barrier to teaching a separate intervention class.

The following list includes literacy programs with evidence of effectiveness for secondary students (Baye, Inns, Lake, & Slavin, 2019; Evidence for ESSA, n.d.b; Hougen, 2015; National Center on Intensive Intervention, 2021; What Works Clearinghouse, 2025a). Importantly, this is not an all-encompassing list. I encourage you to seek out additional information to ensure the selected programs meet district and state guidelines and align with the student population and demographics of your school.

- **Achieve3000 Literacy™:** Provides an online nonfiction literacy library that builds phonemic awareness, phonics, comprehension, vocabulary, and writing skills (You can find more information at www.mheducation.com/prek-12/program/microsites/achieve-3000-literacy.html.)
- **Fast ForWord®:** Provides computer-based instruction to improve thinking skills necessary for literacy and learning (You can find more information at www.carnegielearning.com/solutions/literacy-ela/fast-forword.)
- **Passport Reading Journeys™:** Teaches literacy skills through whole-class, small-group, and computer-adaptive instruction (You can find more information at https://ies.ed.gov/ncee/wwc/Intervention/1448.)
- **Read 180®:** Teaches literacy skills through whole-class, small-group, and computer-adaptive instruction (You can find more information at www.hmhco.com/programs/read-180.)
- **Read Right®:** Provides instruction in literacy skills through books, digital resources, online tutoring, and intensive staff training (You can find more information at www.readright.com.)
- **Reading Plus:** Uses guided, silent reading passages designed to increase vocabulary, comprehension, endurance, and silent reading fluency (You can find more information at www.readingplus.com.)
- **Strategic Adolescent Reading Intervention (STARI):** Teaches literacy through novels, thematic units, and instruction in comprehension (You can find more information at www.serpinstitute.org/stari.)

Few mathematics programs designed for middle and high schools have the research backing necessary for selective national organizations to formally recommend them. The following curricula have been identified as making positive and statistically significant impacts on secondary students' mathematics skills (Evidence for ESSA, n.d.a; What Works Clearinghouse, 2025b). This list is not intended to be exhaustive.

- **ASSISTments:** Incorporates mastery-oriented skill practice and can link to activities in commonly used curricula (You can find more information at www.assistments.org.)
- **Catapult Learning:** Provides mathematics tutoring services and targeted interventions (You can find more information at https://catapultlearning.com.)
- **Math 180®:** Uses a combination of computer-adaptive and teacher-led instruction to accelerate student learning (You can find more information at www.hmhco.com/programs/math-180.)
- **Saga Curriculum:** Teaches mathematics through a traditional or computer-assisted tutoring model (You can find more information at https://saga.org/products/saga-curriculum.)
- **Zearn Math:** Provides mathematics instruction using a concrete, pictorial, abstract (CPA) progression and builds procedural fluency (You can find more information at https://about.zearn.org/tutoring-with-zearn-math.)

Many schools find that designating a time during the day for selected students to receive specialized literacy or mathematics interventions (while other students receive enrichment or an elective class) is an optimum structure for dedicating focus to tiered supports. Scheduling plays a crucial role in effective implementation, and numerous resources exist to assist with scheduling (Durrance, 2023, 2025; Hanover Research, 2014; Massachusetts Department of Elementary and Secondary Education, Rodriguez Educational Consulting Agency, & Novak Educational Consulting, 2020; National Center on Response to Intervention, 2011; Weingarten et al., 2019). Regardless of your school's approach to implementation, you will need guidance, training, coaching, and measures of accountability for effective implementation.

Even if your school has a designated mathematics or literacy intervention program, be cognizant of the teaching strategies found to be most effective with secondary students who need more support in these areas. Teachers responsible for intervention should seek additional professional learning and coaching and take advantage of resources such as *Providing Reading Interventions for Students in Grades 4–9* (Vaughn et al., 2022) or *Principles for Designing Intervention in Mathematics* (National Center on Intensive Intervention, 2016a) to deepen their understanding of methods for supporting students who are struggling. Figures 2.12 and 2.13 (page 60) outline the essential components of literacy intervention and mathematics intervention, respectively.

ESSENTIAL COMPONENTS OF SECONDARY LITERACY INTERVENTION

GOAL OF THE INTERVENTION

To identify missing literacy skills and provide explicit instruction in those areas

TARGET STUDENT GROUP

Identify students based on academic criteria such as course performance (for example, grades and missing assignments), assessments tied to core instruction, academic skill levels (for example, students who score below the 20th percentile on district, state, or standardized assessments or screeners due to low literacy skills), classroom observations, interviews with students and families, and anecdotal teacher input.

ESSENTIAL COMPONENTS

- ☐ Review data to identify students who would benefit from the intervention.
- ☐ Discuss the intervention with relevant stakeholders, including families, students, and teachers.
- ☐ Determine the time of day, location, and instructor for the intervention.
- ☐ Build the intervention time into the schedule so it can be consistently implemented with small groups. (Group size depends on the specific program or curriculum being implemented.)
- ☐ Work with the intervention teacher to conduct a diagnostic assessment to identify each student's specific missing skills. Such assessments might include curriculum-based measures, running records, or the Diagnostic Assessments of Reading™ (DAR). Refer to the State Education Resource Center's (2012) secondary assessment, universal screening, diagnostic, and progress-monitoring tools. The National Center on Intensive Intervention (n.d.b) provides additional diagnostic assessment options.
- ☐ Identify high-quality instructional materials that align with core instruction and that address missing skills.
- ☐ Determine a method for collecting data on each of the following.
    - **Fidelity of implementation:** Have the specific missing skills been identified? Are students receiving literacy intervention with expected frequency? Is the intervention being implemented as designed? Is the intervention connected with core instruction?
    - **Evidence of student progress:** This evidence includes assessments of specific literacy skills being taught (for example, curriculum-based measures of word reading and fluency), embedded curriculum assessments or other school-level literacy assessments (for example, literacy universal screeners), course performance data (for example, grades and missing assignments), English language assessments, classroom observations, interviews with students, and anecdotal teacher input.

Figure 2.12: Essential components of secondary literacy intervention.

continued ▶

ESSENTIAL COMPONENTS OF SECONDARY LITERACY INTERVENTION

☐ Utilize evidence-based approaches for adolescent literacy intervention.

- **Word recognition and word study:**
  - Utilize a diagnostic assessment to determine students' word-reading skills (for example, assessing their knowledge of vowel and consonant combinations). Provide explicit instruction in missing skills in a respectful, grade-appropriate manner (not treating students as if they were in early elementary school).
  - Provide explicit instruction in morphology (teaching morphemes, or the smallest meaning-carrying units within words, including prefixes, suffixes, and root words). Use word analysis routines that include the rationale behind the routine, systematic steps, modeling, guided practice, independent practice, and opportunities to utilize the strategy in multiple contexts. Two example routines include REWARDS (Archer, Gleason, & Vachon, 2000; Klee, Brasch, Neyman, McLaughlin, & Stookey, 2015; Shippen, Houchins, Steventon, & Sartor, 2005) and DISSECT (Lenz, Hughes, 1990; Lenz, Schumaker, Deshler, & Beals, 1984).
- **Fluency:**
  - Incorporate repeated readings that are structured for varying purposes (for example, for expression or prosody and a focus on vocabulary) to prevent them from becoming dull tasks.
  - Select short texts for repeated readings that incorporate recently taught skills, such as breaking down multisyllabic words; that connect to students' content-area classes (when possible); and that increase in difficulty with a specific topic to build students' understanding and reading stamina.
  - Have students chart *cold reads* (words read per minute their first time reading a passage) and then *hot reads* (words read per minute after rereading and studying the passage) to emphasize their progress.
- **Vocabulary:**
  - Preteach the most critical vocabulary to aid students in their core classes or on upcoming challenging reading tasks. Use graphic organizers such as word webs or word maps that include a student-developed definition or a nonlinguistic form of the word to help students connect the word with its meanings.
  - Activate background knowledge using an easier reading passage, videos, images, podcasts, or concept mapping. Prompt students to listen for critical ideas and share reflections with partners.
  - Actively engage students by having them identify examples and non-examples, play games, and use new words in discussions.
  - Provide explicit instruction in word pronunciation—model, note the syllabic breaks, emphasize the stressed syllable, have students practice, and provide feedback.
- **Text comprehension:**
  - Preteach strategies such as close reading (which includes setting a goal for reading a particular passage, annotating it, summarizing it, and reflecting on how the information and ideas connect) in preparation for content-area classes.

- Use think-alouds, anticipation guides, or strategies such as author questioning (asking questions of the author or text while students are reading).
- Teach students to identify the gist of a passage by modeling how to use a specific routine or strategy and how to understand text structures (compare and contrast, problem and solution, and so on).
- Instruct students to determine when they do not understand what they read by asking themselves comprehension questions.
- Provide opportunities for students to practice reading stretch text; this will give them access to complex vocabulary and ideas. Intentionally select challenging text, identify words to preteach, determine when to pause and how to structure discussion time, allow students time to work through the text as a group, and incorporate digital tools for independently reading the stretch text (for example, audio readers and built-in dictionaries).

☐ Develop a plan for fading the intervention.

- How often will the data be reviewed and by whom?
- What are the criteria to exit a student from the literacy intervention?

TIPS FOR IMPLEMENTATION

☐ Select a high-quality instructor with expertise in literacy intervention.

☐ Ensure the intervention time does not prevent students from receiving core instruction.

☐ Incorporate oral and written English language instruction with an awareness of the levels of multilingual learners.

☐ Focus on students' individual strengths and utilize motivational tools such as opportunities to work with peers (book clubs or literature circles), self-selected texts, culturally relevant texts, goal setting, monitoring, and growth mindset teaching.

☐ Emphasize and support relationship building between intervention teachers and students and their families.

☐ Provide all teachers in the building with information about students' literacy needs and strategies for supporting these students.

Source: Baker et al., 2014; Conradi Smith, Jang, & Ostot, 2025; Drake Patrick & Acosta, 2024; Ebbers & Hougen, 2015; Fuchs et al., 2010; Hougen, 2015; Kamil et al., 2008; Marzano, 2004; National Center on Intensive Intervention, n.d.b; O'Connor, 2007; Pyle & Vaughn, 2012; The Reading League, 2024; Scammacca et al., 2007; Shanahan, 2014; Smith et al., 2016; State Education Resource Center, 2012; Torgesen et al., 2007; Vaughn & Fletcher, 2010; Vaughn et al., 2022.

ESSENTIAL COMPONENTS OF SECONDARY MATHEMATICS INTERVENTION

GOAL OF THE INTERVENTION

To identify missing mathematics skills and provide explicit instruction in those areas

TARGET STUDENT GROUP

Identify students based on academic criteria such as course performance (for example, grades and missing assignments), assessments tied to core instruction, academic skill levels (for example, students who score below the 20th percentile on district, state, or standardized assessments or screeners due to low mathematics skills), classroom observations, interviews with students and families, and anecdotal teacher input.

ESSENTIAL COMPONENTS

- ☐ Review data to identify students who would benefit from the intervention.
- ☐ Discuss the intervention with relevant stakeholders, including families, students, and teachers.
- ☐ Determine the time of day, location, and instructor for the intervention.
- ☐ Build the intervention time into the schedule so it can be consistently implemented with small groups. (Group size depends on the specific program or curriculum being implemented.)
- ☐ Work with the intervention teacher to conduct a diagnostic assessment to identify each student's specific missing skills. Such assessments might include curriculum-based measures and student work samples. Refer to the State Education Resource Center's (2012) secondary list of diagnostic and progress-monitoring tools. The National Center on Intensive Intervention (n.d.b) provides additional diagnostic assessment options.
- ☐ Identify high-quality instructional materials that align with core instruction and that address missing skills.
- ☐ Determine a method for collecting data on each of the following.
    - **Fidelity of implementation:** Have the specific missing skills been identified? Are students receiving mathematics intervention with expected frequency? Is the intervention being implemented as designed? Is the intervention connected with core instruction?
    - **Evidence of student progress:** This evidence includes assessments of specific mathematics skills being taught (for example, curriculum-based measures of problem solving and mathematics fluency), embedded curriculum assessments or other school-level mathematics assessments (for example, mathematics universal screeners), course performance data (for example, grades and missing assignments), classroom observations, interviews with students, and anecdotal teacher input.
- ☐ Utilize evidence-based approaches for adolescent mathematics intervention.
    - Provide explicit, systematic instruction.
        - Introduce the relevance and specific objectives of the lesson through an advance organizer.
        - Assess students' background knowledge and prerequisite skills.
        - Use think-alouds to model setting up and solving a problem with correct mathematics vocabulary.
        - Use guided practice, including prompting, scaffolding, and positive corrective feedback, to achieve a goal of at least 85 percent mastery of a concept before moving on.

Figure 2.13: Essential components of secondary mathematics intervention.

- Have students demonstrate their understanding through independent practice while you monitor them and provide feedback.
- Use distributed or cumulative practice to help students maintain newly learned skills.

- Follow a concrete-representational-abstract sequence of instruction.
  - **Concrete:** Utilize three-dimensional manipulatives, such as fraction tiles or algebra tiles, to teach concepts. Then have students use them to solve problems and explain the mathematical procedure underlying the concepts.
  - **Representational, visual, or pictorial:** Use two-dimensional pictures, diagrams, drawings, or virtual representations from a website or application to connect and build on knowledge gained from concrete manipulatives.
  - **Abstract or symbolic:** Draw on skills built through concrete manipulatives and visual representations to guide students' use of numbers and symbols, including memorization of facts and algorithms, to increase their mathematics fluency.
- Provide explicit instruction in mathematics vocabulary and symbols by having word banks, using vocabulary cards, labeling parts of problems, and identifying characteristics of mathematical concepts.
- Use graphic organizers. Organize information and illustrate mathematical concepts through visuals.
- Build fluency. Incorporate additional practice; for example, use computer software, instructional games like bingo, or dice and dry-erase markers to increase students' fluency of operational facts.

☐ Develop a plan for fading the intervention.

- How often will the data be reviewed and by whom?
- What are the criteria to exit a student from the mathematics intervention?

TIPS FOR IMPLEMENTATION

☐ Select a high-quality instructor with expertise in mathematics intervention. Secondary mathematics teachers will be most prepared for learners' diverse needs once they have built a deep understanding from key resources such as the Standards for Mathematical Practice (National Governors Association Center for Best Practices & Council of Chief State School Officers, 2010b) and resources that provide strategies for teaching algebra and problem solving (for example, Star et al., 2015; Woodward et al., 2018).

☐ Ensure the intervention time does not prevent students from receiving core instruction.

☐ Focus on students' individual strengths, and utilize motivational tools such as goal setting, monitoring, and growth mindset teaching.

☐ Emphasize and support relationship building between intervention teachers and students and their families.

☐ Provide all teachers in the building with information about students' mathematics needs and strategies for supporting these students.

Source: Archer & Hughes, 2011; Bundock et al., 2019; Flores & Milton, 2020; Fuchs et al., 2010; Gersten et al., 2009; Miller & Hudson, 2007; National Center on Intensive Intervention, n.d.b, 2016a; National Council of Teachers of Mathematics, 2000; National Mathematics Advisory Panel, 2008; State Education Resource Center, 2012; Vaughn & Fletcher, 2010.

LONG-TERM GOAL FOR TIER 2: Our school will have multiple well-established Tier 2 group interventions led by a variety of personnel with processes in place to check fidelity of implementation and collect progress-monitoring data. These group interventions will be monitored by the Tier 2 team and adapted based on data; student, family, and teacher input; and the unique context. The team will select the appropriate group intervention to best fit a student whose data suggests they need more academic support. This team will monitor the progress of the student over time and determine whether the intervention should be maintained, intensified, or faded.

TIER 2 QUICK-START STEPS

1. Select one Tier 2 group intervention (high-impact tutoring, strategy instruction, or a specialized literacy or mathematics intervention period) based on evidence of need in your school.
2. Analyze data to select a small group of students who will pilot the intervention, considering their specific academic strengths and needs.
3. Implement core features of the intervention. Explore references and related resources to build a deeper understanding of the intervention and specific evidence-based practices. Additional training and coaching ensure the intervention is implemented with fidelity.
4. Adjust and improve implementation based on contextual factors: student data, stakeholder input, and any unintended costs (for example, too much instructional time lost by the student to participate in the intervention, and too much teacher time needed for planning and preparation).
5. Expand implementation to serve more students once the Tier 2 team determines that the intervention is beneficial in your school environment.
6. Solidify the intervention by naming it, documenting processes and core features for implementation, and adding it to the school website or some other school organizational digital platform.
7. Follow these quick-start steps to build the next Tier 2 group intervention into your school's organizational structure.

NOTES

We have discussed three secondary-focused Tier 2 group interventions to support students who are unsuccessful despite having received high-quality, scaffolded Tier 1 instruction from highly trained teachers. Next, we will explore steps for making these interventions more intensive and individualized for students who require support beyond this.

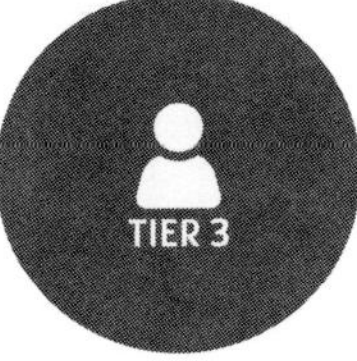

Tier 3 Intensive, Individualized Academic Interventions

Students who demonstrate continued academic difficulties even after strong core instruction and an evidence-based Tier 2 group intervention that was implemented with fidelity may need a more intensive and individualized intervention. The literature suggests that this is typically true for 3–5 percent of the population (Bailey, 2020; Fuchs et al., 2010; National Center on Intensive Intervention, n.d.c; VanDerHeyden & Allsopp, 2014); therefore, this tier should address a small number of students in your building. To strategically allocate limited school resources, teams must reflect on the effectiveness of each preceding tier and ask themselves what percentage of students are successful with their current Tier 1 and Tier 2 practices before seeking to intensify instruction for large numbers of students. See chapter 1 for more information on this issue.

Tier 3 academic interventions differ from Tier 2 in their *intensity* and *individualization*. These are the two key terms you should keep in mind when designing a Tier 3 intervention plan. The Tier 3 team should come together to review data, conduct any additional assessments needed, and build this plan of action. Team members must consider the roles that mental health, executive functioning skills, and behavioral challenges play in the student's academic skills. Along with diagnostic academic data, such as curriculum-based measures, work samples, or running records, this information provides the Tier 3 team with a more comprehensive view of the student's strengths and needs. This leads to a stronger, more relevant, and more impactful plan.

Who provides Tier 3 interventions in a middle or high school, and when do they provide them?

A difficult part of intensifying and individualizing instruction is determining who provides Tier 3 interventions in a middle or high school, and when do they provide them? It is already challenging to identify available time and staff during the school day to offer Tier 2 interventions, and now you must arrange Tier 3! Options might include the following.

- Select high-impact tutoring or strategy instruction as your school's model for providing Tier 2 support and save the literacy or mathematics intervention period for a very small number of students needing Tier 3 intervention.
- Implement a specialized literacy or mathematics intervention period as a Tier 2 intervention and embed Tier 3 interventions into the class for students needing more intensive support.
- Implement Tier 3 interventions as part of a Tier 2 group intervention (for example, high-impact tutoring or strategy instruction).
- Partner with core teachers to embed Tier 3 supports throughout the student's day.

- Utilize extended school services to provide Tier 3 intervention before or after school three or four times per week; though, this is dependent on the student's availability.
- Assign an additional staff member (for example, an instructional assistant or intervention teacher) to provide specific intensified strategies in one or more of the student's current classes.

Let's explore how we could adapt literacy and mathematics interventions to be more intensive and individualized at the secondary level using the strategies for intensifying interventions presented in figure 1.4 (page 24). These strategies for intensification will differ depending on each student's unique strengths and needs identified through diagnostic assessments and observations; therefore, these ideas are to serve as a model of evidence-based intensification. Figure 2.14 features ideas for how you can intensify secondary interventions.

STRENGTH

The Tier 3 team reflects on the strength of the student's current programming.

- Are the materials and instructional practices in content classes based on evidence and implemented with fidelity?
- Are teachers providing appropriate scaffolds (for example, increased wait time, activation of background knowledge, and vocabulary instruction) for the student to access the content?
- Is the Tier 2 intervention based on evidence and implemented with fidelity?

If the student's current programming meets these criteria, the team can increase the intensity and individualization of the student's instruction and intervention using the following dimensions.

DOSAGE

The Tier 3 team may determine that the student would benefit from an increased dosage of instruction. This could be done through small-group instruction that addresses the student's specific needs until they reach mastery. The team will need to identify a time to provide this instruction, considering the student's current schedule and the resources available at the school.

The Tier 3 team can also increase the dosage by giving the student more opportunities to respond. These prompts that require student responses (for example, thumbs-up or thumbs-down, response cards, verbal answers to a peer, or responses written on their individual whiteboard) are typically followed by feedback from the teacher.

Other methods to increase the dosage of an intervention through opportunities to respond and specific feedback include the following.

- Lengthen intervention sessions.
- Create smaller group sizes.
- Reduce distractions (for example, distracting peers or busy hallways).
- Make intervention groups more homogeneous.

 **ALIGNMENT**	The student may have been part of Tier 2 group intervention designed to address general skills (for example, strategy instruction or high-impact tutoring). In this case, the Tier 3 team may determine that the intervention needs to more closely align with the student's specific academic needs or core instruction. Diagnostic assessments, such as curriculum-based measures, running records, and work samples, will clarify the student's specific skill deficits. The team may determine that the student needs a separate intervention period with a curriculum that directly targets the identified area of need. The student's core teachers may also benefit from additional training and coaching on how best to support the student's specific academic needs. Instructional coaches, curriculum specialists, and special education teachers within the school or district may be resources who could offer consultation. Another way to improve alignment of the student's academic needs with grade-level expectations is to focus on prioritized standards. With guidance from a collaborative teacher team and standards resources (such as Achieve the Core's Priority Instructional Content or algebra readiness skill recommendations from the National Mathematics Advisory Panel [2008]), you can identify and target the most crucial competencies. The goal of limiting and prioritizing content is to increase the student's mastery of the most critical knowledge and skills.
 **ATTENTION TO TRANSFER**	You can accelerate student learning by attending to the transfer of new skills. The student may need explicit instruction to understand the connection between the skills being taught during intervention and the work happening during core instruction. It may also be helpful to shift intervention from reteaching or repeating content to instead previewing and preteaching it to implement a just-in-time intervention. This may include sharing a video about an upcoming unit and preteaching vocabulary to increase engagement and background knowledge to help the student be successful during upcoming lessons. This can happen only when intervention and core teachers communicate closely to align language and newly taught skills.
 **COMPREHENSIVENESS**	Accelerating growth is critical for secondary students with significant academic challenges. A key factor in the effectiveness of intervention—especially at the Tier 3 level—is the quality of the instructor. Effective teachers implement comprehensive intervention by integrating strong instructional principles, including explicit instruction, instructional adaptations based on data and analysis of the student's errors, and gradual release. Intervention with integrity requires well-prepared, highly effective teachers. The Tier 3 team may recommend that the student would best be matched with certain teachers, considering their training and relationship with the student.
 **OTHER BEHAVIORAL OR ACADEMIC SUPPORT**	**For students with literacy needs:** Students who have experienced reading problems for a long period of time often have significant challenges with motivation. This is understandable, as their efforts have likely not led to success in the past. Nothing motivates someone more than success; therefore, activities in which the student can feel successful are essential. The following specific activities increase motivation for struggling readers.

Figure 2.14: Strategies for intensifying secondary literacy or mathematics interventions.

continued ▶

OTHER BEHAVIORAL OR ACADEMIC SUPPORT

- Provide choice in the student's topics and types of writing and the types of texts being read. Increase literacy experiences that are relevant to the student's interests, everyday life, and current events.
- Incorporate literature circle discussion,s into instruction.
- Utilize read-alouds to model fluent reading and metacognitive strategies.
- Be aware of the messages that you communicate (intentionally or unintentionally) to students. Focus praise of students on effort rather than on "intelligence" or "ability." Encourage and provide a psychologically safe space for risk taking, complex thinking, and teamwork.
- Increase peer support to model and promote positive behaviors.
- Provide informational feedback and realistic expectations that explicitly communicate step-by-step reading strategies and why the strategies are effective (learning goals), as opposed to feedback that pressures the student to reach a particular outcome (performance goals).
- Partner with the student's other teachers to make complementary materials available at varying reading levels and to support the student's comprehension of texts in the student's other classes. AI programs such as Magic School AI, NotebookLM, or Diffit can be great resources for doing this.

For students with mathematics needs: Language and literacy play important roles in mathematics learning. Multilingual learners or students with oral language or reading difficulties benefit from explicit instruction in mathematics language development, especially with word problems.

Assessments of a student's English proficiency or expressive and receptive language skills can offer insight into the student's specific needs. Partner with speech-language pathologists or multilingual learner specialists for guidance on instructional adaptations (for example, vocabulary checks, repetition, and student-developed glossaries that incorporate their native language). Specific practices to improve mathematics language development include the following.

- Offer explicit instruction and modeling in small, homogeneous intervention groups.
- Provide schema- and strategy-based instruction on word-problem types; emphasize the structures underlying the problems and the metacognitive strategies for solving them.
- Implement scaffolding with culturally responsive practices, such as peer discussion in English or the student's native language. State specific goals for the lesson, and incorporate culturally relevant references into word problems.
- Provide explicit strategy instruction in mathematics writing (for example, Self-Regulated Strategy Development) and journal writing and responding.

For students with behavioral challenges: Difficulties with attention,, social-emotional skills, and so on may play a role in the student's academic struggles. The student may benefit from a targeted behavioral intervention in addition to academic support. Refer to chapter 3 for specific strategies.

Source: Allred & Cena, 2020; Archer & Hughes, 2011; Drake Patrick & Acosta, 2024; Franks & Fraser, 2020; Fuchs et al., 2017; Gambrell & Marinak, n.d.; Kamil et al., 2008; Lariviere, Agrawal, & Wang, 2022; Martin, Sargent, Van Camp, & Wright, 2018; Marzano, 2003; National Center on Intensive Intervention, 2016a, 2019, 2021; National Mathematics Advisory Panel, 2008; Powell et al., 2021; The Reading League, 2024; Scammacca et al., 2007; Scott, 2017; St. Martin et al., 2020; Student Achievement Partners, 2021; VanDerHeyden & Allsopp, 2014; Vaughn et al., 2022; Zagata, Payne, & Arsenault, 2021.

LONG-TERM GOAL FOR TIER 3: Our school will have an established process for convening a Tier 3 team to build a comprehensive Tier 3 plan. Our team will understand the process to intensify interventions for students with significant academic needs. The Tier 3 plan will include methods for monitoring student progress and the fidelity of implementation. Our team will review student progress over time and determine whether the intervention should be maintained, intensified, or faded.

TIER 3 QUICK-START STEPS

1. Identify a student receiving support through a Tier 2 group intervention whose data suggests that they need a more intensive, individualized approach.
2. Bring together a Tier 3 team to review data (for example, diagnostic literacy or mathematics data or academic and behavioral data) and identify what additional information is needed to develop an action plan. Tap into specialists (for example, school psychologists or literacy or mathematics specialists) to help guide this process. Include the student and their family in this process.
3. Based on information gathered and input from the student and their family, build a comprehensive plan with your team that includes intensified Tier 3 interventions. The plan will include the intervention-intensifying dimensions of strength, dosage, alignment, attention to transfer, comprehensiveness, and other behavioral or academic support.
4. Communicate the plan to all stakeholders.
5. Implement core features of the intervention and the overarching plan.
6. Adjust and improve implementation based on data collection (curriculum-based measures, in-class assessments, and feedback from the student, their teachers, and their family).

NOTES

Conclusion

Many students in middle school and high school are performing significantly below grade level. Teachers feel overwhelmed by the pressure to get students to proficiency and to college and career readiness. MTSS can be the framework that empowers your school's teachers to provide the academic support that students need to access high-level learning.

LEARNING OBJECTIVES

- Review fundamental elements of an effective Tier 1 schoolwide positive behavioral and social-emotional support system for secondary students.
- Explore the essential components of five Tier 2 behavioral and social-emotional group interventions for secondary students.
- Examine methods for intensifying Tier 3 behavioral and social-emotional interventions for secondary students.

Shawn struggled as a student in our school system for many years. Even after conducting diagnostic assessments and researching strategies to improve his reading scores, Shawn's teachers and I, the school psychologist, couldn't seem to grow Shawn's literacy skills beyond a second-grade level. His twin brother also struggled academically but was able to read and write near grade level over time. Shawn tragically lost his life to suicide when he was a high school sophomore. I still remember when I first heard that one of the twins had passed. I knew that Shawn's inability to read had always compounded his mental health struggles. I went to the funeral to share my heartfelt condolences to the family of this young man who lost his life too soon. I will never forget the haunting look in Shawn's mother's eyes. Academics matter, but this was a grievous reminder that what really matters are the humans in our classrooms.

This chapter focuses on the behavioral and social-emotional needs of secondary students. It explores U.S. trends, including the prevalence of stress-inducing early childhood experiences, and examines how these potentially traumatic early childhood experiences affect developing brains and bodies and manifest in the classroom. This text lays the foundation for viewing student behavior through a trauma-informed lens, prompting schools to respond preventively and proactively with evidence-based Tier 1 approaches. For students who require a higher level of support, this chapter offers five Tier 2 interventions along with methods to intensify such interventions for those with more complex needs.

The Mental Health Needs of Secondary Students

Our students' behavioral and social-emotional needs are factors we cannot avoid or deny in schools. The mental health crisis is at our front door, and we must respond. On the most recent Youth Risk Behavior Survey (Centers for Disease Control and Prevention, 2024b), adolescents report high rates of poor mental health as well as suicidal thoughts and behaviors (see figure 3.1). These numbers are particularly alarming for students of color, students from poverty, students with disabilities, and LGBTQ+ students.

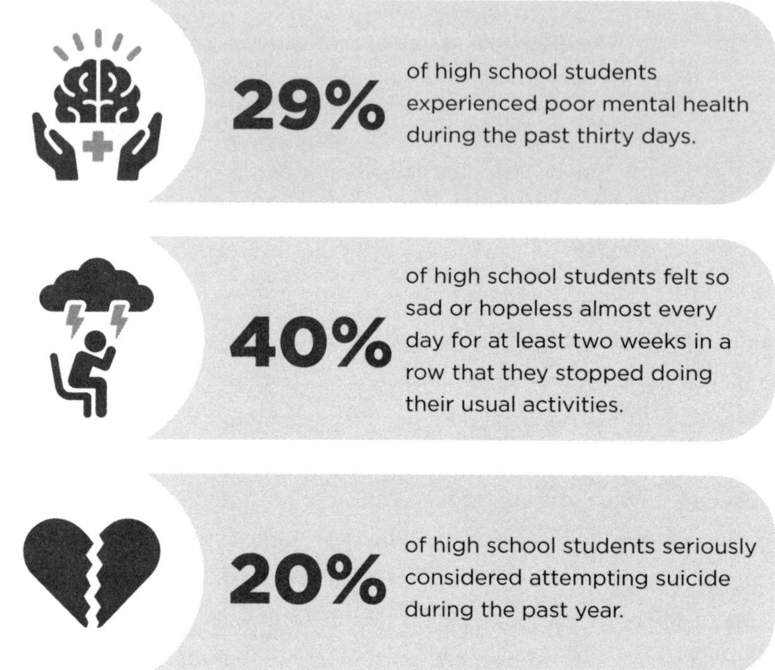

Source: Centers for Disease Control and Prevention, 2024b.

Figure 3.1: Mental health needs of adolescents.

How do we expect to conduct business as usual in a classroom when 40 percent of high school students report they feel sad or hopeless daily and they have stopped doing their usual activities? When students are struggling with anxiety, depression, or other mental health challenges, they are no longer open and available for learning.

When we're planning behavioral supports at school, we can explore what is driving this increase in student mental health problems (and why this matters) by considering the Adverse Childhood Experiences Study. This landmark investigation into adverse childhood experiences found a strong correlation between traumatic events during childhood and negative lifelong physical and mental health outcomes (Felitti et al., 1998).

As shown in figure 3.2, the original study asked participants if they had experienced events such as abuse or exposure to domestic violence, or if they had lived with someone with substance use or mental illness. About 64 percent of adults who participated

ADVERSE CHILDHOOD EXPERIENCES

Physical, emotional, or sexual abuse

Parental divorce

Exposure to domestic violence

Living with someone with mental illness

Living with someone with substance use or criminality

Toxic stress from adverse childhood experiences can produce changes in the brain and the body's stress response system, leading to:

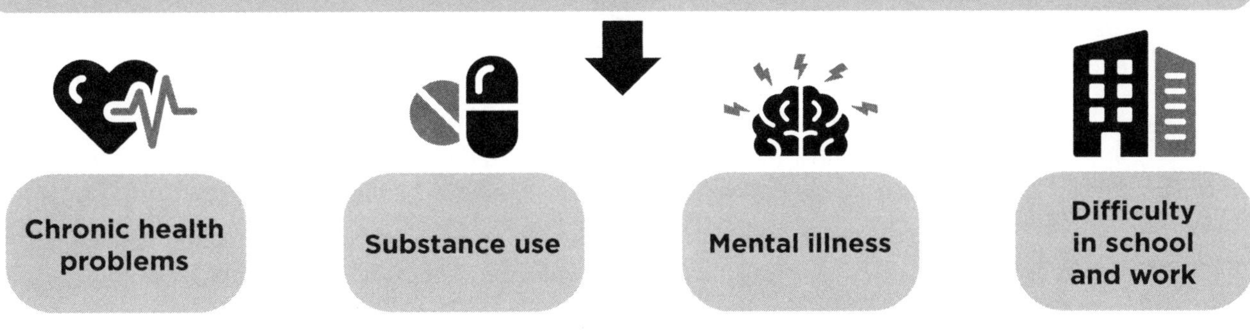

64%

of adults report they experienced at least one adverse childhood experience before they were eighteen.

1 in 6

adults report they experienced four or more adverse childhood experiences.

Source: Centers for Disease Control and Prevention, 2024a.

Figure 3.2: Data from the original Adverse Childhood Experiences Study.

reported having at least one of these experiences, and one in six indicated they had experienced four or more adverse childhood experiences.

Notably, the original study did not include other potentially traumatic conditions students might experience, such as neighborhood danger, bullying, homelessness, and foster care. More recent research finds that these factors increase the rate of exposure to adverse childhood experiences, and minority and lower-income populations are disproportionately affected (Cronholm et al., 2015). We could add other current conditions to the list, such as school experiences interrupted by COVID-19 closures (Felfe et al., 2023) and the impact of social media on teen mental health (U.S. Public Health Service, 2023). The point is many students show up to school holding destructive, unhealthy thoughts about themselves, the world, and the adults around them. Then we, as dedicated educators, try to explain to them why they need to learn a geometry or physics concept. A serious disconnect exists.

Why do these stress-inducing experiences matter? Didn't we all experience tough times as children? Although stress is part of life, there is a range of stress from positive to toxic levels (Center on the Developing Child, n.d.). Many excellent books, videos, and other resources on this topic are available, but here is the gist: When you experience a stressful situation or perceive a threat, your body activates its stress response system, which releases hormones, such as cortisol and adrenaline, to kick you into action. This causes physiological changes in your body—increased heart rate, sweating, and a boost in energy or focus—all of them preparing you to deal with the stressful event. As you work through the situation, you lean on others around you for support and implement your (hopefully) healthy coping strategies, such as taking a break, practicing deep breathing, and talking it out. These strategies help your body return to a state of calm, thereby maintaining a healthy stress response system.

However, when stress becomes extreme or prolonged (such as from adverse childhood experiences listed in figure 3.2) and you lack protective factors (such as strong adult relationships) to buffer the potentially damaging effects of an overactive stress response system, toxic stress can develop. Our bodies are not designed to operate at this heightened state of arousal for long periods of time. Toxic stress can be very damaging to the body—and especially to the developing brain of a child or adolescent. Decades of research have documented the impact that stress-inducing, traumatic events have on people as they grow (Felitti et al., 1998; Hays-Grudo & Morris, 2020; National Child Traumatic Stress Network, 2008). This is relevant to our discussion because childhood exposure to trauma and the associated mental health challenges can manifest in the secondary classroom in many ways, as shown in figure 3.3.

Although trauma is not an excuse for a student's behavior, *it could be a reason.*

Every day, these underlying conditions play out in middle and high schools across the United States. Many students struggle with self-regulation (the ability to control one's thoughts, emotions, and behaviors in pursuit of one's own goals) and executive functioning (for example, time management, organization, memory, and attention; Center on the Developing Child, 2014; Crone, 2009; Hart, Doyle, Cantero, & Garrington, 2022; IRIS Center, 2022a; Murray & Rosanbalm, 2017; Zimmerman, 2002). They may have difficulties with their peers or problems completing tasks. However, when you, as an educator, are under immense pressure to cover your content standards and get students to academic proficiency, it can be difficult to view behavior through this lens of trauma exposure and mental health. Although trauma is not an excuse for a student's behavior, *it could be a reason.*

Considering what we know about the mental health needs of secondary students, these next two sections provide a lens through which educators can view these challenges. Many barriers arise and exist beyond school walls, yet increasing school connectedness and reframing student behavior are two foundational ways to set up secondary students for success.

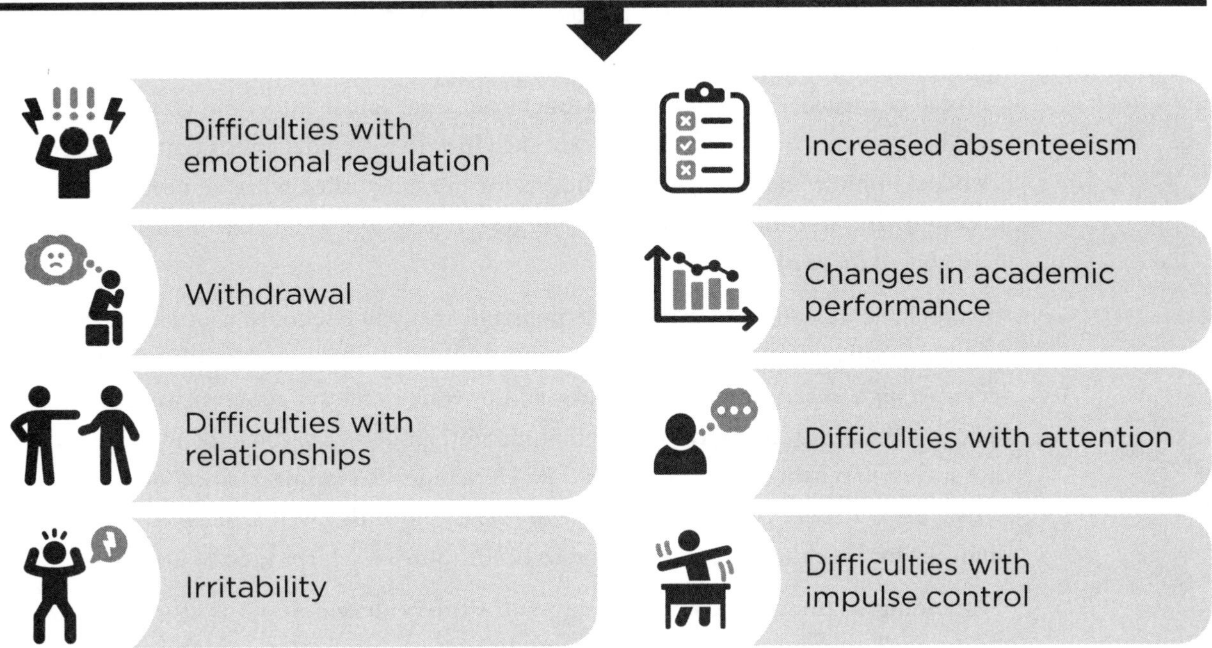

Source: Felitti et al., 1998; Hays-Grudo & Morris, 2020; National Child Traumatic Stress Network, 2008.

Figure 3.3: How adverse childhood experiences can manifest in the classroom.

School Connectedness

But here's the good news: Schools can make an impact! Instead of focusing on the increasing mental health barriers, consider the role that protective factors can play in improving students' mental, physical, and emotional health, ensuring their brains and bodies are open to learning. Protective factors are conditions or elements that can buffer the impact of stressful events and improve lifelong outcomes (La Charite et al., 2023; Simonsen, Goodman, et al., 2021). Protective factors include support from peers, a positive school atmosphere, neighborhood safety, community support, and nurturing parental relationships, to name a few. These conditions can help reduce emotional distress, risky behaviors, and suicidal ideation and promote social competence (La Charite et al., 2023).

Though not all protective factors are within a school's locus of control, school connectedness is one specific protective factor that schools *can* influence. *School connectedness* is "the belief by students that adults and peers in the school care about their learning as well as about them as individuals" (Centers for Disease Control and Prevention, 2009, p. 3). Specific examples of this include having nonparent adults take a genuine interest in the student and feeling a sense of belonging in school (McQuillin, Smith, & Strait, 2011; Morris & Hays-Grudo, 2023). School connectedness is a strong predictor of academic success, including improved attendance, engagement, grades, and high school completion (American Psychological Association, 2014; Blum, 2005a, 2005b; Hernández & Darling-Hammond, 2024a, 2024b; Steiner et al., 2019; Whitlock, 2006).

I recall one teacher sharing how she sought out a particular student in class who she knew had great potential. She privately checked in with the student and communicated her belief in him. She set high expectations for him and asked what he needed to be successful. The student felt seen, the relationship grew, and his behavior and engagement shifted dramatically over time.

Years of research on connectedness demonstrate that when schools maintain effective classroom management, focus on relationship building, engage with families and students, set high expectations for students, and provide necessary academic supports in a physically and psychologically safe environment, students are most likely to experience success in school (Blum, 2005a, 2005b; Hernández & Darling-Hammond, 2024a, 2024b; Steiner et al., 2019). This culture of *care*, along with a well-structured learning environment, sets the stage for learning to occur (Smylie, Murphy, & Louis, 2020).

Attending to these noncognitive factors of student development is crucial to the success of all students. Educators inherently know that it will take more than the abilities to read, write, and compute for students to succeed personally, intellectually, and professionally. School districts across the United States are increasingly seeking techniques that serve the broader purpose of education to better prepare students to meet the intensifying demands of work, life, and citizenship (García, 2014; Hamedani & Darling-Hammond, 2015; Organisation for Economic Co-operation and Development, 2018; Porter, Jackson, Kiguel, & Easton, 2023; Regional Educational Laboratory Appalachia at SRI International, 2020).

Research demonstrates that efforts made in families, schools, and communities can give rise to resilience in children and adolescents (Masten, 2001; Masten & Reed, 2002; National Center for Chronic Disease Prevention and Health Promotion, Division of Adolescent and School Health, 2023), even those considered at risk for negative developmental outcomes. I often think, *Resilience equals hope*. As educators, we have reason to be optimistic that we can change the trajectory of our students.

Get every kid connected!

Therefore, when schools are considering students' behavioral and social-emotional needs, I believe the main goal should be to *get every kid connected*! Connectedness happens through relationships and feelings of belonging that occur when you believe you are a valued member of a group. School connectedness is a powerful tool that schools can leverage to create a positive culture and reduce the likelihood of challenging behavior.

How connected do secondary students feel to their school? The need to belong and feel connected is a driving force for adolescents—and really, all of us! Considering this new understanding of the importance of protective factors, the Youth Risk Behavior Survey began asking young people about two specific protective factors: (1) school connectedness and (2) parental monitoring (Centers for Disease Control and Prevention, 2024b). See their responses in figure 3.4.

PROTECTIVE FACTORS

Connectedness	**55%** of high school students report feeling close to someone at school.
Parental Monitoring	**84%** of high school students report that their parents or other adults in their family most of the time or always know who they are with or where they are going.

Source: Centers for Disease Control and Prevention, 2024b.

Figure 3.4: Protective factors survey responses.

With 45 percent of students lacking connectedness with school (as noted in figure 3.4) and the high prevalence of adverse childhood experiences and associated mental health and learning challenges, it is no surprise that many educators feel that student behavior is deteriorating (Prothero, 2020). In 2023, the EdWeek Research Center conducted a nationally representative survey and found that 64 percent of middle and high school educators feel that students "misbehave" more now than they did in the past (Kurtz, Lloyd, Harwin, Daniels, & Guo, 2023). So, what do we do?

A Reframing of Student Behavior

Beyond increasing school connectedness, we must reframe how we, as educators, view student behavior. How we frame problems affects how we create solutions. By seeking to understand the underlying drivers of behavior, we change the way we respond. Let's explore how this might play out with a secondary student. Imagine Grayson is a student in your fifth-period class. He often puts his head on his desk, overreacts to correction, argues with peers, misses a lot of school, and fails some of his classes. You may describe him as "difficult," "unmotivated," or "apathetic." You may feel that he should know how to behave in school by now.

How we frame problems affects how we create solutions.

Unfortunately, most students will not come to you and articulate, "Look, I can't concentrate today because I'm having intrusive, perseverating thoughts about my adverse childhood experiences. I feel angry because I did not sleep well last night due to my dad and stepmom fighting about money. Then I had to take care of my little sister this morning, so I missed the bus. And a group of boys are bullying me on Snapchat, using their existing power imbalance to exclude and isolate me." As a teacher, wouldn't this be helpful for you to know?

> We must first *believe* that we can impact student behavior and learning.

The tendency to place the onus on the student and to view them as having some character flaw removes the role, and maybe even the responsibility, the school has to influence the student's learning. We must first *believe* that we can impact student behavior and learning. Schools can implement approaches to influence students' learning and feelings of connectedness and also provide successful interventions for students' social-emotional skills, which benefit our society as a whole by improving the community's workforce and economic stability and reducing the need for social services and the justice system (García, 2014; Murray & Rosanbalm, 2017; Porter et al., 2023).

When considering a disengaged or disruptive student, ask yourself the questions in figure 3.5.

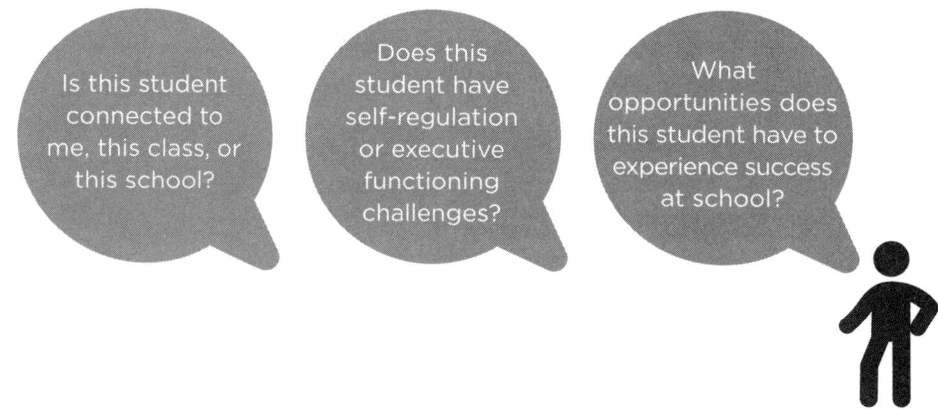

Figure 3.5: Important questions to ask about a disengaged or disruptive student.

There is a strong chance that questions such as these will point to an underlying factor in the student's apparent apathy or lack of motivation. It seems as if we have to become behavior whisperers. Behavior is a form of communication, and we must hone our ability to interpret what really might be driving student behavior and not take behavior at face value. This helps us respond in productive, intentional ways rather than taking a student's behavior personally and reacting in critical or punitive ways (Minahan & Rappaport, 2012; Skiba & Rausch, 2006; Young et al., 2012).

If you were Grayson's teacher in the previous scenario and you investigated the questions in figure 3.5, you might discover that Grayson does not feel connected to anyone at school, reads significantly below grade level, struggles to stay organized, and does not receive any academic or behavioral support at school. Rather than assuming Grayson lacks motivation, is apathetic, and deserves the low grades he gets in class, a well-established tiered system of supports might do the following.

- Provide academic scaffolds in core classes to ensure Grayson's reading level does not prohibit him from accessing grade-level tasks.
- Utilize effective Tier 1 classroom practices such as:
  - Increased opportunities to respond in class
  - Reinforcement for meeting behavioral expectations
  - A continuum of responses to minor behaviors
- Add Grayson to a Check & Connect® group intervention to build a connection with a trusted adult who will monitor his grades, attendance, and behavior.
- Add Grayson to a small-group, social-emotional intervention focused on coping with difficult emotions.

This does not mean teachers have to become therapists. Behavioral and social-emotional learning can be viewed as another set of life skills that teachers can teach. By creating a positive school culture that is welcoming and inclusive, with relationships and care as priorities, you can increase school connectedness.

Having a clear system can lessen teachers' feelings of ambiguity, confusion, and doubt.

As with other areas addressed in this book, you can approach behavioral and social-emotional learning through a framework of increasing intensity, or MTSS, based on the needs of each student. Having a clear system can lessen teachers' feelings of ambiguity, confusion, and doubt by giving them a clear path for supporting students (Heath & Heath, 2010). A behavioral and social-emotional system proactively addresses culture and climate to set students up for success and then ensure support for those who need more. At the secondary level, this system would involve Tier 1 schoolwide supports, Tier 2 group interventions, and Tier 3 intensive, individualized interventions. Let's explore how each of these levels could look in middle and high schools.

Tier 1 Positive Behavioral Interventions and Supports

Though we need expanded research and resources for many aspects of secondary MTSS, the evidence for Tier 1 behavioral and social-emotional support is clear. A rich body of literature supports PBIS's effectiveness for middle and high schools (Flannery et al., 2018; Flannery & Kato, 2017; Flannery & Sugai, 2009; Freeman et al., 2016; Santiago-Rosario, McIntosh, Izzard, Cohen Lissman, & Calhoun, 2023). PBIS implemented with fidelity has been found to do the following.

- It reduces office discipline referrals (Caldarella, Shatzer, Gray, Young, & Young, 2011; Flannery, Fenning, Kato, & McIntosh, 2014; Freeman et al., 2016; Gage, Lee, Grasley-Boy, & Peshak George, 2018; McDaniel & Bloomfield, 2020; Morrissey, Bohanon, & Fenning, 2010; Sprague et al., 2001).

- It reduces days of instruction missed for in-school or out-of-school suspension (Bradshaw, Mitchell, & Leaf, 2010; Gage, Katsiyannis, Carrero, Miller, & Pico, 2020; Gage et al., 2018; Lee, Gage, McLeskey, & Huggins-Manley, 2021; McDaniel & Bloomfield, 2020; Nelson, Martella, & Marchand-Martella, 2002; Scott & Barrett, 2004; Smolkowski, Strycker, & Ward, 2016).
- It reduces the number of student expulsions or referrals to alternative schools or law enforcement (Lee et al., 2021).
- It reduces student dropout rates (Freeman et al., 2015; Malloy, Bohanon, & Francoeur, 2018).
- It improves attendance (Caldarella et al., 2011; Freeman et al., 2015, 2016; Johnson et al., 2013; Pas, Ryoo, Musci, & Bradshaw, 2019; Smolkowski et al., 2016).

Figure 3.6 summarizes the fundamental components of an effective Tier 1 schoolwide positive behavioral support system for secondary students.

ESSENTIAL TIER I COMPONENTS OF PBIS

OUTCOMES

- Reduced office discipline referrals
- Reduced days of instruction missed for in-school or out-of-school suspension
- Reduced number of student expulsions or referrals to alternative schools or law enforcement
- Reduced student dropout rates
- Improved attendance

SCHOOLWIDE SYSTEMS

- Tiered system of supports that are increasingly intensive
- Teaming with all relevant stakeholders, including students
- Training and coaching
- Problem-solving routines that guide a team through data analysis and action planning

SCHOOLWIDE PRACTICES

- Establish context-specific behavioral and social-emotional goals that are culturally equitable.
- Develop a shared vision for encouraging context-appropriate behavior and responding to context-inappropriate behavior.
- Create three to five schoolwide expectations of behavior, explicitly define these for common areas, and establish predictable routines throughout the building.
- Explicitly teach these expectations and other necessary social-emotional and behavioral skills to all students.
- Provide reinforcements to students meeting expectations.
- Define a continuum of responses to context-inappropriate behavior that includes providing explicit feedback, reteaching, and discouraging the behavior.

CLASSROOM PRACTICES

- Strategic arrangement of the physical environment
- Development of a classroom teaching matrix that includes expectations, rules, and routines
- Active supervision
- Defined strategies for encouraging appropriate behavior, including a high ratio of positive to negative interactions
- Continuum of response strategies for inappropriate behaviors
- Student engagement strategies and high rates of opportunities to respond

SCHOOLWIDE DATA

- Routine data analysis should guide implementation and evaluate outcomes.
- Implementation data may include the PBIS Tiered Fidelity Inventory, culture and climate surveys, office referral trends, social-emotional screeners, and so on.
- Student data may include attendance, office referrals, course performance, individual or group progress monitoring, and so on.

ADDITIONAL CONSIDERATIONS AND ADAPTATIONS

- *Culturally responsive PBIS* maintains high expectations for all students, engages students' cultures and experiences to enhance learning, and provides all students with high-quality instruction and resources.
- *Trauma-informed practices* integrate an understanding of the pervasiveness of early trauma exposure and its impact on policies, practices, and procedures. These practices foster resilience and minimize responses to behavior that may cause retraumatization.
- *Restorative practices* create learning communities with a sense of belonging, identify conflict as an opportunity to strengthen relationships, and develop accountability and problem-solving skills.
- *Social-emotional learning* supports healthy relationships by including self-awareness, self-management, responsible decision making, relationship skills, and social awareness in the instruction and culture of the school.

Source: Center on Positive Behavioral Interventions and Supports, n.d.a, 2024, 2025; Flannery et al., 2018; Flannery & Kato, 2017; Freeman et al., 2016; Hernández & Darling-Hammond, 2024b; Leverson, Smith, McIntosh, Rose, & Pinkelman, 2021; Midwest PBIS Network, 2021; National Child Traumatic Stress Network, 2017; Santiago-Rosario et al., 2023; Schreiber, Miller, & Dressler, 2022; Simonsen, Robbie, et al., 2021.

Figure 3.6: Essential Tier 1 components of PBIS.

It can be a big undertaking to establish a strong plan for secondary-level Tier 1 behavioral and social-emotional support, including the components listed in figure 3.6. Fortunately, extensive practical resources exist to guide secondary schools (including those found on PBIS.org); these resources feature strategies for de-escalating student behavior, practice guides on data-based decision making, and tips for classroom management.

Working through self-assessment tools, such as the PBIS Tiered Fidelity Inventory (Center on Positive Behavioral Interventions and Supports, 2025) found on PBIS.org, can assist teams in reflecting on current implementation and identifying specific areas for next steps. I encourage schools and teams leading this work to seek training and coaching.

Although culturally responsive PBIS is listed as an additional consideration in figure 3.6 (page 78), it is imperative to create a positive school culture. School connectedness is enhanced by ensuring your school is culturally responsive. Responsive environments are sensitive to the diverse cultures of their students (Hernández & Darling-Hammond, 2024a, 2024b; Leverson et al., 2021). This responsiveness is particularly crucial if school staff, leadership, and decision-making teams differ significantly from the student population in socioeconomic status, native language, race, religion, and so on.

MTSS teams must explore the role that bias plays in expectations and discipline. Consider the idea of context-appropriate behavior through the lens of different cultures and with input from diverse stakeholders; this way, you can ensure you recognize and minimize bias in expectations of and responses to student behavior. For example, I bring my own set of beliefs about the way students should behave in school, and I need to recognize that I lack the experience of many of my students of color, students with disabilities, students who are new to the country or to the English language, students from significant poverty, or students who practice a religion that the majority of their peers do not practice. Students who are not from the dominant culture may experience unintentional slights throughout the school environment (Leverson et al., 2021) that affect their feelings of connectedness.

When culturally responsive practices guide a school, they can improve students' feelings of belonging—the protective factors necessary for students to be open and available for learning (Hernández & Darling-Hammond, 2024a, 2024b). Recognizing this, I recall one school team that sought to increase student voice in its policies and practices. They learned that many of their Muslim students were fasting during Ramadan, yet they had to go to the cafeteria each day during lunchtime and be surrounded by peers gobbling up their lunches. Though the students were following the rule without complaint, the school wanted to recognize and respect all its students. The school leadership adjusted this rule and began allowing fasting students to go to another teacher's classroom during lunch to minimize the stress they may have been experiencing in the lunchroom. This simple adjustment made a big statement, communicating to those students, "You matter, and you belong here."

Creating a culturally responsive school is key to increasing connectedness, which ultimately benefits all. Though it is not within the scope of this book to dig deeper into this topic, I encourage your team to seek out training and coaching to improve efforts around equitable practices.

Classroom Practices

PBIS provides guidance in analyzing office referrals and other data to strategically intervene with challenging behaviors (Safran & Oswald, 2003). Through this data analysis, MTSS teams commonly find that most behavioral office referrals originate in the classroom. Schoolwide practices and systems are foundational to effective Tier 1 core instruction, but too often, they center PBIS work on what happens in common areas such as the hallways, lunchroom, and bus loop and never quite get to what is happening in classrooms.

Effective classroom practices are an indispensable component of effective Tier 1 core instruction! These practices ensure students are set up for success and prevent Tiers 2 and 3 interventions from being overrun by students who simply need clear expectations, structures, consistency, and predictability in the classroom. Let's briefly unpack each of the evidence-based classroom practices (Center on Positive Behavioral Interventions and Supports, 2024; Midwest PBIS Network, 2021) from figure 3.6 (page 78).

- **Strategic arrangement of the physical environment:** This includes having an intentional, organized classroom layout that corresponds to the learning activity and allows for movement.
- **Development of a classroom teaching matrix that includes expectations, rules, and routines:** A classroom teaching matrix explicitly communicates positively stated behavioral expectations with examples of what these look like in the classroom, along with clear expectations for routines such as turning in homework and accessing help from the teacher.
- **Active supervision:** During active supervision, teachers actively move and interact throughout a space and position themselves to scan the full area, even as they are talking to an individual or group.
- **Defined strategies for encouraging appropriate behavior, including a high ratio of positive to negative interactions:** These strategies include providing instruction, practice, and feedback on the defined expectations and reinforcing students when they meet these expectations. Specific examples include behavior precorrection (for example, "Remember, during this next activity, we can be respectful to one another by using a quiet voice to work with our table partner") and behavior-specific praise (for example, whispering to a student, "I noticed how responsible you were this morning when you arrived to class on time with your materials ready to go. Thank you!"). You want to maintain a high ratio of positive feedback to corrective feedback. This means increasing positive interactions with students who receive a lot of corrections or negative interactions.

- **Continuum of response strategies for inappropriate behaviors:** Teachers must have more options for responding to minor inappropriate behaviors than "Stop it" or "Go to the office." Therefore, it is helpful to build a continuum of response strategies. These could include the following.
  - Physical proximity, or shifting your physical presence closer to a student who is not following directions
  - Planned ignoring, or being aware of minor inappropriate behavior but strategically not intervening at that time
  - Behavior redirection, which you do by restating the expectation (This works best when you describe what to do, such as "Please save conversations for group work, which starts in five minutes" rather than what not to do, such as "Don't talk when I am talking.")
  - A private signal designed to prompt a student to demonstrate the desired behavior
  - Praise of other students in the class who are demonstrating the correct behavior, such as "I see group 1 quietly beginning their self-reflection. Nice work."
  - Praise approximation (For example, if a student answers a question but adds an inappropriate comment, you may acknowledge and respond to the appropriate answer and ignore the inappropriate portion.)
  - Specific error correction done in private in the hallway or after class
  - Choices in the order or manner in which a student completes a task and when they can take a break from the task
  - A conference outside of class where you ask a student why the behavior is occurring, clarify the expectation, give them feedback, and develop a plan
- **Student engagement strategies and high rates of opportunities to respond:** Strategies for increasing students' opportunities to respond and stay engaged include encouraging group responses, increasing think time or allowing students to discuss something with a partner first, and having students write their answers on small whiteboards.

Consider this: How often do teachers feel that they struggle with student behavior in the classroom? Would you say monthly? Weekly? Every fifteen minutes? And how often do teachers receive training or coaching on how to prevent disruptive student behavior? In many schools, this may happen for only three hours once per year! And this often occurs during a half day of isolated professional learning. This leaves teachers in a very difficult position, feeling unsupported, alone, and inadequate. MTSS is the structure that can provide teachers with the support and backing they need.

When your school MTSS team reviews schoolwide behavioral data, they can brainstorm ideas to improve classroom practices, such as providing choice in professional learning opportunities, initiating a peer-mentoring coaching system, or even establishing yearlong schoolwide collaborative efforts (within a professional learning community, for example) focused on supporting student behavior. Whatever the approach, you must not overlook classroom practices when building a strong Tier 1 system for behavior.

Common Misunderstandings of PBIS

Even with substantial evidence of its effectiveness, PBIS sometimes gets a bad rap at the secondary level. This appears to be driven by myths or misunderstandings such as the following.

- **PBIS does not include consequences for inappropriate behavior:** It is true that PBIS increases focus on teaching, modeling, and reinforcing positive behavior. When proactive, preventive strategies are in place, fewer students will demonstrate problem behaviors. However, having a schoolwide, structured system for responding to context-specific inappropriate behaviors and creating a continuum of response strategies for inappropriate behaviors are *also* important pieces of PBIS work. The MTSS team can help build a systematized response to inappropriate behaviors (for example, one minor rule violation in class equals a discussion with the teacher, two minor rule violations in class equals a phone call to the student's family, and so on). If team members are intentional and proactive and they engage stakeholders (students, teachers, and families) from the beginning, they can create an approach that is connected to the vision and goals of the school, rather than a haphazard, reactive, and simply punitive approach.
- **Students shouldn't get rewarded for behavior that is expected:** Students come to school with varying social-emotional skills. Some students are exposed to trauma, come from disadvantaged backgrounds, or have delays in their development. Cultural backgrounds differ as well. Reinforcement of positive behaviors is a strategy that, when done well, increases the likelihood that expected behaviors will continue. Think about it—adults also enjoy rewards for good behavior! Everyone appreciates receiving praise from their boss, earning a discount on their car insurance for safe driving, or racking up points or "miles" for using and paying off credit cards. Humans are wired to respond to reinforcements.
- **PBIS takes too much time to implement:** Although building the system requires some initial work, PBIS ultimately can improve the school culture and climate, reduce discipline referrals, and increase teaching time (Van Camp, Wehby, Copeland, & Bruhn, 2021). Effectively implemented PBIS is an investment that ultimately reduces the time teachers and administrators

spend responding to inappropriate behaviors, allowing them to focus on instruction and student learning (Flannery et al., 2014; Oswald, Safran, & Johanson, 2005; Solomon, Klein, Hintze, Cressey, & Peller, 2012).

- **PBIS does not work with secondary-level students:** A big barrier to PBIS is it can seem like an ineffective approach when poorly implemented. PBIS pieces work together to have an impact—clear expectations, reinforcements for positive behaviors, effective classroom practices, a continuum of responses to minor behaviors, clear and consistent responses to major behaviors, and a focus on creating a culture of care and connectedness. Placing too much emphasis on one practice and overlooking others can lead to problems. Research shows that when PBIS is implemented with fidelity, secondary teachers report an increase in academic engagement, a reduction in disruptive behaviors, and more positive attitudes toward school (Flannery et al., 2014; Oswald et al., 2005; Solomon et al., 2012; Van Camp et al., 2021).

To bring to light some of these misconceptions, stakeholders should consider the following questions.

- What is the purpose of school discipline?
  - To change student behavior?
  - To maintain safety?
- What is a possible *unspoken* purpose of school discipline?
  - Is there an element of retribution—in other words, is discipline creating suffering as a "just punishment"?
  - Is it to get rid of "problem students" so adults don't have to deal with them?
  - Is it to serve as a supplemental law enforcement agency, providing consequences for behavior?
  - Is it to assert adult authority by making it clear to students that adults are "in charge"?

Although PBIS involves building a continuum of consequences for minor behaviors and solidifying and systematizing responses to more significant behaviors, the disadvantages of traditional punitive approaches, including exclusionary practices of in-school and out-of-school suspension, must be considered (Civil Rights Data Collection, 2021; Nese et al., 2021; Skiba, Arredondo, & Williams, 2014; Thapa, Cohen, Guffey, & Higgins-D'Alessandro, 2013; Young et al., 2012).

- Punitive approaches are not effective methods for changing most behaviors.
- Punitive approaches do not teach students alternative behaviors for preventing future problem behaviors.

- Punitive approaches inhibit learning and create stress and possible retraumatization for some students.
- Punitive approaches provide an aggressive model for students.
- Punitive approaches do not eliminate reinforcement of problem behaviors.
- Punitive approaches are often disproportionately utilized for students with disabilities and students of color.

This does not mean that schools don't need discipline or consequences, but it does mean that *they need more options*! Consequences must be intentional. Punishing a student over and over and hoping they will be sent to an alternative school or eventually move is not an effective system for students who demonstrate challenging behaviors or for the teachers who serve them. As I heard one principal announce to his staff, "These are our students, and no one is coming to save us."

Considering these factors, it would benefit a school or district to identify the purposes of its disciplinary measures. This allows decision-making teams to build their practices and procedures with these ideals in mind rather than responding in a reactive and emotional manner. Upon reflection, your MTSS team may find that the following purposes of discipline better represent their true vision for the school community.

- Protect students from harm.
- Provide opportunities for students to learn from their mistakes.
- Foster a positive learning community.
- Keep students in school.
- Implement a graduated set of age-appropriate responses to misconduct.

Tier 2 Behavioral and Social-Emotional Group Interventions

Even with effective Tier 1 core instruction in place, there will be a subset of students who need additional support. This is where Tier 2 comes in. Within a tiered system of supports, student behavior will tell you when Tier 1 expectations, instruction, and reinforcement are not enough. This will be the sign to increase one or more of the following (Center on Positive Behavioral Interventions and Supports, 2024; Simonsen, Robbie, et al., 2021).

- Instruction on skill development (for example, self-regulation)
- Predictability and structure
- Opportunities for goal setting, praise, precorrection, and feedback to support growth

These additional supports increase the likelihood that students will be able to meet Tier 1 expectations. Using the EWIMS model (see chapter 1, page 17), your MTSS team can use early warning indicators to identify which students need additional supports.

LONG-TERM GOAL FOR TIER I: Our school will have a functioning MTSS team that routinely analyzes schoolwide behavioral and social-emotional data to determine how best to establish schoolwide expectations, systematize reinforcements and disciplinary responses, structure professional learning, and maintain ongoing communication with school staff to ensure effective classroom practices are in place.

TIER I QUICK-START STEPS

1. Solidify a teaming model and clarify which team is responsible for reviewing Tier 1 schoolwide data and ensuring behavioral and social-emotional supports are in place for students in your school.
2. As a team, discuss the purpose of discipline in your school and how this intersects with other mission statements, goals, or initiatives. Determine methods for seeking input from the larger faculty, families, students, and the community. Brainstorm how best to share these proposed goals with these stakeholders and establish the vision to guide your work.
3. As a team, work through the PBIS Tiered Fidelity Inventory (Center on Positive Behavioral Interventions and Supports, 2025) or some other validated self-assessment to prioritize action steps for Tier 1 behavioral and social-emotional supports.
4. Determine what data the MTSS team will review (for example, office referral data, culture and climate surveys, and attendance). Utilize a data-based decision-making process to ensure the students' behavioral and social-emotional needs are systematically supported.
5. Set MTSS team meetings for the school year and determine how best to assign roles and organize data, agendas, and notes. Identify methods for monitoring implementation.

NOTES

Since Tier 2 typically serves 10–15 percent of students (which can be a large number at a middle or high school), the goal of Tier 2 is to serve groups of students through structured interventions that can be efficiently implemented and monitored. Therefore, it is helpful to view Tier 2 as *group interventions.*

Even though not all Tier 2 interventions will involve bringing together a group of students, they are still considered group interventions because they are structured and used consistently with minimal individualization for students. Many of these interventions (such as Class Pass and self-monitoring) would be implemented within a student's regular schedule; however, an intervention such as small-group social-emotional instruction requires a designated time in the school day with a staff member. Scheduling plays a key role in implementation, and specific plans depend on a school's student population, identified priorities, and available resources.

The Function of Student Behavior

The first step to ensuring a Tier 2 group intervention is a good fit for a student is to consider the challenging behavior's function (Crone, Hawken, & Horner, 2015; Ingram, Lewis-Palmer, & Sugai, 2005; Strickland-Cohen & Simonsen, 2022; Young et al., 2012). The *function of behavior* is the underlying need or desire driving the main behavior of concern. Research demonstrates that behavioral and social-emotional interventions are most successful when they are function based (Jeong & Copeland, 2020; Lloyd, Barton, Pokorski, Ledbetter-Cho, & Pennington, 2019; Strickland-Cohen & Simonsen, 2022; Walker, Chung, & Bonnet, 2018). If you select interventions without considering the suspected function of a student's behavior, the behavior may worsen or become more resistant to change.

The function of behavior is typically determined through a review of data, observations, and interviews, with the most intensive approach to data collection being a complex functional behavioral assessment or formal functional analysis. (I discuss functional behavioral assessments in more detail in the Tier 3 section.) For the purposes of Tier 2, you should prioritize efficiency. Therefore, your Tier 2 team may use a more informal approach, including reviewing available data, conducting brief observations, and seeking input from current or previous teachers, the student, and the student's family to identify a *suspected* function of behavior.

Skill and Performance Deficits

When considering the function of behavior, it's important to determine whether the behavior stems from a skill deficit (also called an *acquisition deficit*) or a performance deficit. A *skill deficit* means the student demonstrates inappropriate behaviors because they lack the knowledge and skills necessary to demonstrate the desired behavior. This sometimes is referred to as a "can't do" behavior. A *performance deficit* means the student has the necessary skills yet lacks self-awareness, motivation, or necessary reinforcement for demonstrating the desired behavior. This is referred to as a "won't do" behavior.

Let's say you have a student who isn't turning in assignments. Relevant skill deficits might include academic or organizational weaknesses. These are skills to be *taught*. Performance deficits suggest the student has the academic skills to complete the assignments and the organizational skills to keep up with the assignments but lacks the necessary reinforcement to finish and submit them. In this case, an intervention plan would include motivational strategies and supports to increase the desired behavior. Sometimes, teachers assume student behaviors are due to performance deficits and overlook the skill deficits that may also drive the behaviors (Djabrayan Hannigan & Hannigan, 2024; Minahan & Rappaport, 2012; VanDerHeyden & Witt, 2008). Figure 3.7 illustrates this dynamic.

Figure 3.7: How to respond to skill deficits versus performance deficits.

After determining whether the behavior of concern is due to a skill deficit or a performance deficit (or both), you should further explore if the function of the student's inappropriate behavior is to *avoid* or *obtain* one of the following: attention, tangibles or activities, or sensory conditions (IRIS Center, 2025b; Strickland-Cohen & Simonsen, 2022; Umbreit, Ferro, Liaupsin, & Lane, 2007). For example, some adolescent student behaviors may be motivated by peer attention. A student might find the reinforcement they get for making their peers laugh more desirable than the reinforcement they receive for listening to the teacher's instructions. In this case, the suspected function of the inappropriate behavior would be to *obtain peer attention*, and the team may determine that the student has the skills to participate in class appropriately, but the reinforcement for doing so (learning something new, receiving praise from the teacher, and getting good grades) is insufficient compared to the reinforcement of the disruptive behavior (peers laughing and giving attention to him). So, this would be a performance deficit.

Another student might find a reading assignment so frustrating that they would rather demonstrate acting-out behaviors to be removed from class than attempt the difficult task or risk being embarrassed by their reading abilities. The function of this behavior would be to *avoid an activity*, along with a skill deficit in reading, which should also be addressed (see chapter 2 for strategies to support reading skills). Figure 3.8 illustrates this dynamic.

Figure 3.8: What is driving the behavior?

Replacement Behaviors

Interventions selected based on the suspected function of behavior typically provide an alternative or more socially appropriate first step that still meets the function of behavior. These are called *replacement behaviors* and are strategic tools for improvement (Crone et al., 2015; O'Neill, Albin, Storey, Horner, & Sprague, 2015). Replacement behaviors might feel counterintuitive at first, but they are designed to be faded over time as the student comes closer to reaching the desired behavior. For the student who demonstrates disruptive behaviors to get out of a reading assignment, you could add a structured break system, like Class Pass, that allows the student to request a break when they feel frustrated or overwhelmed. Requesting a break is a replacement behavior for the disruptive behaviors they demonstrated in class. It is a more appropriate method that still meets the same need—avoiding the task.

Educators often wonder, *Why would we let a student continue to avoid a task if that was causing the problem in the first place?* This intermediate step of creating a replacement behavior is like a baby step toward the desired behavior. It helps *shape* student behavior. Over time, the number of breaks allowed can be reduced to fade the intervention as you get closer to the desired behavior of the student remaining in class with minimal disruptions.

You can't lose sight of this goal and get stuck viewing behavior through a negative lens and leading with a punitive mindset. In addition to beginning this break system, it is also important to build just-in-time literacy scaffolding into the lesson and, if available, schedule the student into a literacy intervention class. These supports can increase the student's access to grade-level instruction and lessen their need to avoid the task. Combined, these interventions create a more comprehensive approach to address this example of disruptive student behaviors.

Traditional approaches might have involved sending the student to the office when they displayed these disruptive behaviors. An unintended effect of this type of punitive response is that it actually reinforces the behaviors. It would allow the student to continue to escape the activity and miss the opportunity to practice responding more appropriately to frustration. Plus, missing instruction would only put them further behind academically, compounding the underlying original skill deficit. Figure 3.9 illustrates this dynamic.

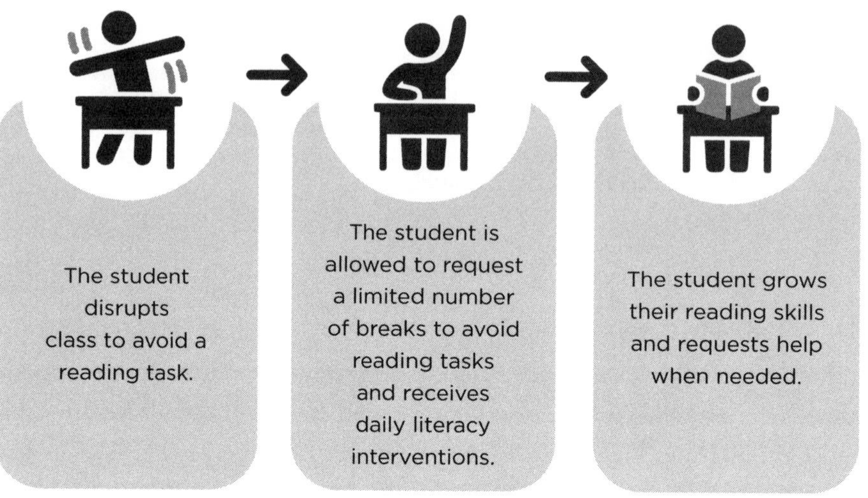

Figure 3.9: How to shape student behavior through replacement behaviors.

To take this concept further, Jessica Djabrayan Hannigan and John Hannigan (2024) define *replacement behaviors* as "a way to help students think about the unproductive behavior they want to replace and how to do it effectively" and state, "We want students to have an inner toolkit of replacement behaviors they can instinctively pull from to demonstrate each targeted life skill" (p. 43). Offering replacement behaviors in class can help students build their own repertoire of appropriate behaviors to draw from in the future.

Functional Behavior Pathway

Optimize the effectiveness of a Tier 2 intervention by considering the suspected function of behavior. You can visualize the reading task scenario through the graphic of a brief functional behavior pathway in figure 3.10. It is not within the scope of this book to provide detailed training in conducting brief or complex functional behavioral assessments; therefore, I encourage your team to tap specialists in the building or district who have expertise on this topic to provide more training and guidance.

Tier 2 Intervention Match

Once a Tier 2 team has identified the suspected function of behavior for students who need additional support, it selects the Tier 2 intervention that is the best match. In the following sections, I discuss the essential components of the following five Tier 2 behavioral and social-emotional group interventions for secondary students.

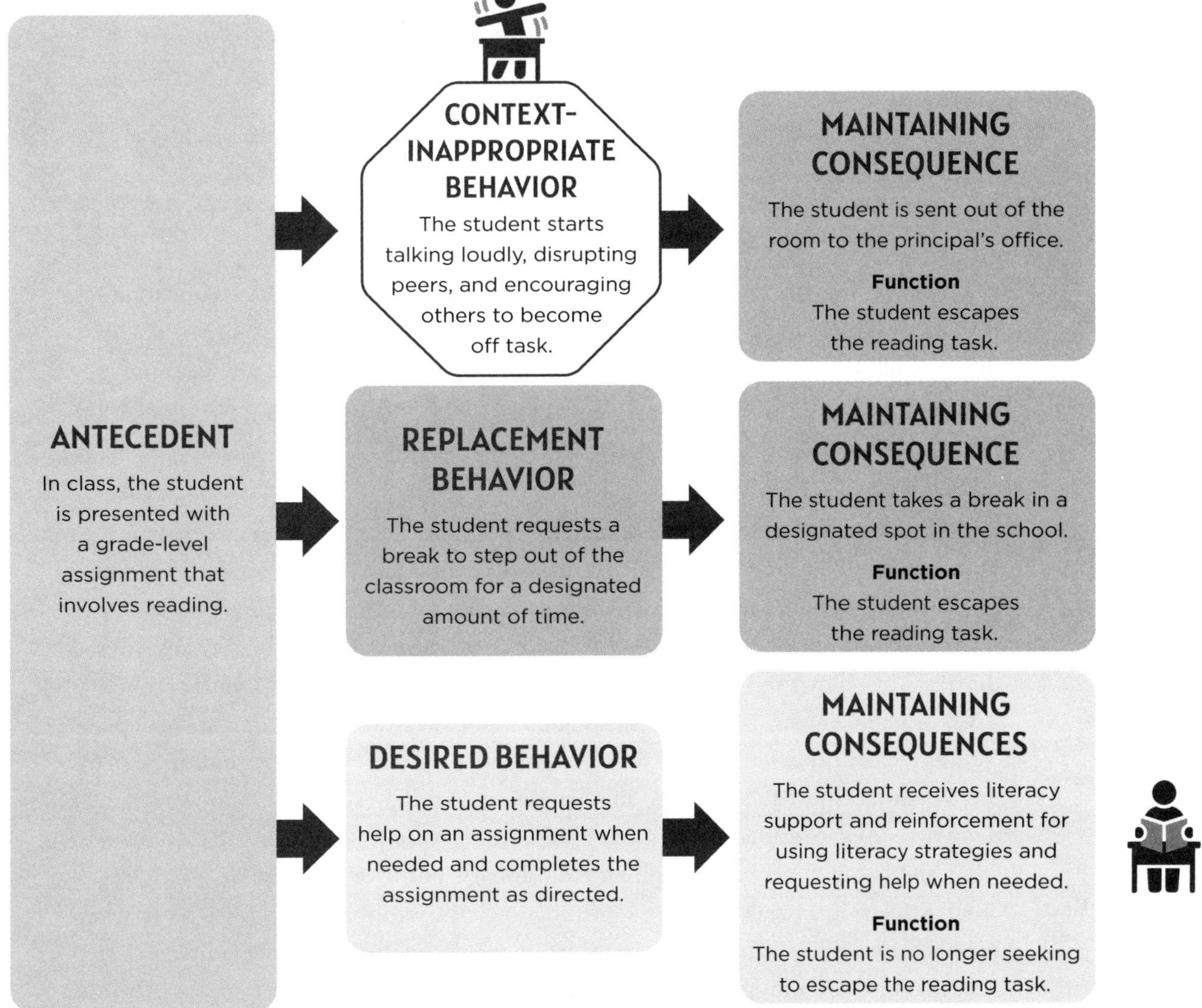

A SYSTEM OF INTERVENTION IN ACTION

SETTING EVENTS

- The MTSS team reviews student grades, attendance, behavior, and credit obtainment.
- The MTSS team assigns identified students interventions based on suspected function of behavior.
- The MTSS team ensures teachers have professional learning to effectively implement scaffolds and interventions.

ANTECEDENT	BEHAVIOR	CONSEQUENCE
• The student begins receiving intervention to improve their reading skills. • The teacher integrates just-in-time literacy scaffolds into lessons.	• The Tier 2 Class Pass intervention is implemented with fidelity. • The student receives small-group Tier 2 instruction in social-emotional skills, including coping with frustration and requesting help.	The teacher reinforces the student for requesting help and practicing newly taught literacy strategies.

Figure 3.10: Sample functional behavior pathway.

Pay close attention to the specific bullet points in the Tier 2 intervention summaries, as they are critical, evidence-based recommendations for effective implementation.

1. Class Pass
2. Self-monitoring
3. Behavior contract
4. Check & Connect
5. Small-group social-emotional instruction

Class Pass

Class Pass is a great introductory intervention to implement at the secondary level. Class Pass is rated highly acceptable by both teachers and students (Collins et al., 2016; Cook, Collins, et al., 2014), meaning they believe the intervention is practical and they are likely to use it in the classroom. Class Pass involves formalizing a system of break cards to use during the most challenging part of a student's day, along with earning incentives for unused breaks.

For students with a performance deficit, whose suspected function of behavior is to escape or avoid an activity, Class Pass provides an alternative, more socially acceptable method for escaping a task or the environment. Plus, Class Pass increases a student's tolerance for remaining in class since they can earn privileges or incentives for any unused breaks. This allows the student to still meet their need of avoidance with an alternative, or replacement, behavior. Although some educators may at first struggle with this approach because they feel that it enables the student, it is important to remember that this is just the first step in changing the student's behavior. You can fade it over time. Also consider which student behavior is preferable—(1) being disruptive in class and being removed through an exclusionary, punitive response or (2) appropriately requesting a break and then returning to class. Additionally, taking a break when one is frustrated or agitated is a healthy self-regulating behavior. As adults, we often step out of the room, go to the restroom, or seek a break when we're upset in a relationship or at work. This is a life skill!

Figure 3.11 shows the essential components of Class Pass. Remember that each step of this intervention must be explicitly taught and practiced. The teacher and student need to clearly understand how the student should request a break (for example, raise one finger) and how the teacher will communicate their response (for example, give a thumbs-up or thumbs-down). There are numerous adaptations to these steps, so consider the context and seek teacher and student input.

Figure 3.12 (page 95) provides an example of a Class Pass break card. Note the very explicit directions. It is important to document, teach, and practice these predetermined expectations. Once these expectations are clear for all, you can shorten the break card to only include the number of breaks that are allowed and the time of day or class periods when breaks can be requested. The instructional component of the document can remain with the student and be reviewed as needed.

ESSENTIAL COMPONENTS OF THE CLASS PASS INTERVENTION

GOAL OF THE INTERVENTION

To create a structured system for a student to request a break from a less preferred task or environment in a socially acceptable way, rather than behaving inappropriately to escape the task or environment

SUSPECTED FUNCTION OF BEHAVIOR

The student demonstrates inappropriate behavior to escape a task or the environment (for example, to avoid an academic assignment, the student becomes disruptive, and the teacher sends them into the hallway or to the office).

ESSENTIAL COMPONENTS

- ☐ Review data to identify the student or students who would benefit from the intervention.
- ☐ Discuss the intervention with relevant stakeholders, including families, students, and teachers.
- ☐ Set the number of break cards a student will receive (for example, three per day).
- ☐ Establish the period of time during which the break will occur (for example, during one particularly challenging class each afternoon after lunch).
- ☐ Determine the amount of time that will be provided for the break (for example, three to seven minutes) and how this will be monitored (for example, by setting a timer).
- ☐ Determine activities for the break with student input (for example, sit and listen to music in a separate space in the classroom, or journal or draw in an adjacent classroom or a specific break space in the building).
- ☐ Identify an incentive (a preferred item or activity, such as time at the end of the day to play basketball) for unused break cards. Increase the significance of the reward based on the number of unused break cards.
- ☐ Determine a method for collecting data on each of the following.
    - **Fidelity of implementation:** Are the break cards provided each day? Is the student allowed to take the breaks? Does the student take each break as defined? Does the student return appropriately after each break? Is the student given the incentive for unused breaks?
    - **Evidence of student progress:** This evidence includes the following.
        - Number of breaks used (For example, at the end of the period or day, the student communicates with the teacher and documents the number of breaks used in a shared spreadsheet.)
        - Pre- and post-behavior rating scales, office referral data, in-class direct behavior ratings, self-monitoring, classroom observations, interviews with students, and anecdotal teacher input

Figure 3.11: Essential components of the Class Pass intervention.

continued ▶

ESSENTIAL COMPONENTS OF THE CLASS PASS INTERVENTION

- ☐ Explicitly teach appropriate steps for the Class Pass breaks.
  - **For the student:** Recognize triggers such as feelings of frustration, anxiety, or boredom when in class. Have them raise one finger and wait for the teacher to give them a thumbs-up or thumbs-down, cross out one break on their Class Pass card, take the break as defined, and then return to class and to the activity.
  - **For the teacher:** Determine how to respond when the student requests a Class Pass break; how to prompt the student to take a break if they show signs of agitation, anxiety, or frustration; how to receive the student once they return from the break; how to monitor progress; how to provide incentives for unused breaks; and how to provide feedback to the student about their progress.
- ☐ Develop a plan for fading the intervention.
  - How often will the data be reviewed and by whom?
  - What are the criteria for reducing the number of breaks made available?
  - What are the criteria for discontinuing the intervention?

TIPS FOR IMPLEMENTATION

- ☐ Ensure the student is academically capable of completing the tasks they are being asked to do.
- ☐ Adjust the reinforcements for unused breaks and timelines for receiving these reinforcements as needed.

Source: Collins et al., 2016; Cook, Collins, et al., 2014.

An important piece of any intervention is data collection. Monitoring will guide a Tier 2 team in deciding how best to adapt the intervention. For Class Pass, this information helps the team determine the number of breaks the student needs, times when the student might most need the breaks, the fidelity of implementation, and when to fade the intervention. Figure 3.13 shows an example Class Pass fidelity and progress-monitoring form.

Self-Monitoring

Self-monitoring is a Tier 2 intervention designed for students who struggle to maintain attention and stay engaged or who demonstrate mildly disruptive behaviors such as calling out, talking to peers, and frequently seeking the teacher's attention. This intervention works best for students who demonstrate inappropriate behaviors such as performance deficits, meaning students know how to demonstrate appropriate behaviors but need to increase their self-awareness and self-management.

CLASS PASS

Date: *1/10/26* Name: *Jimmy P.*

I can tell I need a break when:

- My teeth clench.
- I need to start pacing.
- I begin to cry.
- I want to put my head down.
- My stomach gets upset.
- I'm very fidgety and uncomfortable.
- Other: *I feel like I want to call my grandma.*

I can request a break by:

- Raising one finger and waiting quietly for the teacher
- Watching for the teacher to give me a thumbs-up or a thumbs-down
    - If I get a thumbs-up, I can take my break.
    - If I get a thumbs-down, I will practice taking deep breaths and counting to myself. After at least five minutes, I can request a break again.
- After I have taken my break, I cross out one break on my Class Pass break card and return to the activity.
- During my break, I can quietly go to the designated break spot without bothering others and choose from the following.
    - Listen to music, journal, or draw.
    - Practice progressive muscle relaxation.
    - Play an educational game on a tablet.
    - Work on a sudoku or crossword puzzle.
    - Request to speak to a support person.
    - Other: *I can walk to get a drink of water and then come directly back.*

Time of day or class periods when breaks may be requested:
I have three breaks I can use anytime during fourth, fifth, or sixth period.

Number of breaks taken (cross out one each time you take a break):

~~**Break**~~ ~~**Break**~~ **Break**

Figure 3.12: Class Pass break card example.

Visit ***go.SolutionTree.com/RTI*** *for a free blank reproducible version of this figure.*

Fidelity of Implementation

Name: *Jimmy P.*

Date:	*January 10*	*January 11*	*January 12*	*January 13*	*January 14*
Were the break cards provided each day?	(Yes) No	(Yes) No	(Yes) No	(Yes) No	Yes No *Jimmy was absent.*
Was the student allowed to take the breaks?	(Yes) No	(Yes) No	(Yes) No	(Yes) No	Yes No

Figure 3.13: Class Pass progress-monitoring form example.

continued ▶

Did the student take each break as defined?	(Yes) No	(Yes) No	(Yes) No	(Yes) No	Yes No
Did the student return appropriately after each break?	(Yes) No	Yes (No)	(Yes) No	(Yes) No	Yes No
Was the student given the incentive for unused breaks?	(Yes) No	Yes No *N/A*	(Yes) No	(Yes) No	Yes No

Class Pass Breaks

Date:	*January 10*	*January 11*	*January 12*	*January 13*	*January 14*
Number of Class Pass breaks available	*3*	*3*	*3*	*3*	*3*
Number of Class Pass breaks used	*2*	*3*	*1*	*1*	*Jimmy was absent.*
Number of Class Pass breaks unused	*1*	*0*	*2*	*2*	
Rewards earned for unused Class Pass Breaks	*Jimmy earned one school ticket, which can be saved up to spend at the school store.*		*Jimmy assisted the media specialist at the end of the day.*	*Jimmy assisted the media specialist at the end of the day.*	
Teacher rating of the behavior being measured (completing work as assigned, asking questions about unclear assignments): 1 = Low occurrence 5 = High occurrence	1 2 3 (4) 5	(1) 2 3 4 5	1 2 3 4 (5)	1 2 3 4 (5)	1 2 3 4 5
Other notes: *Tuesday was a tough day this week, but Jimmy did a great job engaging in class on Wednesday and Thursday! I was proud of him for taking his breaks appropriately and returning to his assignment promptly.*					

*Visit **go.SolutionTree.com/RTI** for a free blank reproducible version of this figure.*

Numerous studies support self-monitoring as a tool to reduce off-task behavior and increase academic engagement (Avina, Boyle, Duble Moore, Hicks, & Wiggins, 2022; Bruhn, McDaniel, & Kreigh, 2015; Cook & Sayeski, 2022; Graham-Day, Gardner, & Hsin, 2010; Sheffield & Waller, 2010).

Teachers rate self-monitoring as unintrusive and easy to implement. Secondary teachers appreciate the independent nature of the intervention. Plus, the beauty of this intervention is that self-monitoring is an important life skill. As adults, we self-monitor if we are trying to quit smoking, exercise more frequently, or change other habits. This intervention encourages the development and practice of this skill for students.

My son was once placed on a self-monitoring intervention in middle school. He came home and told me, "Mom, I started checking myself today!" When I probed further, he explained that his teacher asked him to begin marking each time he called out in class on a sticky note. I must admit, he is an enthusiastic, bright, and talkative kid, so I understood his teacher's interest in this intervention. His teacher reached out to me that evening, and we discussed ways I could support this intervention. After only a few weeks, we decided to discontinue the intervention as she (and my son) had noticed a marked improvement in the number of callouts during class. This was a helpful, short-term approach that ultimately improved his self-regulation skills and ability to self-monitor—both of which will benefit him in the future.

Figure 3.14 (page 98) describes the essential components of self-monitoring. Self-monitoring forms can vary considerably based on the monitored behavior and student and teacher preferences. Figures 3.15 (page 100) and 3.16 (page 100) provide two example student self-monitoring cards.

Collecting data on the implementation of a self-monitoring intervention will guide your Tier 2 team in determining when adaptations need to occur. The team can verify that the student understands the goal and target behaviors by the accuracy of their self-monitoring. Fidelity data ensures the intervention was implemented as intended, while summary data provides an overall snapshot of the behavior's frequency of occurrence. Figure 3.17 (page 101) shows an example self-monitoring fidelity and progress-monitoring form.

ESSENTIAL COMPONENTS OF THE SELF-MONITORING INTERVENTION

GOAL OF THE INTERVENTION

To increase a student's self-awareness and self-management by prompting the student to self-reflect on their behavior through a structured self-monitoring system

SUSPECTED FUNCTION OF BEHAVIOR

The student has the skills to be successful but demonstrates off-task or inappropriate behavior due to difficulties with self-awareness or self-management.

ESSENTIAL COMPONENTS

- ☐ Review data to identify students who would benefit from the intervention.
- ☐ Discuss the intervention with relevant stakeholders, including families, students, and teachers.
- ☐ The specific behaviors to be monitored (for example, on- or off-task behaviors) and definitions of the behaviors
    - For example, a definition of *on-task behavior* could be "sitting up and facing the teacher or writing"; a definition of *off-task behavior* could be "digging through a book bag, staring off into space, or talking to a peer."
    - Students can self-monitor the target behavior (the behavior you want to reduce, such as calling out), or they can self-monitor the goal behavior (the behavior you want to increase, such as staying on task), depending on the type of behavior being targeted.
- ☐ When the self-monitoring will take place (for example, during a particularly challenging class or for fifteen minutes at the beginning of each period)
- ☐ The method for prompting self-monitoring (for example, a sound in the classroom, a device on the student that buzzes at predetermined intervals, a physical cue from the teacher, or independent student self-monitoring of when the target behavior occurs)
- ☐ The frequency with which the student will be prompted to self-monitor (for example, every five minutes or during independent student monitoring when the target behavior occurs)
- ☐ The goal set with the student (for example, on task for at least 75 percent of instances measured, or no more than three callouts during class)
- ☐ The self-monitoring chart to mark the behavior once prompted (for example, a tally on a sticky note with the target behavior listed, a self-monitoring card with intervals for marking, or a digital tool such as a Google Form)
- ☐ How to periodically check the student's accuracy in self-monitoring by reviewing whether their self-monitoring chart matches the teacher's reflection

Figure 3.14: Essential components of the self-monitoring intervention.

- ☐ The reinforcement a student will receive for matching the teacher's monitoring
- ☐ The reinforcement a student will receive for meeting the set goal
- ☐ A method for collecting data on each of the following
  - **Fidelity of implementation:** Does the student self-monitor during the designated time? Does the teacher perform random checks to see if the student's self-monitoring matches their monitoring? Does the student receive reinforcement when their self-monitoring matches the teacher's monitoring? Does the student receive reinforcement for meeting the set goal?
  - **Evidence of student progress:** This evidence includes the following.
    - Frequency of the target behavior during self-monitoring (for example, the percentage of time the student rates themselves as on task or off task, or the number of callouts per period)
    - Frequency with which the teacher's and student's self-monitoring charts match
    - Pre- and post-behavior rating scales, office referral data, in-class direct behavior ratings, work completion, classroom observations, interviews with students, and anecdotal teacher input
- ☐ Explicitly teach appropriate steps for self-monitoring.
  - **For the student:** Understand the behavior being monitored, steps for controlling this behavior, and when and how to self-reflect and mark their behavior on the chart.
  - **For the teacher:** Initiate the prompting system, periodically conduct monitoring with the student to assess the accuracy of their self-monitoring, reflect on the student's self-monitoring at the end of class, and reinforce appropriate behaviors and improvement.
- ☐ Develop a plan for fading the intervention.
  - How often will the data be reviewed and by whom?
  - What are the criteria for fading the intervention by extending the amount of time between self-monitoring prompts (for example, moving to ten or fifteen minutes between prompts)?
  - What are the criteria for discontinuing the intervention?

TIPS FOR IMPLEMENTATION

- ☐ Ensure the student is academically capable of completing the tasks they are being asked to do.
- ☐ Add the step of having the student graph positive or on-task behaviors to increase their motivation (for example, digitally or on graph paper in a notebook).
- ☐ Utilize a commercial tool to simplify self-monitoring prompting and data collection (for example, MotivAider or the I-Connect app from Apple).

Source: Avina et al., 2022; Bruhn et al., 2015; Cook & Sayeski, 2022; Sheffield & Waller, 2010; Wills & Mason, 2014.

Date: *October 15*

Name: *Leah M.*

Behavior goal and description (Yes): *Leah will come to class prepared—sitting in her seat and have notebook and pencil out when the bell rings; have homework completed and ready to submit.*

Non-examples of the behavior (No): *Not in seat when the bell rings; missing homework, notebook, or pencil.*

Self-Monitoring Chart

(Mark *yes* or *no* at each designated interval or prompt.)

Monitoring Frequency	Monday	Tuesday	Wednesday	Thursday	Friday
Yes	✓	✓		✓	
No			✓		✓

Rate of behavior: I demonstrated my goal behavior during *mathematics class* in *three* out of *five* instances, which is *60* percent.

Did the student's self-monitoring match the teacher's monitoring during periodic checks? (Yes) No

Did the student meet the goal of *80 percent* this week? Yes (No)

Figure 3.15: Student self-monitoring card—Example 1.

Visit ***go.SolutionTree.com/RTI*** *for a free blank reproducible version of this figure.*

Date: *September 20*

Name: *Jkeyah B.*

Goal: *Use quiet and collaborative methods (such as writing it down or raising my hand) when I have a thought or question during class.*

Target behavior I'm trying to reduce: *Call outs during English class*

Tally marks for each time the target behavior occurred: ||||

Rate of behavior: I demonstrated the target behavior *4* times during the *55-minute* time period.

Did my self-monitoring match the teacher's monitoring during periodic checks? Yes (No)

Did I meet the goal of: *less than 5 call outs during English class*? (Yes) No

Figure 3.16: Student self-monitoring card—Example 2.

Visit ***go.SolutionTree.com/RTI*** *for a free blank reproducible version of this figure.*

Fidelity of Implementation

Name: *Jkeyah B.*

Date:	*September 16*	*September 17*	*September 18*	*September 19*	*September 20*
Did the student self-monitor during the designated time?	**(Yes)** No	**(Yes)** No	**(Yes)** No	**(Yes)** No	**(Yes)** No
Did the teacher perform random checks to see if the student's self-monitoring matched their monitoring?	**(Yes)** No	Yes **(No)**	**(Yes)** No	Yes **(No)**	**(Yes)** No
Did the student's self-monitoring match the teacher's monitoring during periodic checks?	**(Yes)** No	Yes No	**(Yes)** No	Yes No	**(Yes)** No
Did the student receive reinforcement when their self-monitoring matched the teacher's monitoring?	**(Yes)** No *Ms. Boards praised Jkeyah.*	Yes No	**(Yes)** No *Ms. Boards praised Jkeyah.*	Yes No	**(Yes)** No *Ms. Boards praised Jkeyah.*
Did the student receive reinforcement for meeting the set goal?	Yes **(No)** *Jkeyah didn't meet her goal today.*	**(Yes)** No	**(Yes)** No	**(Yes)** No	**(Yes)** No

Frequency of the Behavior (Percentage or Total Number)

Date:	*September 16*	*September 17*	*September 18*	*September 19*	*September 20*
Behavior being measured: *Call outs during class.*	*7*	*3*	*2*	*3*	*4*

Other notes:

Jkeyah's goal is to use quiet and collaborative methods when she has a thought or question during class. She is trying to reduce her call outs to less than five during this class period. Ms. Boards and Jkeyah met briefly at the end of each class period to reflect. After class on Monday, Ms. Boards reminded Jkeyah about the importance of writing down her questions, whispering to a peer to clarify, or raising her hand when she had questions. Jkeyah did a good job using these strategies the rest of the week.

Figure 3.17: Self-monitoring fidelity and progress-monitoring form example.

*Visit **go.SolutionTree.com/RTI** for a free blank reproducible version of this figure.*

Behavior Contract

A behavior contract is another group intervention that researchers find to be effective with secondary students (Bowman-Perrott, Burke, de Marin, Zhang, & Davis, 2015; Din, Isack, & Rietveld, 2003; Schrieber, Ware, & Dart, 2023; Simonsen, Fairbanks, Briesch, Myers, & Sugai, 2008). Researchers Stefanie R. Schrieber, Mary E. Ware, and Evan H. Dart (2023) note that behavior contracts can be especially applicable for secondary students, since these contracts are flexible, involve goal setting, provide explicit clarification of rules, and can be done collaboratively with the student, giving the student agency and voice. Behavior contracts work best for students with a performance deficit, who know how to demonstrate the expected skills but may need additional support and motivation to do so. Figure 3.18 outlines the essential components of a behavior contract.

ESSENTIAL COMPONENTS OF A BEHAVIOR CONTRACT INTERVENTION

GOAL OF THE INTERVENTION

To increase a student's motivation to demonstrate a targeted skill through the development of a behavior contract and reinforcement system with student input

SUSPECTED FUNCTION OF BEHAVIOR

The student has the skill (for example, they are able to attend school, complete assignments, or get to class on time) but needs more reinforcement to demonstrate the skill.

ESSENTIAL COMPONENTS

- ☐ Review data to identify students who would benefit from the intervention.
- ☐ Discuss the intervention with relevant stakeholders, including families, students, and teachers.
- ☐ The specific behavior goals to be monitored (To maintain the efficiency of a behavior contract at the Tier 2 level, goals typically connect to the schoolwide expectations and are the same for all students receiving the group intervention. If a Tier 2 team feels they need to add a particular behavior that falls under these expectations, then they must specifically define the behavior. For example, if a team wants to define "being responsible," they may add a specific challenge for the student, such as arriving to class on time, and then operationally define this behavior: *On time* means sitting in their seat when the bell rings; *late* means not arriving to class until after the bell rings or entering the classroom as the bell rings. They could specify that to earn the reward on Friday, the student must be on time to class four out of five days.)
- ☐ The reinforcement or reward the student can earn for meeting the expectations (For example, they and a friend get to play basketball for fifteen minutes after lunch on Friday.)

Figure 3.18: Essential components of a behavior contract intervention.

To create a strong behavior contract, enlist the student to identify ideas for a reasonable goal for improving the behavior, and then brainstorm ideas for reinforcements. The key is to think creatively and encourage the student to open their mind to reinforcements they may not have considered before. Oftentimes, educators are surprised by the reinforcements students find motivating. Some students might enjoy working toward school swag (for example, sweatshirts and water bottles), while others may enjoy spending time with a trusted adult during the school day, and others may want to earn discounted prom tickets or free tickets to a school ball game. The goal is to identify reinforcements that can be motivating enough to change habitual negative behaviors. This creates a student-centered plan of action. Behavior contracts can vary considerably. Figure 3.19 (page 104) shows an example behavior contract.

- ☐ How the teacher reviews, precorrects, and prompts the contract with the student (For example, each day the teacher is with the student, they will remind the student of the contract, expectations, and reinforcement.)
- ☐ How to write up the contract and obtain the student's and teacher's (and possibly family's) signatures
- ☐ A method for collecting data on each of the following
    - **Fidelity of implementation:** Is the contract developed with input from the teacher and the student (and if possible, the family)? Does the teacher regularly review, precorrect, and prompt the contract? Does the student document their behavior on the monitoring sheet? Does the teacher provide the reinforcement as defined?
    - **Evidence of student progress:** This evidence includes the following.
        - Frequency of the target behavior (For example, if you are tracking the number of days that the student is on time to class each week, the student could mark *yes* or *no* on a chart on the teacher's desk each time they arrive to class.)
        - Pre- and post-behavior rating scales, office referral data, in-class direct behavior ratings, course performance data (for example, grades and missing assignments), classroom observations, interviews with students, and anecdotal teacher input
- ☐ Explicitly teach appropriate steps for the behavior contract.
    - **For the student:** Clarify the specifics of the negotiated contract. Discuss tips for meeting the expected behavior (for example, help them determine during which breaks they have time to go to their locker and when they do not). Provide guidance on how to document their behavior and initiate the reinforcement at the designated times.
    - **For the teacher:** Clarify the specifics of the negotiated contract, including the expected behavior and reinforcement. Discuss how they will review, precorrect, and prompt the contract each day they are with the student.

continued ▶

ESSENTIAL COMPONENTS OF A BEHAVIOR CONTRACT INTERVENTION

☐ Develop a plan for fading the intervention.
- How often will the data be reviewed and by whom?
- What are the criteria for reducing the frequency of the reinforcement?
- What are the criteria for discontinuing the intervention?

TIPS FOR IMPLEMENTATION

☐ The contract should be written in the positive—what the student *should do* rather than what they *should not do*.

☐ The contract must be built collaboratively with the teacher's and the student's (and ideally, the family's) input.

☐ If the student does not know how to demonstrate the expected behavior, then this behavior should be explicitly taught.

Source: Adapted from Bowman-Perrott et al., 2015; Din et al., 2003; Schrieber et al., 2023; Simonsen et al., 2008.

	Schoolwide expectations or behavior goal: • *Be responsible.* • *Show up to class on time, which means be in my seat with my materials out, when the bell rings.* • *Specifically, be on time for fourth period (Mrs. Lindsey's class), defined as no more than two tardies during this first quarter.*
	Challenges to overcome to reach my goal: • *I sometimes want to talk to my friends between classes.* • *I can't find what I need in my locker.*
	Strategies to help me reach my goal: • *Work with Ms. Jackson (youth service coordinator) to organize my backpack and locker.* • *Set a timer between classes that shows a countdown of five minutes.* • *Plan to arrive at my classroom when there is one minute remaining to allow time to get to my seat and get out my materials.* • *Remind myself that I can talk to my friends more once school is out.*
	Reinforcement options: • *Choose from the treat basket for each week I am on time all five days (zero tardies).* • *Get one homework pass per month if I have no more than one tardy.* • *Join the "No Tardy Party" in October if I have no more than two tardies during the first quarter.*

Student signature: *Caleb B.*

Teacher signature: *Mrs. Lindsey* *Ms. Jackson*

Figure 3.19: Behavior contract form example.

Visit ***go.SolutionTree.com/RTI*** *for a free blank reproducible version of this figure.*

The behavior contract requires some type of simple monitoring to document the frequency at which the student demonstrates the behavior goal. For example, if a student is working to reduce their tardies, they could keep a weekly chart at the teacher's desk. When the student enters the room each day, they can circle *yes* or *no* on the chart based on whether they were on time (with their goal being to arrive on time to class four out of five days). Figure 3.20 shows an example of how to easily monitor this type of behavior.

Name: Caleb B.					
Date:	August 15	August 16	August 17	August 18	August 19
Did I meet my goal today?	(Yes) No	(Yes) No	(Yes) No	(Yes) No	(Yes) No
Did I earn my reward this week?	(Yes) No				

Figure 3.20: Behavior contract monitoring form example.

Visit ***go.SolutionTree.com/RTI*** *for a free blank reproducible version of this figure.*

Fidelity of implementation should always be considered by the Tier 2 team monitoring the intervention. Figure 3.21 shows an example data collection form for a behavior contract, noting the essential elements of implementation and providing a section to summarize the student's progress.

Fidelity of Implementation					
Name: Caleb B.					
Date:	August 15	August 16	August 17	August 18	August 19
Was the contract developed with input from the teacher and the student (and if possible, the family)?	(Yes) No				
Did the teacher regularly review, precorrect, and prompt the contract?	(Yes) No	(Yes) No	(Yes) No	(Yes) No	(Yes) No
Did the student document their behavior on the monitoring sheet?	(Yes) No	(Yes) No	(Yes) No	(Yes) No	(Yes) No

Figure 3.21: Behavior contract fidelity and monitoring form example.

continued ▶

Did the teacher provide the reinforcement as defined?	Yes No	Yes No	Yes No	Yes No	(Yes) No Caleb has been on time each day this week, so he got to pick out of Mrs. Lindsey's treat basket.

Frequency of Reaching Their Goal (Percentage or Total Number)					
Week	**1**	**2**	**3**	**4**	**5**
Behavior being measured:	5/5	4/5	5/5	5/5	4/5
Other notes: *Caleb has worked hard to be on time and prepared. His grades are showing improvement since last year. We are proud of the effort he is putting into being responsible!*					

Visit ***go.SolutionTree.com/RTI*** *for a free blank reproducible version of this figure.*

Check & Connect

Considering the power of relationships, a strong intervention option to build into your school's MTSS is Check & Connect® (https://checkandconnect.umn.edu). The formal program of Check & Connect was developed by the Institute on Community Integration at the University of Minnesota. This intervention accomplishes many important goals. It keeps students in school, reduces office behavior referrals, and improves tardiness and attendance (Anderson, Christenson, Sinclair, & Lehr, 2004; Christenson et al., 2008; Maynard, Kjellstrand, & Thompson, 2014; Rumberger et al., 2017; Sinclair, Christenson, Evelo, & Hurley, 1998; Sinclair, Christenson, & Thurlow, 2005).

Check involves an adult who regularly meets with the student and systematically monitors their grades, attendance, and behavior. *Connect* refers to the adult mentoring the student and connecting the student, their teachers, and their family to solve problems and facilitate engagement. Figure 3.22 shows the essential components of Check & Connect.

A key activity of Check & Connect includes systematically monitoring data points that have been found to correlate with a student's successful progression through middle and high school (for example, course performance, attendance, and behavior). This data drives the conversation between the mentor and the student, their family, and others. You may use various monitoring methods tailored to your specific school contexts.

ESSENTIAL COMPONENTS OF THE CHECK & CONNECT INTERVENTION

GOAL OF THE INTERVENTION

To have a well-matched mentor monitor a student's grades, attendance, and office behavior referrals to coach them and reinforce positive behaviors

SUSPECTED FUNCTION OF BEHAVIOR

The Check & Connect intervention centers on relationship building. It is multifaceted and, therefore, can serve a multitude of student needs. If a student has a skill deficit, a mentor can identify the specific skill the student may need to learn (for example, organization) and provide support and coaching in that skill. If a student has the skill (for example, they are able to attend school, complete assignments, or get to class on time), Check & Connect can give them the reinforcement to demonstrate the skill. If a student seeks attention from adults, this intervention provides them access to a mentoring adult.

ESSENTIAL COMPONENTS

- ☐ Review data to identify students who would benefit from the intervention.
- ☐ Discuss the intervention with relevant stakeholders, including families, students, and teachers.
- ☐ Identify a mentor who will be a strong match for the student for a minimum of two years; the mentor could be a school employee or volunteer. Determine what resources are needed to train the mentor.
- ☐ Provide an organizational tool or document for collecting and monitoring student success factors (attendance, behavior, and course performance) and notes from meetings with the student and family.
- ☐ Establish a schedule for the mentor to meet weekly with the student to share "check" data and provide explicit performance feedback based on that data.
- ☐ Ensure that at least monthly, the mentor systematically problem-solves with the mentee and discusses the long-term importance of school and staying engaged.
- ☐ Determine methods for the mentor to connect with the student's family to foster a positive relationship and cultivate engagement.
- ☐ Determine a method for collecting data on each of the following.
    - **Fidelity of implementation:** Is the mentor intentionally selected and a good match for the student and their family? Does the mentor systematically monitor the student's course performance, attendance, and office referral data? Does the mentor meet weekly with the student, share "check" data, and provide explicit performance feedback based on that data? Does the mentor meet at least monthly with the student to systematically problem-solve and discuss the long-term importance of school and staying engaged? Does the mentor connect with the student's family to facilitate a relationship and cultivate engagement?
    - **Evidence of student progress:** This evidence includes the following.

Figure 3.22: Essential components of the Check & Connect intervention.

continued ▶

ESSENTIAL COMPONENTS OF THE CHECK & CONNECT INTERVENTION

- Critical student success factors to provide the check for course performance (for example, grades and credits earned), attendance, and behavior
- Pre- and post-behavior rating scales, office referral data, in-class direct behavior ratings, course performance data (for example, grades and missing assignments), attendance, classroom observations, interviews with students, and anecdotal teacher input

☐ Explicitly teach the steps for Check & Connect.

- **For the student:** Clarify the method for meeting regularly with the mentor and what will happen during those check-ins. Communicate the plan for connecting with their family.
- **For the mentor:** Determine the frequency and location of meetings with the student. Provide guidance for coaching and communicating with the student (for example, building a relationship, connecting with the family, clarifying boundaries, and setting goals). Train the mentor on how to maintain an organizational tool or document for collecting and monitoring student success factors (attendance, behavior, and course performance) and notes from meetings with the student and family.

☐ Develop a plan for fading the intervention.

- How often will the data be reviewed and by whom?
- What are the criteria for discontinuing the intervention?
- How will the mentor maintain the relationship once the intervention is discontinued?

TIPS FOR IMPLEMENTATION

☐ An effective mentor-mentee match is crucial. Ideally, students are matched with an adult with whom trust is already established.

☐ Check & Connect works best when the check includes precorrections of common problem behaviors for the student (for example, falling asleep during first period) and explicit performance feedback.

☐ Connecting with the family is a step that is too often dropped during mentoring interventions such as this. Schools should engage in multiple efforts and methods to ensure this essential component is accomplished.

Source: Adapted from Christenson et al., 2012; Institute on Community Integration, n.d.; Rumberger et al., 2017.

To implement Check & Connect, you may find a Mentor Practice Profile and other specialized tools that provide a comprehensive and accurate measurement of fidelity at https://checkandconnect.umn.edu.

Small-Group Social-Emotional Instruction

When considering the suspected function of a student's behavior, the Tier 2 team may determine that it is not an absence of motivation or reinforcement; rather, the student has not yet mastered the social-emotional skills necessary to demonstrate context-appropriate behavior. As secondary educators, we often are quick to assume that a student has the prerequisite skills to be successful. However, there are many reasons why students may not have acquired developmentally appropriate social-emotional skills, including disrupted school experiences, developmental delays or disabilities, trauma exposure, and increased technology usage, to name a few (Centers for Disease Control and Prevention, 2024a; Cerutti, Burt, Moeller, & Seehuus, 2024; Felitti et al., 1998; Hamilton & Gross, 2021; Ross, Kim, Tolan, & Jennings, 2019; U.S. Public Health Service, 2023).

Additionally, even for typically developing adolescents, the brain is under rapid construction. The emotional systems that seek rewards and heighten feelings are often better developed than the "stop and think" systems of the brain that help one plan, organize, and solve problems (Murray & Rosanbalm, 2017; National Academies of Sciences, Engineering, and Medicine, 2019). An expanding body of research indicates that students who participate in social-emotional learning programs exhibit increased prosocial behaviors *and* academic skills (Belfield et al., 2015; Boncu, Costea, & Minulescu, 2017; Duncan et al., 2017; Durlak, Weissberg, Dymnicki, Taylor, & Schellinger, 2011; Hamedani & Darling-Hammond, 2015; Steinberg, 2014; Yeager, 2017). So, how do we teach these skills?

The Collaborative for Academic, Social, and Emotional Learning (CASEL, n.d.) identifies the following social-emotional learning competencies.

- **Self-awareness:** Recognizing and understanding your emotions, strengths, and limitations
- **Self-management:** Managing your own emotions, thoughts, and behaviors in pursuit of your goals
- **Responsible decision making:** Making intentional choices that align with your goals and values
- **Relationship skills:** Creating and sustaining positive relationships with others
- **Social awareness:** Taking others' perspectives and empathizing with others

Numerous social-emotional learning programs exist for middle and high school students, with growing evidence of the effectiveness of such programs (Jones et al., 2022). In the secondary context, these programs may be approached as character education, employability skills or life skills training, positive youth development, violence prevention, and so on. Effective social-emotional learning programs involve explicit instruction in these competencies through lessons, strategies, and routines. CASEL.org is an excellent resource for finding evidence-based social-emotional learning programs for secondary students, some of which are free to utilize. Research and program development are ongoing, and new programs are added routinely. (Visit **go.Solution Tree.com/RTI** to find a list of social-emotional learning programs appropriate for the secondary level.)

When selecting a program, note that effective social-emotional learning programs emphasize the following (CASEL, n.d.; Domitrovich, Syvertsen, & Calin, 2017; Jones et al., 2022).

- *Providing explicit instruction* in social-emotional skills through lessons that follow an organized scope and sequence
- *Making content connections* that bridge the social-emotional learning lessons with vocational skills, civic engagement, or activities such as community service
- *Addressing the beliefs and behavior of the adults in the school* by increasing their understanding of their role in creating a psychologically safe culture and teaching and reinforcing students' social-emotional competencies
- *Improving the school culture* by building in structures and routines across the school to strengthen teacher-student relationships and positive peer interactions
- *Making reforms to the organization* by installing policy and procedural changes that prioritize social-emotional learning and integrate it into all aspects of the school's functioning

Tier 2 group interventions, such as a specific social-emotional learning program or some other behavioral intervention, can be the means by which schools support groups of students who need more than the Tier 1 expectations, predictability, relationships, routines, and reinforcement provided in the classroom and school. In this section, I reviewed five Tier 2 interventions that can be implemented at the middle and high school levels. In the next section, I explore three Tier 3 interventions for those students who need more intensive, individualized support.

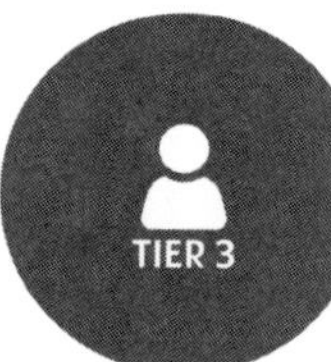

Tier 3 Intensive, Individualized Behavioral and Social-Emotional Interventions

Most students will experience positive behavioral outcomes when strong Tier 1 and Tier 2 plans are in place. However, it is expected that 3–5 percent of students may still require additional support (Center on Positive Behavioral Interventions and Supports, 2024), leading to the need for an intensified layer of support. For the most stubborn or challenging student behaviors, your school may feel like your only options are to assign in-school or out-of-school suspension or to refer the student to an alternative school or possibly special education. This section guides your school to flip the script and adopt a proactive, positive approach to developing intensive interventions rather than relying on punitive, reactive, or exclusionary approaches.

LONG-TERM GOAL FOR TIER 2: Our school will have multiple well-established Tier 2 group interventions led by a variety of personnel with processes in place to check fidelity of implementation and collect progress-monitoring data. These group interventions will be monitored by the Tier 2 team and adapted based on data; student, family, and teacher input; and the unique context. The team will select the appropriate group intervention to best fit a student whose data suggests they need more behavioral and social-emotional support. This team will monitor the progress of the student over time and determine whether the intervention should be maintained, intensified, or faded.

TIER 2 QUICK-START STEPS

1. Select one Tier 2 group intervention (Class Pass, self-monitoring, behavior contract, Check & Connect, or small-group, social-emotional instruction) based on evidence of need in your school.
2. Analyze data to select a small group of students who will pilot the intervention, considering the suspected function of student behavior.
3. Implement core features of the intervention.
4. Adjust and improve implementation based on contextual factors: student data, stakeholder input, and any unintended costs (for example, too much instructional time lost by the student to participate in the intervention, and too much teacher time needed for planning and preparation).
5. Expand implementation to serve more students once the Tier 2 team determines that the intervention is beneficial in your school environment.
6. Solidify the intervention by naming it, documenting processes and core features for implementation, and adding it to the school website or some other school organizational digital platform.
7. Follow these quick-start steps to build the next Tier 2 group intervention into your school's organizational structure.

NOTES

....

....

....

....

....

....

....

....

....

....

....

....

....

....

....

....

....

....

Tier 3 differs from Tier 2 in that the team, assessments, action plan, and data collection methods become more intensive and individualized. Tier 3 intervention is more resource- and time-intensive, so you must be very intentional about identifying the students for this level of support. To begin planning, form a Tier 3 team to focus on intensive, individualized interventions. This team needs to gather information about the student, such as academic, behavioral, and social-emotional data across all life domains. This might involve conducting a record review (for example, reviewing health records, past schools attended, grades, previous testing, attendance, course performance, office referral data, reports from outside agencies, and medical records) and collecting current progress-monitoring data (for example, direct behavior rating or other monitoring from a Tier 2 intervention the student has been receiving, formative assessment data from teachers, and other in-class behavior monitoring from teachers). Once this data is collected, the team can consider how best to develop a comprehensive plan of action.

Key Practices at Tier 3

The Center on Positive Behavioral Interventions and Supports (2024) identifies four key practices for intervening at the Tier 3 level. These practices are the best approaches to take when tackling significant behavioral challenges at the secondary level. Each requires some expertise to implement; thus, it is important for intervention leaders to have a general awareness and then seek out specialists in their school, district, or community to assist.

1. **Functional behavioral assessments:** Research shows that one of the most recommended practices for supporting students at the Tier 3 level—including students in middle and high school—is to conduct a formal or complex functional behavioral assessment to guide the creation of a Behavior Intervention Plan (BIP; Davis, Fredrick, Alberto, & Gama, 2012; Kern, Starosta, Cook, Bambara, & Gresham, 2007; Lane et al., 2007; Lane, Weisenbach, Phillips, & Wehby, 2007; Losinski, Maag, Katsiyannis, & Ryan, 2015). This process is typically led by a specialist with applied behavior expertise. The focus is on identifying cognitive, environmental, social-emotional, and affective factors to understand the drivers of a behavior of concern. Functional behavioral assessments typically involve a review of records, behavior rating scales, and checklists; interviews with the student, their teacher or teachers, and their family; and direct observations to generate hypotheses about the behavior and develop a function-based BIP (IRIS Center, 2025b; O'Neill et al., 2015).

   Comprehensive BIPs include prevention strategies, instructional strategies, strategies for removing reinforcements of the target behavior, identified rewards for the desired behavior, fidelity checks, and the steps to put the BIP into action (Center on Positive Behavioral Interventions and Supports, 2025).

It is outside the scope of this book to train readers on conducting a functional behavioral assessment, but it is important that intervention leaders have a basic understanding of this process and lean on experts in the field who can guide this work.

2. **Wraparound support:** The wraparound service delivery model is a youth- and family-driven approach to support students with behavioral challenges. In a true wraparound model, the family and student determine the vision and goals and identify friends, neighbors, and family members, along with community and school resources, to help them meet these goals. The key principles include family voice and choice, teaming, natural supports, collaboration, community supports, cultural competence, individualization, a focus on the student's strengths, unconditional care and commitment, and an emphasis on outcomes (Bruns, Walker, & National Wraparound Initiative Advisory Group, 2008; Center on Positive Behavioral Interventions and Supports, 2024; National Wraparound Initiative, 2019). This is different from many behavior-planning models in which the school typically selects the goals and action items. The wraparound model is centered on a family- and student-first philosophy and can be an impactful approach to supporting a student with significantly challenging behaviors.
3. **Person-centered planning:** Person-centered planning is similar to the wraparound approach in that it is directed by the individual who needs the support. Person-centered planning is often associated with individuals with diverse cognitive abilities. The person-centered team seeks to identify opportunities for the person to develop relationships with others, participate in their community, increase control over their life, and develop the needed skills to meet these goals (Administration for Community Living, 2024; Center on Positive Behavioral Interventions and Supports, 2024; Kennedy et al., 2001).
4. **Cultural and contextual fit:** Regardless of the Tier 3 approach, it is important to consider the culture and context of the student and school when intensifying supports (Center on Positive Behavioral Interventions and Supports, 2024). This includes the local environment of the neighborhood and community and the race, ethnicity, nationality, language, customs, and experiences of the student. Consideration of these characteristics and how they intersect with the student's peers and school community is critical to any intervention-planning model.

Intensification of Tier 3 Interventions

What type of interventions might you put in place at the Tier 3 level? The strategies for intensifying interventions in figure 1.4 (page 24) can guide you in developing a Tier 3 behavioral system of supports. If you analyze available data to drive decisions and you have a validated Tier 2 intervention in place, you can make adaptations using these research-based approaches to create an individualized Tier 3 intervention plan (Fuchs et al., 2017). Let's take some of the Tier 2 interventions from earlier in this chapter and apply the strategies for intensifying interventions. Figure 3.23 shows examples of how you could intensify a behavior contract.

STRENGTH

There is evidence that supports the effectiveness of a behavior contract for secondary students (Bowman-Perrott et al., 2015; Din et al., 2003; Schrieber et al., 2023; Simonsen et al., 2008), so we will continue this intervention and intensify it.

DOSAGE

This student may benefit from more frequent feedback and possibly different reinforcements. The behavior contract may need to be broken down into shorter intervals, or you could add a bonus reinforcement for exceeding goals (for example, "For every full week you use appropriate language during class with zero profanity, you can choose a friend and, together, help the physical education teacher set up the gym the following Monday morning").

ALIGNMENT

The Tier 3 team may determine that the expectations need to be broken down into smaller, more discrete steps for the student to be successful. Consult with a special education teacher about task analysis (dividing goals into smaller tasks) because they are well versed in this technique. This method can improve the likelihood that a student understands and meets their goals. You could list these subtasks on a card as a guide for the student. For example, to reduce inappropriate language in class, you may give a student a list of steps such as the following.

- Notice if you start to feel frustrated (feel your body tense up or have the urge to blurt something out).
- Pause and practice box breathing.
- Use an alternative phrase such as, "Can I have a minute?" or "This is really frustrating."
- Ask for help or a short break if needed.

ATTENTION TO TRANSFER

The Tier 3 team may involve the student's athletic coach or other classroom teachers in the development, monitoring, and reinforcement of the behavior contract to encourage connection and increase consistency across settings.

COMPREHENSIVENESS

The student may need more explicit instruction in expectations. This can be done through a model-lead-test approach. Other ways to increase the comprehensiveness of a behavioral intervention include the following.

- Make adaptations in the behavior's antecedent—what typically happens before the behavior—to reduce the likelihood that the behavior will occur. For example, give the student a private reminder of the upcoming expectation.
- Reinforce appropriate behavior. For example, provide positive interactions frequently and immediately after improvements in the student's behavior, such as a thumbs-up from across the room.

- Minimize reinforcement of negative behaviors. For example, engage friends and peers who may influence the student by reinforcing their use of appropriate language in class.
- Fade supports. For example, as the student begins increasing the desired behavior, lessen the frequency of support and monitoring in a systematic way.
- Monitor and ensure fidelity of the intervention before making decisions about its effectiveness, and consider whether all components are implemented as intended.
- Work with related services and the student's family to improve consistency and encourage other connected adults to support the goals of the intervention.

The Tier 3 team may decide that the student is missing some skills that are required to be successful with the identified goals. In addition to the behavior contract, they could add an element of weekly instruction in social-emotional skills, such as self-management (including organizational skills) or responsible decision making (including recognizing times to talk to peers and times to stay focused).

Source: Bowman-Perrott et al., 2015; Din et al., 2003; Fuchs et al., 2017; National Center on Intensive Intervention, 2015, 2019; Schrieber et al., 2023; Simonsen et al., 2008.

Figure 3.23: Strategies for intensifying a behavior contract.

You can also adapt Check & Connect to serve as a Tier 3 intervention. Figure 3.24 shows an intensified version of Check & Connect utilizing recommendations from the University of Minnesota and the strategies for intensifying interventions.

Research supports Check & Connect's effectiveness with secondary students. It keeps students in school reduces office behavior referrals or improves tardiness and attendance (Anderson et al., 2004; Christenson et al., 2012; Maynard et al., 2014; Sinclair et al., 1998, 2005); the meeting before, this intervention will remain in place and be intensified based on the student's unique needs.

To ensure Check & Connect is being implemented with fidelity, school personnel should seek out formal training from the University of Minnesota's Institute on Community Integration.

If the mentor was previously meeting with the student weekly, the Tier 3 team may increase the frequency to twice weekly, daily, or even twice daily, depending on availability. Meeting with the student.s twice daily can offer more opportunities to provide precorrection, positive interactions, and specific performance feedback.

Another option would be to increase the length of these sessions, allowing more time to share "check" data and provide performance feedback based on that data. Increasing the dosage may also mean the team increases reinforcement for meeting goals. For example, if a student is working to improve their work completion, they could complete all assignments for that day or week and receive a predetermined reward such as lunch with their mentor or tickets to a school ball game. Reinforcements work best when they are strategically selected with the student

Figure 3.24: Strategies for intensifying Check & Connect.

continued ▶

Strategy	Adaptation
 **ALIGNMENT**	It is important to reflect on matching the mentor and student to ensure they have a positive and supportive relationship. Interviews with the mentor, the student, and the student's family may provide insight into this. Additionally, the mentor may benefit from more specialized training to improve their ability to connect with the student and family and provide explicit performance feedback.
 **ATTENTION TO TRANSFER**	The Tier 3 team may determine that teachers of the student's other classes need to become more involved in the intervention. It can also be helpful to engage other school staff who are connected with the student, such as a cafeteria worker, a bus driver, a coach, an instructional assistant, or a front-office staff member. The mentor and student could share set goals and the skills they are addressing and brainstorm strategies for support during other times in the school day. These conversations may also lead to adaptations to the student's goals or ideas for improving the mentor's methods. It is helpful to seek out contexts in which the student is already succeeding (for example, in one particular class or with one particular teacher) and share ideas to try in other classes.
 **COMPREHENSIVENESS**	The mentor should ensure they are utilizing best practices when providing explicit performance feedback by increasing their use of modeling and think-alouds and having students explain it in their own words.
 **OTHER BEHAVIORAL OR ACADEMIC SUPPORT**	Small-group instruction may be an additional piece that the student needs to be successful. This could involve instruction in relationship-building skills (for example, making friends) or self-awareness (for example, having a growth mindset).

Source: Adapted from Christenson et al., 2012; Fuchs et al., 2017; Institute on Community Integration, n.d.; National Center on Intensive Intervention, 2019.

The Tier 3 team may determine that the student's increasing behavioral and social-emotional needs would best be addressed by intensifying their social-emotional instruction. Figure 3.25 outlines ideas for adapting social-emotional instruction utilizing the strategies for intensifying interventions.

Tier 3 interventions are complex and require more time and resources to plan, implement, and monitor. One can easily feel overwhelmed when first learning about this level of support. Remember to start small—with one student—and seek out other professionals in your school and community with expertise to assist. This process will become clearer and feel more doable with time and practice.

 **STRENGTH**	Research shows that instruction in social-emotional learning can increase prosocial and academic skills (Belfield et al., 2015; Boncu et al., 2017; Duncan et al., 2017; Durlak et al., 2011; Yeager, 2017), so the Tier 3 team may maintain this intervention and intensify and individualize it.
 **DOSAGE**	The Tier 3 team can increase the dosage of small-group social-emotional instruction by incorporating occasional one-on-one sessions or fully moving to individual counseling or therapy. This can be more readily achieved if the school has established partnerships with community mental health organizations.
 **ALIGNMENT**	Depending on the specific skills being taught during social-emotional instruction, the student may benefit from identifying steps they can take to self-regulate or de-escalate during difficult situations. It is important for educators working with this student to be aware of these steps so they understand how to support these actions. Specifically, it might benefit the student to reflect on and document the following. • **Warning signs:** Ways they can tell that they are losing control (for example, feeling jittery and clenching their jaw) • **Behavior concerns:** Behaviors they show when they are feeling stressed (for example, putting their head down and withdrawing from the activity) • **Triggers:** Things that make them feel unsafe or upset (for example, being corrected in front of others and receiving an assignment they can't read well) • **Self-regulation tools:** Things that might help them calm down (for example, requesting to take a break outside the classroom and talking to their support person) • **Conditions to avoid:** Things that do not help when they are feeling upset (for example, humor, sarcasm, and a loud tone of voice)
 **ATTENTION TO TRANSFER**	To increase the likelihood that the student will transfer newly taught skills across contexts, it is helpful to share specific strategies being taught with the student's family, teachers, and coaches, as well as others. For example, the student or a staff member could provide a copy of the steps the student intends to follow to self-regulate or de-escalate as described in the previous row. All adults should be encouraged to prompt and reinforce these practices.
 **COMPREHENSIVENESS**	The student may need additional instruction in identified skills, such as videos demonstrating how self-regulating behaviors (for example, taking a break and practicing deep breathing) impact the mind and body. Modeling and practicing self-regulating behaviors together—or co-regulation—can allow the student to experience what it feels like to calm down. Those working with the student should notice and encourage steps toward self-regulation. For example, if the student requests a break to cool down, encouraging them to take the break and giving them positive feedback after they do so will increase the likelihood that the student can learn and practice this skill. This positive feedback might sound like the following: "Today, I noticed you were trying to avoid getting upset by requesting to take a break. I am proud of you for trying to handle things differently."

Figure 3.25: Strategies for intensifying social-emotional instruction.

continued ▶

OTHER BEHAVIORAL OR ACADEMIC SUPPORT

If the student is receiving academic intervention to support their reading skills, it will be helpful for them to practice these social-emotional skills in that context. For example, you could prompt the student to practice their self-regulating behaviors (for example, taking a deep breath) when they feel frustrated while practicing a challenging reading task. In the regular classroom, the student could practice the skill of requesting help when they receive an assignment that is difficult for them to read. These practices help align academic and behavioral strategies.

Source: Belfield et al., 2015; Boncu et al., 2017; Duncan et al., 2017; Durlak et al., 2011; Fuchs et al., 2017; Hart et al., 2022; National Center on Intensive Intervention, 2019; Wisconsin Department of Public Instruction, n.d.; Yeager, 2017.

Conclusion

If our ultimate goal as educators is to create collaborative, communicative problem solvers of the future, we must recognize that behavioral and social-emotional skills are the foundation. Although numerous relevant factors are out of your school's locus of control, there are *many* elements you can influence. MTSS can be your school's framework for a solid, intentional approach to serving the behavioral and social-emotional needs of your students.

LONG-TERM GOAL FOR TIER 3: Our school will have an established process for convening a Tier 3 team to build a comprehensive Tier 3 plan. Our team will understand the process to intensify interventions for students with significant behavioral and social-emotional needs. The Tier 3 plan will include methods for monitoring student progress and the fidelity of implementation. Our team will review student progress over time and determine whether the intervention should be maintained, intensified, or faded.

TIER 3 QUICK-START STEPS

1. Identify a student receiving support through a Tier 2 group intervention whose data suggests that they need a more intensive, individualized approach.
2. Bring together a Tier 3 team to review data (for example, functional behavioral assessments) and identify what additional information is needed to develop an action plan. Tap into specialists (for example, school psychologists, mental health therapists, or certified behavior analysts) to help guide this process. Include the student and their family in this development.
3. Based on information gathered and input from the student and their family, build a comprehensive plan with your team that includes intensified Tier 3 interventions. The plan will include the intervention-intensifying dimensions of strength, dosage, alignment, attention to transfer, comprehensiveness, and other behavioral or academic support.
4. Communicate the plan to all stakeholders.
5. Implement core features of the intervention and the overarching plan. Explore references and related resources to build a deeper understanding of the intervention and specific evidence-based practices. Additional training and coaching ensure the intervention is implemented with fidelity.
6. Adjust and improve implementation based on data collection (student data and feedback from the student, their teachers, their family, and others).

NOTES

LEARNING OBJECTIVES

- Review fundamental qualities of an effective Tier 1 schoolwide college-and-career-readiness system for secondary students.
- Explore the essential components of three Tier 2 college-and-career-readiness group interventions for secondary students.
- Examine methods for intensifying college-and-career-readiness interventions for secondary students.

Tyreon was an eighth-grade student who struggled with reading. His teachers often viewed him as a troublemaker. Despite his academic and behavioral challenges, he had high hopes of graduating and becoming a successful adult. He was always determined to succeed and prove his doubtful teachers wrong. At his high school graduation, he told me, "They thought I couldn't. They looked at me, saw where I lived, and thought I couldn't. They don't know what is inside of me. So, I had to show them that I could."

This chapter delves into college and career readiness by reviewing U.S. trends and the methods that secondary schools can use to help students graduate and reach positive postsecondary outcomes. For students who are not on track for college and career readiness, this chapter offers three Tier 2 group interventions designed specifically for secondary schools. For those few students who may need more intensive support to become college and career ready and graduate, it offers one individualized Tier 3 model.

The College-and-Career-Readiness Needs of Secondary Students

Our goal at the secondary level is to prepare students for their future. How can we ensure students attend school, grow academically, progress and complete school, and enroll in college and persist to graduation or successfully enter the labor market? These objectives are ambitious and consequential. Future careers provide students with more than an income; they also provide personal fulfillment, social connections, and structure in their lives. From a community or societal perspective, economic competitiveness and an engaged, productive citizenry depend on thriving individuals and families. Our communities are highly dependent on our educational system to help meet this demand.

Nearly all school districts integrate college and career readiness into the fabric of their secondary schools. Many of them initiate this work much earlier, at the preschool or

Future careers provide students with more than an income; they also provide personal fulfillment, social connections, and structure in their lives.

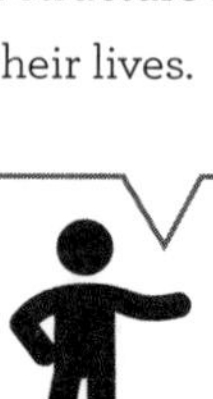

elementary level, since early career exposure leads to a more successful postsecondary transition (Association for Career and Technical Education, 2018; Mann, Denis, & Percy, 2020; Tillery, Cech, & Mania, 2022; Warner, Yarnall, Ball, & Jonas, 2020). This may include service-learning projects, career interest assessments, career mapping, guidance lessons on career or social development, career information infused into content instruction, school-based or student-led businesses, themed middle and high schools, college visits, or career fairs. Plus, work-based learning experiences that bridge the gap between education and employment—apprenticeships, job shadowing, internships, and so on—are used to increase student engagement and connect classroom learning to future careers (Johnson, White, Charner, Cole, & Promboin, 2018; National Center for Innovation in Career and Technical Education, n.d.; Regional Educational Laboratory Appalachia at SRI International, 2020; Rumberger et al., 2017; Southern Regional Education Board, 2020; Visher & Stern, 2015).

College readiness and career readiness have big implications for a student's future. Figure 4.1 outlines the median annual earnings (in dollars) for full-time, year-round workers, twenty-five years old and older, by educational attainment rate (U.S. Census Bureau, 2025).

	Some high school, no completion	**High school completion (includes equivalency)**	**Some college, no degree**	**Associate degree**	**Bachelor's degree**	**Master's degree**
All surveyed	$39,340	$48,810	$55,570	$59,530	$81,090	$97,060

Source: Adapted from U.S. Census Bureau, 2025.

Figure 4.1: Median annual earnings (in dollars) for full-time, year-round workers, twenty-five years old and older, rated by educational attainment.

The more schooling we complete, the higher income we will likely earn. Note that even *some* schooling or an associate degree can impact access to certain careers and lead to higher future earnings and economic growth (Aghion, Boustan, Hoxby, & Vandenbussche, 2009; Federal Reserve Bank of New York, 2025; Lochner & Moretti, 2004).

High school graduation rates continue to increase across the United States; the average rate was 87 percent in 2021–2022; although, rates are lower for students with disabilities, multilingual learners, youth experiencing homelessness, youth in foster care, and those who are economically disadvantaged (National Center for Education Statistics, 2024b). Rates of on-time completion of postsecondary education at two-year and four-year institutions substantially vary by state but have generally remained stable at average rates of 36.5 percent and 57.9 percent, respectively, as last measured in 2019 (Solberg et al., 2022).

Disproportionality exists across both college and career readiness and access. Low numbers of students from historically marginalized groups, multilingual students, students from low-income households, and those who would be first-generation college students enroll in and persist in college (Bailey & Dynarski, 2011; Mann et al., 2020; Tierney, Bailey, Constantine, Finkelstein, & Hurd, 2009). In 2022, college enrollment rates for eighteen- to twenty-four-year-olds were as follows: Asian (61 percent), White (41 percent), Black (36 percent), two or more races (36 percent), and Hispanic (33 percent; National Center for Education Statistics, 2024a).

In 2024, the national average ACT composite score was 20.9 for White students, while it was 16.0 for Black students, 17.4 for Hispanic or Latine students, 24.1 for Asian students, and19.7 for students who identify as two or more races (ACT, 2024). Gaps also exist in career and technical education for many groups of students (Advance CTE, 2019; Donini-Lenhoff & Brotherton, 2010; Mann et al., 2020). On average, 12 percent of White students participate in dual enrollment, while only 7 percent of Black students and 8 percent of Hispanic or Latine students do (Fink et al., 2023; Xu, Fink, & Solanki, 2019).

Students from economically disadvantaged backgrounds are less likely to graduate from college *regardless* of academic level.

This disproportionality in college and career readiness is not due to students in particular subgroups having lower academic skills. In fact, students from economically disadvantaged backgrounds are less likely to graduate from college *regardless* of academic level (Bailey & Dynarski, 2011; Belley & Lochner, 2007; Ellwood & Kane, 2000; Page & Scott-Clayton, 2016; Roderick et al., 2008). This is a complex problem with no simple solution. However, research identifies specific action steps that secondary schools can employ to address these inequalities. These include disaggregating data on college and career readiness, acknowledging existing gaps, obtaining stakeholder input on programming, providing early access (for example, seventh, eighth, and ninth grade) to college-preparatory courses, ensuring students have the academic preparation for college-level work, helping students and families understand the steps for entering college, and creating a postsecondary culture (Advance CTE, 2019; Fink et al., 2023; National Academies of Sciences, Engineering, and Medicine, 2017; Page & Scott-Clayton, 2016; Tierney et al., 2009). In addition to the guidance provided in this book, school leaders should explore their unique contextual data and actively seek strategies for addressing the needs of particular populations that may not be reaching high levels of college and career readiness in their school.

Viewing college and career readiness through the lens of tiered support is a relatively new approach—an integration of the power of a tiered system of support and best practices in college and career readiness. More leaders in the field now recommend that secondary schools integrate college and career readiness (as part of the larger goal of graduating with a diploma) into their existing PBIS or MTSS framework (Daye, 2019; Flannery et al., 2018; Flannery & Sugai, 2009; Johnson et al., 2009; Koselak, 2011; Stoiber & Gettinger, 2016). In the rest of this chapter, I explore how a tiered approach to college and career readiness provides a framework for educators to guide students toward a successful postsecondary transition.

College Readiness

When my daughter was eighteen years old, I jumped in to help her navigate the transition from high school to college, which was her aspiration. Not only did she need the academic skills to handle the demands of college courses, but she also needed to be able to maneuver through multiple applications, forms, assessments, visits, fees, and more. This is surprisingly complicated—even for a parent who has worked in high schools for many years.

How do secondary schools guide students toward college readiness? First, consider how college readiness is measured in the United States. There is variation from state to state, but most include some combination of seat time and course performance along with standardized assessments, including Advanced Placement tests, International Baccalaureate tests, and the SAT, the ACT, and other college-entrance exams. Competency-based assessments and grade point averages are more recent approaches being adopted to measure college readiness. Notably, all these measures are academic in nature and don't consider the complex path one must follow to be accepted to and ultimately graduate from an institute of higher education. In fact, every year, at least 10–40 percent of high school students who apply and are accepted to college do not attend in the fall (Arnold, Fleming, DeAnda, Castleman, & Wartman, 2009; Castleman & Page, 2014; Friedman, 2019). Numerous barriers exist, such as financial and logistic challenges, information gaps, poor academic preparation, concerns about fitting in, and low graduation rates (Bound, Lovenheim, & Turner, 2010; Dynarski, Nurshatayeva, Page, & Scott-Clayton, 2023; Hoffman, Vargas, & Santos, 2008; Linkow, Miller, Parsad, Price, & Martinez, 2021; Page & Scott-Clayton, 2016).

Researcher Elisabeth Barnett (2016) describes the power of a momentum chain, in which a secondary school creates an accumulation of momentum points of college-preparatory experiences that increase the likelihood a student will attend and persist in college. Rather than providing one specific event or experience, we must build a postsecondary culture through repeated exposures to and partnerships with postsecondary institutions to impact each student's school experience. This creates forward motion toward a successful postsecondary transition. Numerous resources, reminders, and college-going experiences (such as college tours or guest speakers who share information with students) can play important roles in increasing the number of students who not only graduate from high school academically ready but also are prepared to traverse any obstacles that come between them and a college degree (Advance CTE, 2024; Barnett, 2016; Farrington et al., 2012; García, 2014; Hamedani & Darling-Hammond, 2015; Page & Scott-Clayton, 2016; Warner et al., 2020).

Career Readiness

The world of work is rapidly changing, and what it means to be "career ready" is constantly shifting, meaning schools must continuously evolve to prepare students for the job market of the future. Career readiness means equipping *all* students with not just academic skills but interpersonal competencies and durable skills (for example, communication, collaboration, self-awareness, self-regulation, and critical thinking). Secondary schools also bolster career readiness by offering industry certifications. These nationally recognized credentials, such as certified welder and certified nursing assistant, signal to future employers that the students have mastered job-readiness skills (Advance CTE, 2018; National Academies of Sciences, Engineering, and Medicine, 2017; Regional Educational Laboratory Appalachia at SRI International, 2020; Shechtman, Yarnall, Stites, & Cheng, 2016; Smith, Lee, Carr, Weatherill, & Lancashire, 2020; Southern Regional Education Board, 2020; Warner et al., 2020).

Teaching employability skills—in addition to academic knowledge—is essential in secondary schools.

Interpersonal competencies, often called *employability skills* when viewed through the lens of college and career readiness, include three overarching dimensions: (1) applied knowledge, (2) effective relationships, and (3) workplace skills (Perkins Collaborative Resource Network, n.d.b). Employability skills enable students to pursue and be successful in diverse postsecondary pathways. Many of the specific skills embedded across these dimensions, such as comprehending written material, analyzing information, and using technology, are built into daily academic instruction. I discuss other skills, such as relationship skills and self-regulation, in chapter 3 as part of social-emotional learning. The importance of college and career readiness reminds educators that teaching employability skills—in addition to academic knowledge—is essential in secondary schools.

In the early 2000s, there was a particular emphasis on "college for all"; however, *college and career readiness* includes an *and* instead of an *or*, which is understandable, considering that high-quality career-readiness programs and pathways overlap and can even elevate college readiness (Brodersen, Gagnon, Liu, & Tedeschi, 2021; Kreamer, 2025). The commitment to career readiness was solidified with federal legislation and funding through the Strengthening Career and Technical Education for the 21st Century Act (Perkins V) in 2018 and the incorporation of career and technical education (CTE) requirements into the Every Student Succeeds Act in 2015 (Advance CTE, 2018; College and Career Readiness and Success Center, 2013, 2017; García, 2014; Perkins Collaborative Resource Network, n.d.a; Shechtman et al., 2016; Taylor et al., 2018; Warner et al., 2020).

At the secondary level, CTE can be viewed as the structure that includes the programs, career pathways, courses, and employability skills students need to pursue postsecondary training or higher education to enter a career field. The days of viewing career readiness as low-level classes designed for entry-level jobs are over. Instead, most students, families, and communities recognize the value of guiding young people toward highly trained technical careers (for example, dental hygienist, aesthetician, electrician, emergency medical technician, and mechanic).

Historically, some students were identified for a college-ready track, while some were led toward an "inferior" career track. Middle and high school reform continues to address this history of "tracking" and seeks to reduce the student experience of being automatically channeled down a particular vocational path based on one's academic or behavioral history. Instead, redesigned programs that include a focus on college *and* career readiness seek to provide rigorous academic learning opportunities, along with high-quality career exploration, that guide students through high school, postsecondary training, college, and beyond. Strong career-readiness programs ensure coursework is intentional and employability skills are addressed to ultimately help students prepare for postsecondary success, whether that involves higher education or other postsecondary training (College and Career Readiness and Success Center, 2013; Oakes, 2005).

Tier 1 College and Career Readiness

To assist schools in establishing an effective Tier 1 plan for college and career readiness, the Regional Educational Laboratory Appalachia at SRI International (2020) collected up-to-date evidence-based practices in *Paving the Pathway to College and Careers.* This group identified the following Tier 1 strategies as key in preparing students for their postsecondary transition.

- **Expose students to the norms and expectations of higher education settings:** Structure virtual or in-person visits with universities, community colleges, and technical schools, and invite alumni or other community members to speak to students.
- **Explore careers and postsecondary degrees:** Host career fairs, utilize career inventories, establish and advise students toward diverse career pathways, create individualized learning plans, offer career-focused dual enrollment courses, and establish work-based learning opportunities, including service learning, mentoring, internships, and work-study programs.
- **Connect with students' families to create postsecondary awareness:** Host virtual and in-person family events that are inviting and supportive.
- **Assist with the admissions process:** Integrate activities that guide students through the application process. Coach students on writing emails and college essays, prompt students and families with important timelines, assist students with résumé building, and help students access fee waivers for applications.
- **Assist with postsecondary assessments:** Establish schoolwide assessments, help students obtain fee waivers to take additional assessments, and provide testing boot camps.

- **Provide financial guidance:** Support completion of the FAFSA process, and assist families in understanding financial aid and the costs of various postsecondary options.
- **Prepare students for the social-emotional aspects of a postsecondary transition:** Establish a school culture that creates connectedness, encourage students to have a growth mindset, help students set postsecondary goals, and develop a timeline of activities to reach these goals.

School leaders should dig deeper into the preceding guide, resources such as the U.S. Department of Education's work-based learning tool kit (National Center for Innovation in Career and Technical Education, n.d.), or guidance from reputable organizations such as Advance CTE, the Association for Career and Technical Education, and the College and Career Readiness and Success Center at the American Institutes for Research to build a comprehensive Tier 1 college-and-career-readiness approach.

With this national emphasis on college and career readiness, there is a surplus of information on the topic. The downside of having so many resources is that it can feel overwhelming and bewildering to navigate them. Numerous national centers, frameworks, guides, and methods of measurement exist with many overlaps but no clear consensus. The intention of this chapter is to provide brief introductions to evidence-based practices as a quick-start guide to help schools overcome the abundance of information on college and career readiness, with a particular focus on how to intervene with students who are not on track to be college and career ready.

Tier 2 College-and-Career-Readiness Group Interventions

Like many academic and behavioral supports shared throughout this book, the three Tier 2 group interventions in the following list may benefit *all* students. You might even have some version of these strategies already in place in your building. The purpose of this section is to explore how you can leverage these evidence-based approaches specifically to support students who may not be on track to reach college and career readiness.

1. Nudging
2. Career academies with targeted supports
3. Dual enrollment and early college high schools with targeted supports

Nudging

We begin with the simplest of three recommended practices for supporting students in becoming college and career ready and reaching graduation. *Nudging* refers to providing ongoing prompts through text messages or other formats that cue students to complete postsecondary-related tasks. Though the idea of nudges may seem simple, these well-timed reminders from the school make a big impact on college-going behaviors,

LONG-TERM GOAL FOR TIER I: Our school will have a functioning MTSS team that routinely analyzes college-and-career-readiness data to determine how best to establish college-and-career-readiness structures and activities in partnership with postsecondary institutions and local industries with the goal that all students meet criteria for college and career readiness. Our team will structure professional learning and maintain ongoing communication with school staff to ensure effective practices are in place.

TIER I QUICK-START STEPS

1. Solidify a teaming model and clarify which team is responsible for reviewing Tier 1 schoolwide data and ensuring college-and-career-readiness structures and activities are in place for students in your school.
2. As a team, discuss the purpose of college and career readiness and the belief and expectation that all students can be college and career ready. Determine methods for seeking input from the larger faculty, families, students, and community partners. Brainstorm how best to share these proposed goals with these stakeholders and establish the vision to guide your work.
3. As a team, review the rich repository of reputable online college-and-career-readiness resources. Reflect on current implementation. The team may utilize the Self-Study Guide for Career Readiness in Secondary Schools (Regional Educational Laboratory Appalachia at SRI International, 2020) to consider what is working and not working with your career-readiness program implementation. Consider the effectiveness of college-readiness implementation using survey and outcome data. Prioritize action steps for Tier 1 college-and-career-readiness structures and activities.
4. Determine what data the MTSS team will review on an ongoing basis (for example, percentage of students who meet college-readiness benchmarks and career-readiness benchmarks; course performance; standardized assessment scores; graduation rates; postsecondary measures, including college-going and postsecondary training and employment rates; and culture and climate surveys). Utilize a data-based decision-making process to ensure the students' college-and-career-readiness needs are systematically supported.
5. Set MTSS team meetings for the school year and determine how best to assign roles and organize data, agendas, and notes. Identify methods for monitoring implementation.

NOTES

....

....

....

....

....

....

....

....

....

....

....

....

....

....

....

....

....

....

especially when implemented using evidence-based practices (Avery, Castleman, Hurwitz, Long, & Page, 2020; Castleman & Page, 2015; Page & Scott-Clayton, 2016; Seftor, 2022). Career-ready nudges have not been the focal point of as much research, yet this strategy can also encourage the completion of career-focused activities (Joy & O'Hara, 2022; O'Hara, Sparrow, & Joy, 2022).

Behavioral science tells us that nudges can be effective because they interrupt procrastination, tap into student impulsiveness to immediately respond, and encourage positive actions toward a goal (Armstrong et al., 2009; Kraft & Rogers, 2015; Lavecchia, Liu, & Oreopoulos, 2014; York & Loeb, 2018). Nudges may be automated or generated and personalized by a peer or counselor. Many schools use platforms to streamline the process and allow for two-way interactions with students. AI chatbots are also effective tools for nudging (Nurshatayeva, Page, White, & Gehlbach, 2021; Page & Gehlbach, 2017). The beauty of nudging is that unlike more time- and resource-intensive group interventions, nudging is a low-cost, efficient intervention tool that requires minimal training.

Specific areas to target with nudging could include the following (Castleman & Page, 2015; ideas42, Nudge4, & Heckscher Foundation for Children, 2016; Linkow et al., 2021).

- Financial assistance, such as how and when to complete the FAFSA process, and information about timelines, planning for fees, registration, and housing applications
- College-entrance or career-related assessments, such as upcoming dates, how to register, access to fee waivers, or opportunities for tutoring or assessment practice
- Mentoring to encourage a growth mindset
- Success strategies listing available resources, including support for student-specific obstacles (for example, transportation and clean clothes)
- Who to reach out to when more help is needed

As with other interventions, nearly all students would benefit from this strategy. The purpose of this section is to discuss how to intentionally utilize nudging for students who need additional support to take the necessary steps toward an intentional career path or students who are less likely to make the transition into higher education. Your Tier 2 team may choose to use nudging as a Tier 2 intervention for students who are underrepresented in postsecondary training or higher education, students from poverty, students who would be first-generation college students, students who do not see themselves as "college material," and so on. Nudging is especially impactful for students who are at a tipping point for taking an action, as in those who might not independently take the next step but are close to it (Koomar, 2024).

General nudging, such as announcements of upcoming assessment dates or college visits, may be appropriate for the larger student body, as you can do this with minimal effort. Then, to maximize efficiency, a tiered model could help schools utilize more personalized, student-specific, two-way nudging for smaller, targeted groups of students. Intensified nudging is most impactful when followed up with small-group or individualized assistance. This sophisticated level of nudging is more time- and resource-intensive, so it should be reserved for fewer students.

It is critical to learn from others' experiences, as some studies find that it is difficult to scale up nudging (Linkow et al., 2021). This may partially be because solely one-way messaging platforms prevent the student from responding directly. Nudges may be ineffective if they come from an organization or person who does not have a strong relationship with the student, if the counselors or advisers have too large of a caseload to provide the follow-up that some students need, or if the nudging content is general and unspecific to the context and the student (Castleman, 2021). Considering these frequent pitfalls, figure 4.2 outlines evidence-based tips for implementing nudging as a Tier 2 college-and-career-readiness group intervention.

Career Academies With Targeted Supports

Multiple means of measuring the qualities of a career-ready student exist, such as the completion of a career pathway (an aligned series of courses and training in a specific postsecondary industry), assessments that validate the skills gained from the completion of a career pathway, course performance, and assessments of employability skills. We also know numerous strategies for increasing the likelihood that secondary students will be career ready as described in the Tier 1 section of this chapter. However, few interventions meet the rigorous requirements to be considered evidence-based programs (having strong, moderate, or promising evidence for career readiness as defined by the Every Student Succeeds Act [ESSA]; What Works Clearinghouse, n.d.). With this scarcity in evidence-based career-readiness programs, career academies stand out as one proven model.

Career academies are small learning communities in which a cohort of students and teachers remain together for multiple classes each year following a program of study focused on a particular career theme (for example, health care, communications, technology, aviation, or law). These academies work in partnership with local industries and higher education institutions and center on careers that are considered relevant and timely based on the labor market and community needs (National Career Academy Coalition, n.d.). Career academies bring meaningful context to student learning.

Although many students could benefit from participating in a career academy model, this approach could be strategically leveraged as a Tier 2 group intervention for students who have academic or behavioral challenges or for those who are more likely to drop out of school (Fink et al., 2023; Fletcher, 2023; Fletcher, Dumford, Hernandez-Gantes, & Minar, 2020; Kemple & Snipes, 2000; What Works Clearinghouse, 2015).

ESSENTIAL COMPONENTS OF NUDGING AS A TIER 2 INTERVENTION

GOAL OF THE INTERVENTION

To provide personalized, student-specific, two-way prompts and reminders to a targeted group of students and follow those up with small-group or individualized assistance to help the students reach college and career readiness

TARGET STUDENT GROUP

Consider students who seem to be at a tipping point for taking the next steps toward college and career readiness, students from poverty, students who would be first-generation college students, students who do not see themselves as "college material," students who are underrepresented in postsecondary training or higher education, and so on.

ESSENTIAL COMPONENTS

- ☐ Identify a nudging coordinator, and establish time during their workday for these activities.
- ☐ Review data to identify students who would benefit from the intervention.
- ☐ Partner with local higher education institutions, community technical schools, industry leaders, other community members, families, and students to identify partners and priorities for this intervention.
- ☐ Identify sources of funding if a platform will be utilized to automate the nudges. Ideally, choose a platform that allows for two-way communication.
- ☐ Determine whether the school will provide nudges for all students and then how to intensify nudges and follow up with students who need additional support.
- ☐ Based on priorities and timelines, identify initial nudges to be sent out.
- ☐ Create processes and structures for sending out nudges.
- ☐ Continuously seek input to adapt and improve how nudges are sent, what information is shared, and how best to follow up with the targeted student group to determine the impact and effectiveness of nudges.
- ☐ Determine a method for collecting data on each of the following.
    - **Fidelity of implementation:** Has a nudging coordinator been selected and provided time for coordinating these activities? Have a small group of students been identified to receive more individualized nudging? Are nudges succinct, action oriented, and specific to students' interests and needs? Do the nudges originate from a person who has a relationship with the students? Are families and students receiving the nudges? Are nudges designed as two way so students can respond and receive follow-up responses? Do the nudges indicate who students can talk to if they need more assistance? Does the students' contact person at school have sufficient capacity in their caseload to provide follow-up support to students when needed?

Figure 4.2: Essential components of nudging as a Tier 2 intervention.

continued ▶

ESSENTIAL COMPONENTS OF NUDGING AS A TIER 2 INTERVENTION

- **Evidence of student progress and effectiveness of the nudges:** This evidence includes attendance, retention, credits earned, percentage of students completing college-and-career-readiness activities (for example, taking assessments, attending speaker sessions or postsecondary visits, completing the FAFSA process, and applying to colleges or other postsecondary training), graduation rates, and postsecondary measures, including college-going or other postsecondary training and employment rates.

TIPS FOR IMPLEMENTATION

- ☐ Seek input from all stakeholders (students, teachers, families, school and district administrators, higher education institutions, and community partners).
- ☐ Details matter. Consider the context and unique behavior obstacles of your student population. Monitor the tone of nudges to keep them inclusive, supportive, motivating, and relevant.
- ☐ Include students and their families in text messaging.
- ☐ Have the nudges originate from a staff member with whom the student and family have a relationship.
- ☐ Use caution to keep nudges succinct so as not to overwhelm students and families with too much information at one time. Keep texts focused on single, discrete tasks, framing the messages to encourage students to take immediate action. Here's an example: "Hi, Tyreon. Register for next week's orientation to ________ University at this link: . . ."
- ☐ Use an interactive platform for nudging that allows two-way messages so students can respond directly to the texts for support. Some platforms feature AI technology to provide automatic replies on basic information or connect the student with a staff member when needed.
- ☐ Embed links to directly access specific forms (for example, the FAFSA form and college-entrance assessment applications).
- ☐ Include information on how students and families can access more assistance when needed. This may involve issues beyond college- or career-specific topics, such as resources for physical or mental health needs.
- ☐ Ensure nudges are timely by sending them during key decision times (for example, before upcoming college visits, speakers, assessments, and essay-writing sessions).

Career academies capitalize on increasing connectedness by seeking to create a family-like atmosphere in which students work more closely with a small group of teachers and peers. Historically, such programs may have been reserved for students through a selective process requiring high scores on academic assessments. However, a student's previous academic achievement should not prevent them from accessing a career academy of interest.

Career academies can be beneficial for multilingual learners, students with disabilities, or other students with academic or behavioral challenges as long as schedules are flexible and allow for the additional support they may need. Interestingly, the National

☐ Consider including voice notes or phone calls as alternative or additional means of nudging families that may have low literacy levels. These will be most powerful when offered in a student and family's native language.

☐ Increase personalization of nudges by using the student's name, the name of the school, and their specific postsecondary goals, area of interest, and motives. Consider this example: "Tell us, Honette, which of these makes you most excited about having a construction career: using your hands to build and fix things, helping to bring new products or improvements to the community, or being part of a team?"

☐ Include growth-minded nudges to promote the student's belief in their ability to attend higher education and fit in at that level. Here's an example: "Hello, Berkley. On a scale of 1–10, how are you feeling about completing the application to ______ University? 1 = I feel very nervous, 5 = I feel OK, and 10 = I've got this." The text response to answers of 1–3 might be "This can be a challenging time for lots of students. We believe in you. Reach out to Mr. Hutchins to talk through this more at this link: . . ." For 4–6, the response might be "Hang in there! We believe in you, and we know this can be a lot. Mr. Hutchins is always here to help. Reach out to him anytime at this link: . . ." For 7–10, the response might be "Awesome! We believe in you. Mr. Hutchins is always here to help. Reach out to him anytime at this link: . . ."

☐ Consider pairing the student with a near-age mentor who is enrolled in college or technical school to provide them with encouragement and increase their sense of belonging. If possible, select a peer mentor who has similar characteristics to the student.

☐ Continue nudges and access to active college counseling throughout the summer after graduation to increase the likelihood that students who have applied and have been accepted will overcome challenges in the summer months that could alter or derail matriculation in the fall.

☐ Partner with advisers in higher education organizations to continue nudges into the first year of college.

Source: Arnold et al., 2009; Avery et al., 2020; Castleman, Arnold, & Wartman, 2012; Castleman & Page, 2015, 2017; Hoxby & Turner, 2013; ideas42 et al., 2016; Joy & O'Hara, 2022; Koomar, 2024; Linkow et al., 2021; O'Hara et al., 2022; Oreopoulos & Dunn, 2012; Page & Gehlbach, 2017; Rumberger et al., 2017; Seftor, 2022; What Works Clearinghouse, 2015.

Gang Center and the Office of Juvenile Justice and Delinquency Prevention specifically note career academies as a recommended practice to reduce delinquent behaviors and increase protective factors (Development Services Group, 2015; National Gang Center, 2021). Too often, these particular groups of students participate less often in career academies (Hemelt, Lenard, & Paeplow, 2017). Therefore, schools need to make intentional efforts to engage families of multilingual learners, or other families that may have barriers to engaging in their child's education, to increase awareness of and access to career academies.

Students who may not traditionally qualify to participate and succeed in a career academy will likely need additional targeted supports. For example, students may benefit from frequent check-ins by a staff member with whom they have a good relationship; this staff member may check their progress, offer organizational tips, or connect them with needed services, such as financial support for associated fees or assistance with transportation to an event. A student might be supported with high-impact tutoring to do well in a career academy core class or social-emotional group to improve their ability to self-regulate. The goal would be to continue providing the career academy opportunity to high-performing students but also engage students who need additional support to be college and career ready and graduate.

Launching career academies can be quite an undertaking. Those who work in secondary schools know how challenging it can be to change their complex system. Any adjustment made has implications across departmental structures, schedules, human resources, and undeniably, the political, symbolic, or historical elements that make up the school (Bolman & Deal, 2021). Therefore, it is important to learn from others who have already journeyed down this road. Figure 4.3 explores how to utilize career academies as a Tier 2 intervention; it shares recommendations from research and schools that have been implementing career academies for many years.

Dual Enrollment and Early College High Schools With Targeted Supports

One of the most effective approaches we can take to keep students in high school and increase attendance, academic achievement, college readiness, and college access, enrollment, and attainment is to give them opportunities to receive college credit (Berger et al., 2013; Edmunds, Unlu, Furey, Glennie, & Arshavsky, 2020; Edmunds et al., 2017; Haxton et al., 2016; Seftor, 2022; Song & Zeiser, 2019). In the past, this approach may have been reserved for advanced students, but we now know it can be especially beneficial for students who are often underrepresented in higher education, including those who do not score well on admissions or screening assessments, students from poverty, first-generation college-going students, immigrant students, or students from ethnic or racial minority populations (An, 2013; Barnett, 2016; Barnett, Bucceri, Hindo, & Kim, 2013; Edmunds et al., 2020; Edwards, Hughes, & Weisberg, 2011; Fink et al., 2023; Karp, Calcagno, Hughes, Jeong, & Bailey, 2007; Mehl, Wyner, Barnett, Fink, & Jenkins, 2020; Xu et al., 2019; Zinth & Barnett, 2018).

These opportunities benefit students by exposing them to college-level courses through community and technical colleges or four-year institutions while they are in an environment that can provide support when needed. Additionally, these college credits are typically offered at a reduced price and lessen the likelihood that students will need to take remedial courses once enrolled in college (Kim & Bragg, 2008; What Works Clearinghouse, 2017a).

ESSENTIAL COMPONENTS OF CAREER ACADEMIES AS A TIER 2 INTERVENTION

GOAL OF THE INTERVENTION

To have selected students take part in a small learning community with a cohort of their peers and a selected group of teachers for at least part of their school day. This career academy should include intentional academic and behavioral support and last for two or more years in classes with rigorous academic content that is tied to a particular career theme.

TARGET STUDENT GROUP

Include students who may be considered at risk for academic or behavioral challenges or for dropping out of school based on attendance, office referrals, and course performance. Assignment to each career academy will be based on student interest and willingness to participate.

ESSENTIAL COMPONENTS

- ☐ Identify a career academy coordinator as a primary point of contact. This increases consistency for building relationships and community partnerships and clarifies whom families can reach out to for information. Provide time during the coordinator's workday for activities. One way to do this is to add a release period to one career academy teacher's schedule, during which they meet with students and coordinate the program.
- ☐ Review data to identify students who would benefit from the intervention.
- ☐ Partner with local higher education institutions, the chamber of commerce, community technical schools, industry leaders, other community members, families, and students to identify a career academy theme built around interests and labor market demands.
- ☐ Brainstorm logistic adaptations necessary to establish a career academy, such as adjusting the master schedule, the current organization of staff, and the method for placing students in classes.
- ☐ Work with district and community leaders to identify funding opportunities and establish partnerships.
- ☐ Identify a cohort of teachers to assign to the career academy.
- ☐ Develop the scope and sequence for the career academy; this includes college-preparatory and CTE courses integrated into the master schedule.
- ☐ Create processes and structures for participating students to access academic or behavioral support when needed in order to be successful in the career academy (for example, high-impact tutoring, strategy instruction, or a small social-emotional group).
- ☐ Build in career academy–specific field trips, guest speakers, internships, mentorships, work-study programs, and job-shadowing opportunities.
- ☐ Establish recruitment events at least one semester before students begin the career academy.
- ☐ Determine a method for collecting data on each of the following.

Figure 4.3: Essential components of career academies as a Tier 2 intervention.

continued ▶

ESSENTIAL COMPONENTS OF CAREER ACADEMIES AS A TIER 2 INTERVENTION

- **Fidelity of implementation:** Has a career academy coordinator been established? Has time been built into their day for completion of these activities? Have stakeholders been identified and engaged in the development of the career academy? Are students scheduled with a small cohort of students and teachers for a portion of their day that includes college-preparatory and CTE courses? Will this cohort last at least two years? Are opportunities provided to increase access to higher education or other postsecondary training in the career academy? Are work-based experiences (for example, internships and work-study programs) integrated into the career academy? What percentage of high-performing students are participating in the career academy? What percentage of students identified as needing additional support participate in the career academy? Are multilingual students, students with disabilities, or students with other academic or behavioral challenges receiving additional opportunities for support?
- **Evidence of student progress and effectiveness of the career academy:** This evidence includes attendance, retention, credits, course performance, standardized assessment scores, graduation rate, and postsecondary measures, including college-going or other postsecondary training and employment rates.

TIPS FOR IMPLEMENTATION

Scheduling and organizational tips:

☐ Start small! Use an iterative process before expanding.

☐ Assign one counselor for each career academy.

☐ Arrange the schedule so that career academy teachers teach career academy students only (or primarily).

☐ Utilize teacher looping.

☐ Maintain a sustainable number of students in career academies. (Some experienced schools find it best to have no more than 150 students enrolled per grade level.)

☐ Ensure that only students in the academy are assigned to career academy courses.

☐ Ensure that the career academy lasts at least two to three years, through twelfth grade.

☐ Provide career academy students with access to advanced coursework, dual-credit opportunities, and other college-readiness explorational and informational options.

☐ Seek to provide students with financial compensation or course credit for work-study programs or internships that occur outside the school day.

Partnership tips:

☐ Seek support from all stakeholders (students, teachers, families, school, and district administrators and community partners). An advisory board that meets quarterly is an effective method for seeking support.

☐ Plan for the financial requirements of implementing career academies. These costs continue beyond the first year. Seek grants and community partnerships to assist with costs.

☐ Partner with feeder middle (or elementary) schools to offer introductory and exploratory opportunities aligned with high school career academies.

☐ Make teacher and student participation in career academies voluntary, and seek family support.

☐ Integrate opportunities for students to earn valuable industry certificates that can help them be hired in the future.

☐ Encourage all career academy teachers to participate in decision making, professional learning, curriculum planning, and brainstorming about instructional practices during shared planning time.

☐ Utilize a senior or capstone project as a culminating activity, and engage industry and community partners in the evaluation.

Student-specific tips:

☐ Some states require at least 50 percent of career academy students to have academic or behavioral challenges (for example, students with disabilities, multilingual learners, or students with one or two office referrals).

☐ For each career academy, monitor participation, perspectives, and impact to ensure effectiveness and avoid unintentionally building a system of tracking that benefits particular groups of students (for example, those of a specific gender, socioeconomic status, or ethnic or racial background) while others are disadvantaged.

☐ Consider the implications for the non–career academy students and teachers throughout implementation. One effective schoolwide model included building a general ninth-grade academy and multiple tenth- to twelfth-grade career academies.

☐ Publicly recognize student achievement (for example, growth in academic, behavioral, or employability skills) throughout the school year.

☐ Increase connectedness by hosting career academy social events. For example, have students from each academy work with the art teacher to create logos and T-shirts.

☐ Identify students who may benefit from additional connection and support that would be a good fit for the career academy. Proactively encourage participation by building relationships and fostering trust with these students and their families.

Source: Elliott, Hanser, & Gilroy, 2002; Fink et al., 2023; Fixsen et al., 2005; Fletcher, 2023; Fletcher & Tan, 2024; Guha et al., 2014; Hernández & Darling-Hammond, 2024b; Kemple & Snipes, 2000; Kemple & Willner, 2008; Kistler, Childs, & Dougherty, 2024; Lanford & Maruco, 2019; Lyon & Palmer, 2021; McPartland, Balfanz, Jordan, & Legters, 1998; Rumberger et al., 2017; Seftor, 2022; Stern, Dayton, & Raby, 2010; What Works Clearinghouse, 2015.

Dual enrollment, in which a secondary student takes college courses, has become "an on-ramp to college programs of study that lead to family-supporting, career-path jobs for students who might not otherwise pursue education after high school" (Fink et al., 2023, p. 1). Other acceleration options exist in secondary schools, such as Advanced Placement and International Baccalaureate, but this conversation through the lens of intervention focuses on dual enrollment and early college high schools. State or local requirements, such as a particular score on college admissions exams, may be preventing some students who could succeed in dual enrollment from accessing these opportunities. School leaders may need to advocate for policy changes or request waivers when appropriate. Alternative student criteria for accessing dual credit might include the following (Zinth & Barnett, 2018).

- Incoming juniors
- Students with high grade point averages
- Students who score near preset cut scores
- Students with good attendance
- Students who demonstrate high engagement (for example, seeking help when needed and participating actively in class)
- Students who demonstrate higher-order thinking in class or have strong reading or writing skills based on in-class assessments

Early college is an elevated model of dual enrollment described as "small schools that will blur the line between high school and college" (Edmunds et al., 2017, p. 297). In essence, it is dual enrollment on steroids! Early college and other similar models allow students to earn high school credits while also earning an associate degree or up to two full years of college credit for a four- or five-year program.

Providing access to dual enrollment or early college for students who have academic or behavioral challenges or who are at risk of dropping out of school will have success only if the school builds in necessary structures for support. These may include providing individual or small-group support for students who need encouragement, front-loading material, and increasing structure for classes (for example, establishing a schedule of task completion for online classes or providing direct instruction in navigating management systems). As discussed in chapter 2, these types of scaffolds keep expectations high by incorporating the support that students need to be successful. Figure 4.4 outlines tips for implementing dual enrollment or early college high school as a Tier 2 intervention.

The strategies shared in this chapter could be your school's Tier 2 group interventions if you intentionally design them to provide additional support for students not on track for college and career readiness. In this next section, I discuss how to intensify these interventions for those few students who may still need more support.

ESSENTIAL COMPONENTS OF DUAL ENROLLMENT AND EARLY COLLEGE HIGH SCHOOLS AS TIER 2 INTERVENTION

GOAL OF THE INTERVENTION

To have selected students take college-level classes while receiving intentional academic and behavioral support to successfully earn college credit while in high school

TARGET STUDENT GROUP

Include students who have traditionally been underrepresented in higher education, including first-generation college-going students, students from poverty, multilingual students, those from racial or ethnic minority groups, students who may be considered at risk for academic or behavioral challenges, or students may drop out of school based on attendance, office referrals, and course performance.

ESSENTIAL COMPONENTS

- ☐ Identify a dual enrollment or early college champion as a primary point of contact, and ensure time is built into their day for related activities. Having one point of contact increases consistency for relationship building, clarifies whom families can reach out to for information, and establishes who will be responsible for coordinating with higher education institutions.
- ☐ Review data to identify students who would benefit from the intervention.
- ☐ Partner with community and technical colleges and institutions of higher education to establish dual enrollment or early college opportunities.
- ☐ Work with district and community leaders to identify funding and methods of support. Consider creating a memorandum of agreement with higher education partners in order to efficiently share resources such as staff, transportation, access to the campus library, tutors, or counselors.
- ☐ Inventory current college-credit course offerings and align the newly developed courses with existing high-interest college degree programs.
- ☐ Determine whether the courses will be taken at the high school, college, community college, or regional satellite campuses, depending on contextual needs and available resources.
- ☐ Determine plans for reducing barriers to dual enrollment or early college access (for example, students who cannot afford tuition, fees, or books or do not have transportation to campus).
- ☐ Reach out to underserved students and share information with them before they are in high school. Do this to build trust with families and leverage community partners to whom families feel connected.
- ☐ Embed dual enrollment or early college access into programs that currently exist in the school (for example, career pathways or career academies).
- ☐ Utilize career exploration strategies (see Tier 1) such as strong academic advising, individual planning, and ongoing checkpoints in partnership with college advisers to more clearly design an aligned plan for each student through degree completion.

Figure 4.4: Essential components of dual enrollment and early college high schools as Tier 2 interventions.

continued ▶

ESSENTIAL COMPONENTS OF DUAL ENROLLMENT AND EARLY COLLEGE HIGH SCHOOLS AS TIER 2 INTERVENTION

☐ Establish built-in time and staffing for monitoring student progress in dual enrollment or early college courses and providing individual or small-group support for students. These students may need encouragement, additional scaffolding, front-loaded material, or more structure for classes (for example, establish a schedule of task completion for online classes or direct instruction on navigating management systems).

☐ Create processes and structures for participating students to access academic or behavioral support when needed in order to be successful in dual enrollment or early college (for example, high-impact tutoring, strategy instruction, or a small social-emotional group).

☐ Determine a method for collecting data on each of the following.

- **Fidelity of implementation:** Has a dual enrollment or early college champion been identified, and have they begun building partnerships with higher education institutions? Do the college-credit courses align with existing high-interest college degree programs? Are admissions opportunities open for multilingual students, students with disabilities, or students with other academic or behavioral challenges? Have students, including those who are traditionally underrepresented in higher education, been actively recruited and encouraged to participate? Is strong academic advising and individual planning occurring and helping students design a plan to degree completion? Is there a process for monitoring student progress and providing support for each student to be successful in the college-credit course?
- **Evidence of student progress and effectiveness of the dual enrollment or early college opportunities:** This evidence includes the number of students who participate, credit hours attempted versus completed, student performance by course modality (online, at the high school, or on a college campus), attendance, retention, standardized assessment scores, graduation rate, and postsecondary measures, including college-going or other postsecondary training and employment rates.

TIPS FOR IMPLEMENTATION

☐ Believe in the potential of every student to be successful in dual enrollment and early college opportunities. Communicate these beliefs to students and families before high school, as early as the preschool and elementary levels.

☐ Seek support and input from all stakeholders (students, teachers, families, school and district administrators, and community partners) along the way to gain insight and ideas for improvement.

☐ Increase open access by utilizing criteria such as grades as an alternative to admissions tests or other screenings for student participation. If testing is required in your state or district, reduce barriers for families by having all students take key assessments at their home school, hosting boot camps to refresh relevant academic skills, providing opportunities for retesting, and arranging for students with disabilities to receive appropriate accommodations.

☐ Ensure that academic courses leading up to dual enrollment or early college opportunities are rigorous and build strong study habits that prepare students for the high expectations of college-level courses.

☐ Work with district-level leaders and feeder middle schools to review the sequencing of classes (especially in mathematics) to ensure all students have opportunities to get on a path to take accelerated courses in high school.

- ☐ Review student data and actively reach out to individual students who have the potential to pursue dual enrollment or early college opportunities but are not currently enrolled. Provide these students with encouragement and prompting.
- ☐ Structure the school schedule to align with partner higher education organizations (for example, make it semester based to facilitate dual enrollment at a local university or community technical schools).
- ☐ Seek methods to offer college-credit opportunities at low or no cost for students whose families cannot afford these opportunities.
- ☐ Provide authentic exposure to college culture by having courses that include enrolled college-age students and that are taught by college faculty.
- ☐ Share videos with middle school students and families to explain upcoming dual enrollment or early college opportunities.
- ☐ Monitor student success to identify concerns with instructional quality or professional learning needs.
- ☐ Monitor participation, perspectives, and impact to avoid unintentionally building a system of tracking that benefits particular groups of students (for example, those of a specific gender, socioeconomic status, or ethnic or racial background) and hinders others.
- ☐ Utilize some of the following specific strategies that other schools have found to be helpful.
- ☐ Allow eighth-grade students one day per semester to shadow juniors and seniors who are taking college courses and report on their observations as a class assignment.
- ☐ Celebrate students who complete associate degrees while in high school by publicly awarding these degrees and posting student pictures along with other athletic, attendance, and GPA accomplishments.
- ☐ Train community leaders or family members who could become leaders in their local community to share information on college access with families.
- ☐ Partner with higher education organizations to host a breakfast for high school and college advisers to increase connections and conversations.
- ☐ Partner with higher education organizations to host events for grades K–12 (for example, STEAM days) to increase family and school connections to campuses.
- ☐ Scaffold access by allowing sophomores to take college-level courses within the high school setting while allowing juniors and seniors to take college-level courses on a college campus.
- ☐ Have students sign a Family Educational Rights and Privacy Act (FERPA) waiver to allow higher education advisers and faculty to share information with high school staff on the students' course performance. This will assist the high school in providing needed support.
- ☐ Assign a participating high school senior to mentor juniors by checking in with them weekly or twice monthly and offering tips and encouragement.

Source: An, 2013; Barnett, 2016; Barnett et al., 2013; Berger et al., 2013; Edmunds et al., 2017; Edwards et al., 2011; Fink et al., 2023; Giani, Alexander, & Reyes, 2014; Haxton et al., 2016; Karp et al., 2007; Mehl et al., 2020; Page & Scott-Clayton, 2016; Rumberger et al., 2017; Seftor, 2022; Struhl & Vargas, 2012; What Works Clearinghouse, 2017a.

LONG-TERM GOAL FOR TIER 2: Our school will have multiple well-established Tier 2 group interventions led by a variety of personnel with processes in place to check fidelity of implementation and collect progress-monitoring data. These group interventions will be monitored by the Tier 2 team and adapted based on data; student, family, and teacher input; and insights from community partners. The team will select the appropriate group intervention to best fit a student whose data suggests they need more support to be college and career ready and graduate. This team will monitor the progress of the student over time and determine whether the intervention should be maintained, intensified, or faded.

TIER 2 QUICK-START STEPS

1. Select one Tier 2 group intervention (for example, nudging, career academies, dual enrollment, or early college) based on evidence of need in your school.
2. Analyze data to select a small group of students who will pilot the intervention, considering the students' unique needs.
3. Seek community partners and input from students, teachers, and families. Implement core features of the intervention. Explore references and related resources to build a deeper understanding of the intervention and specific evidence-based practices. Additional training and coaching ensure the intervention is implemented with fidelity.
4. Adjust and improve implementation based on contextual factors: student data, stakeholder input, and any unintended costs (for example, any negative impacts on students who are not part of the intervention and any unintentional trends of tracking that may arise).
5. Expand implementation to serve more students once the Tier 2 team determines that the intervention is beneficial in your school environment.
6. Solidify the intervention by naming it, documenting processes and core features for implementation, and adding it to the school website or some other school organizational digital platform.
7. Follow these quick-start steps to build the next Tier 2 group intervention into your school's organizational structure.

NOTES

....

....

....

....

....

....

....

....

....

....

....

....

....

....

....

....

....

....

Tier 3 Intensive, Individualized College-and-Career-Readiness Interventions

Even with a strong Tier 1 plan for college and career readiness and a well-implemented Tier 2 group intervention, a small number of students may need an individualized plan to reach college and career readiness and graduate. In this section, I present one specific approach for intensifying support.

As noted in *Preventing Dropout in Secondary Schools* (Rumberger et al., 2017), one evidence-based method to aid students who need this level of support is to assign a school advocate. This model of intervention might be appropriate as a Tier 3 intervention for students who are significantly off track for graduation, students for whom other interventions have been unsuccessful, or those who have substantial personal obstacles. This advocate could be in a certified or noncertified position. They could be a school employee or a non-school employee who receives training and supervision from the school. What matters most is that the individual has the interpersonal skills and knowledge (and belief in students) to provide resources and guidance. In essence, this is a mentor for students who may meet any of the following conditions.

- The student is significantly off track for reaching college or career readiness.
- The student is chronically absent.
- The student has not passed core classes.
- The student has behavioral challenges.
- The student is pregnant.
- The student has experienced trauma or homelessness.

Ideally, the advocate will be similar in culture and language to the student. This mentoring works best when the advocate can be available outside school hours; therefore, schools would need to establish clear compensation and job duties to ensure this position is implemented effectively. The school can also assist the advocate by:

- Opening access to relevant student data
- Allowing them time to learn from more experienced advocates
- Connecting them with teachers to create mutual trust
- Providing ongoing professional learning
- Establishing a system for the advocate's documentation
- Providing a list of services that the school offers to students (literacy intervention, social-emotional learning groups, and so on)

To implement this approach, some school districts have partnered with organizations such as local colleges or community colleges, Big Brothers Big Sisters, or AmeriCorps to identify advocates. A school may seek funding from grants, community partners, or school or district Title I funds to pay a staff member to serve in this capacity. A school could even share an advocate with another school. Research shows this approach can look different depending on the needs of the students and the available resources at the school, but providing students this focused advocate can increase their progress in school and the likelihood that they will graduate, access postsecondary credits, and attend postsecondary education (Corrin, Parise, Cerna, Haider, & Somers, 2015; Dynarski, Gleason, Rangarajan, & Wood, 1998; Larson & Rumberger, 1995; Rodríguez-Planas, 2012; Sinclair et al., 2005).

The impact of this approach is illustrated by the sustained relationship it fosters. One staff member, who served as an advocate, shared with me that their relationship with a student became so meaningful that years after the student graduated from school and started college, she reached out to share an update on her life. The influence of this advocate stayed with this student long after she left the classroom.

Following the strategies for intensifying interventions, the Tier 2 team could come together, review data, and determine how best to intensify the strength, dosage, alignment, attention to transfer, comprehensiveness, or other behavioral or academic support to build a Tier 3 plan. Figure 4.5 outlines specific strategies to intensify college-and-career-readiness interventions by assigning an advocate.

Conclusion

Considering the crucial nature of college and career readiness, implications of our work as educators at the secondary level cannot be overemphasized. Our goal is to set students up to succeed in a career and in life. MTSS can be the framework we use to strategically structure support to help all students become college and career ready.

STRENGTH

Research shows that assigning an advocate can increase a student's progress in school and their likelihood that the student will graduate access postsecondary credits, and attend postsecondary education (Corrin et al., 2015; Dynarski et al., 1998; Larson & Rumberger, 1995; Rodríguez-Planas, 2012; Sinclair et al., 2005). Advocates would monitor the student's attendance, behavior, and course performance and be the go-to person for the student.

DOSAGE

This approach works best when the advocate maintains contact with the student and family year-round and for a minimum of one year. Schools must ensure advocates are assigned a reasonable number of students, depending on the time available. This may be one or two students or up to twenty students if time is built into the advocate's day. The advocate could meet with the student weekly (or daily during especially challenging times for the student). These meetings can taper off based on the student's needs.

ALIGNMENT

Seek an advocate who is similar to the student in culture and language and is connected to the student's community. Ensure the advocate believes in the potential of the student and works to connect with the family to identify the unique supports the student may need (such as accessing SNAP benefits, coordinating transportation for the student to get to outside counseling appointments, and obtaining a computer for them to take home for homework).

ATTENTION TO TRANSFER

The advocate can meet with individual teachers to share the student's current functioning and barriers, and ideas for support. Plus, the advocate can communicate teacher efforts for students and their families to strengthen relationships. To increase the generalization of newly learned skills—meaning the student learns to demonstrate the skills in other contexts—the advocate may need to provide explicit guidance on how to apply various strategies (for example, getting organized or requesting assistance).

COMPREHENSIVENESS

Advocates should use evidence-based mentoring practices, such as the following.

- Build positive, trusting relationships with the student and their family.
- Assist the student in identifying barriers and developing a specific action plan broken into multiple steps to reach a goal.
- Provide explicit instruction in skills the student is missing (for example, setting up a system for keeping up with due dates, organizing email, and completing a multistep project).
- Utilize strategies such as thinking aloud, modeling action steps such as checking grades, planning to study for a test, or deciding how to deal with a difficult peer.
- Have the student repeat back strategies in their own words.

OTHER BEHAVIORAL OR ACADEMIC SUPPORT

The advocate can guide the student toward other academic or behavioral supports (for example, a social-emotional learning group or strategy instruction). They can also help the student establish a motivational plan focused on the postsecondary goals and seek reinforcements to reach short-term goals.

These goals should be obtainable, and the advocate can provide actionable feedback and encourage reflection as part of the goal-setting process. It may also be helpful to loop in peers who can model and promote positive behaviors.

Source: Corrin et al., 2015; Dynarski et al., 2008; Larson & Rumberger, 1995; Midwest Comprehensive Center, 2018; National Center on Intensive Intervention, 2019; Rodríguez-Planas, 2012; Rumberger et al., 2017; Sinclair et al., 2005.

Figure 4.5: Strategies for intensifying college-and-career-readiness interventions by assigning an advocate.

LONG-TERM GOAL FOR TIER 3: Our school will have an established process for convening a Tier 3 team to build a comprehensive Tier 3 plan. Our team will understand the process to intensify collage-and-career-readiness interventions based on the student's unique needs. The Tier 3 plan will include methods for monitoring student progress and the fidelity of implementation. Our team will review student progress over time and determine whether the intervention should be maintained, intensified, or faded.

TIER 3 QUICK-START STEPS

1. Identify a student receiving support through a Tier 2 group intervention whose data suggests that they need a more intensive, individualized approach.
2. Bring together a Tier 3 team to review data (for example, personal or family needs of the student) and identify what additional information is needed to develop an action plan. Tap into specialists (for example, youth service center employees, school psychologists, mental health therapists, or community agency representatives) to help guide this process. Include the student and their family in this development.
3. Based on information gathered and input from the student and their family, build a comprehensive plan with your team that includes intensified Tier 3 interventions. The plan will include the intervention-intensifying dimensions of strength, dosage, alignment, attention to transfer, comprehensiveness, or other behavioral or academic support.
4. Communicate the plan to all stakeholders.
5. Implement core features of the intervention and the overarching plan.
6. Adjust and improve implementation based on data collection (progress-monitoring data and feedback from the student, their teachers, their family, and others).

NOTES

Epilogue

MTSS offers secondary schools an evidence-based framework to support students' academic, behavioral, social-emotional, and college-and-career-readiness needs. However, many secondary educators lack the support and readily available resources needed to fully align an MTSS framework with the unique realities of middle and high school settings.

Now that you have explored how MTSS applies to the secondary context and investigated secondary-specific interventions, you may be asking, "Where do I even start?"

Most teams will find that they are not ready to launch a full-scale MTSS implementation. Instead, they may benefit from eating the elephant one bite at a time, so to speak. Start small. Begin with baby steps that busy, stressed educators can believe in. Many schools I have worked with have found that this strategic method increases their likelihood of success. For example, one school identified PBIS Tier 1 implementation as their ideal first step because teachers were interested in clarifying expectations for students and improving common areas within the building. Perhaps educators in your school or district are motivated to address students' increased mental health needs, to learn strategies for reducing anxiety, or to adopt innovative methods for connecting with students. Other ideas for entry points include the following.

- A schoolwide plan for tiered support in literacy based on concerning academic data and resources available from the English department's leadership
- A schoolwide plan for a Tier 1 positive behavioral support system for a freshman academy based on office referral data and a dedicated assistant principal who is motivated to make a change
- One Tier 2 behavioral group intervention (for example, Check & Connect) based on needs identified through office referral data and teacher interviews

- Tier 2 academic group intervention time added to the schedule for a targeted area (for example, mathematics) based on trends identified from college readiness exams
- One Tier 2 academic group intervention (for example, high-impact tutoring) for a selected group of students identified through early warning indicators (for example, grades and college-and-career-readiness data)

These potential on-ramps illustrate an implementation model that is more sensitive to available resources and student populations. Start by examining your school's strengths and challenges to determine the best entry point for your context. Your initial MTSS team can utilize an MTSS fidelity tool as a self-assessment to map current resources and align initiatives to guide your next steps. Tools such as the Self-Assessment of MTSS Implementation (Stockslager et al., 2022), the PBIS Tiered Fidelity Inventory (Center on Positive Behavioral Interventions and Supports, 2025), the Multi-Tiered Systems of Support Needs Assessment: Secondary Version (McIntosh & Goodman, 2016), or the Self-Study Guide for Implementing High School Academic Interventions (Smith et al., 2016) are assessments with strong psychometric properties that will guide your team in identifying existing structures as well as missing pieces.

And here is a tip: Be tough on yourself when completing these self-assessments. The strongest teams seek input from people in varying positions and with different, even conflicting, perspectives. This gives leaders a true understanding of the experiences of all stakeholders and ultimately creates a stronger action plan. Key questions for your MTSS team to consider include the following.

- What pieces do we already have in place?
- What existing systems are working well?
- What structures that are in place need improvement or adjustment?
- What criteria have we established to identify students who need additional academic or behavioral support or who are not on track to reach college and career readiness?
- What groups of students are served or supported well?
- What groups of students are not served or supported well?
- Do all stakeholders have a voice in our work (students, families, teachers, and the community)?
- How do we evaluate the impact of initiatives in our building? What additional evaluation methods do we need?

Starting small works well if the MTSS team approaches the work with an iterative continuous improvement process and a long-term vision for scaling up. Bring in your early adopters. Let the process grow and develop. This will lessen frustration from educators who can ultimately stall implementation because the framework feels too large or disconnected from their current priorities and situation. Too often, we say that we don't have teachers' buy-in, but this likely stems from top-down mandates that lack context specificity. Instead, starting small allows systems to grow from within. The answer to your question, "Where do I even start?," is *start small.*

Secondary educators are compassionate, dedicated individuals who want great things for their students. They deserve the support they need to be good at their jobs and serve the students who are placed before them. I hope this book becomes a toolbox that you refer to again and again to successfully initiate, iterate, grow, and sustain your MTSS.

References and Resources

Abell, M. M., Bauder, D. K., & Simmons, T. J. (2005). Access to the general curriculum: A curriculum and instruction perspective for educators. *Intervention in School and Clinic, 41*(2), 82–86. https://doi.org/10.1177/10534512050410020801

Achieve the Core. (n.d.a). *Instructional practice guide.* Student Achievement Partners. Accessed at https://achievethecore.org/page/1119/instructional-practice-guide on August 9, 2024.

Achieve the Core. (n.d.b). *Understand the shifts* [Search results]. Accessed at https://achievethecore.org/category/677/understand-the-shifts on August 9, 2024.

ACT. (n.d.a). *Supports for English learners.* Accessed at www.act.org/content/act/en/products-and-services/the-act/registration/accommodations/policy-for-el-supports-documentation.html on January 2, 2026.

ACT. (n.d.b). *Policy for requesting accommodations for the ACT test.* Accessed at www.act.org/content/act/en/products-and-services/the-act/registration/accommodations/policy-for-accommodations-documentation.html on January 2, 2026.

ACT. (2024). *ACT profile report: National—Graduating class 2024.* Author. Accessed at www.act.org/content/dam/act/unsecured/documents/2024-act-national-graduating-class-profile-report.pdf on January 6, 2026.

Administration for Community Living. (2024, September 19). *Person-centered planning.* Accessed at https://acl.gov/programs/consumer-control/person-centered-planning on September 11, 2025.

Advance CTE. (2018, July). *Ensuring career pathway quality: A guide to pathway intervention.* Author. Accessed at https://careertech.org/wp-content/uploads/2023/01/18-138-AdvanceCTE-ProgramEvaluationAnd-InterventionGuide071318_1.pdf on September 12, 2025.

Advance CTE. (2019, January). *Making good on the promise: Building trust to promote equity in CTE.* Author. Accessed at https://careertech.org/wp-content/uploads/sites/default/files/files/resources/Building_Trust_Promote_Equity_CTE_Jan_2019.pdf on September 11, 2025.

Advance CTE. (2024, October 21). *The modernized National Career Clusters® framework guidebook.* Author. Accessed at https://careertech.org/wp-content/uploads/2024/11/Guidebook_-National-Career-Clusters-Framework-1.pdf on September 12, 2025.

Aghion, P., Boustan, L., Hoxby, C., & Vandenbussche, J. (2009, March). *The causal impact of education on economic growth: Evidence from the United States.* Brookings. Accessed at www.brookings.edu/wp-content/uploads/2016/07/2009_spring_bpea_aghion_etal.pdf on September 12, 2025.

Allensworth, E. M., & Easton, J. Q. (2005, June). *The on-track indicator as a predictor of high school graduation.* Consortium on Chicago School Research. Accessed at https://consortium.uchicago.edu/sites/default/files/2018-10/p78.pdf on September 12, 2025.

Allensworth, E. M., & Easton, J. Q. (2007, July). *What matters for staying on-track and graduating in Chicago Public Schools.* University of Chicago Consortium on School Research. Accessed at https://consortium.uchicago.edu/publications/what-matters-staying-track-and-graduating-chicago-public-schools on September 12, 2025.

Allensworth, E. M., Gwynne, J. A., Moore, P., & de la Torre, M. (2014, November). *Looking forward to high school and college: Middle grade indicators of readiness in Chicago Public Schools.* University of Chicago Consortium on Chicago School Research.

Allensworth, E. M., & Schwartz, N. (2020, June). *School practices to address learning loss.* EdResearch for Recovery. Accessed at https://annenberg.brown.edu/sites/default/files/EdResearch_for_Recovery_Brief_1.pdf on September 12, 2025.

Allred, J. B., & Cena, M. E. (2020). Reading motivation in high school: Instructional shifts in student choice and class time. *Journal of Adolescent and Adult Literacy, 64*(1), 27–35.

American Psychological Association. (2014). *School connectedness.* Accessed at www.apa.org/pi/lgbt/programs/safe-supportive/school-connectedness on September 12, 2025.

Americans With Disabilities Act of 1990, 42 U.S.C. § 12101, et seq. (1990).

An, B. P. (2013). The impact of dual enrollment on college degree attainment: Do low-SES students benefit? *Educational Evaluation and Policy Analysis, 35*(1), 57–75. https://doi.org/10.3102/0162373712461933

Ander, R., Guryan, J., & Ludwig, J. (2016, March). *Improving academic outcomes for disadvantaged students: Scaling up individualized tutorials* (Policy Proposal No. 2016-02). The Hamilton Project. Accessed at www.hamiltonproject.org/assets/files/improving_academic_outcomes_for_disadvantaged_students_pp.pdf?_ga=2.133158795.461868053.1725983853-407620611.1725983853 on September 12, 2025.

Anderson, A. R., Christenson, S. L., Sinclair, M. F., & Lehr, C. A. (2004). Check & Connect: The importance of relationships for promoting engagement with school. *Journal of School Psychology, 42*(2), 95–113.

Archer, A. L. (2015). *Explicit vocabulary instruction: Words for everyone, elementary.* Pacific Northwest.

Archer, A. L., Gleason, M. M., & Vachon, V. (2000). *REWARDS reading excellence: Word attack and rate development strategies.* Sopris West.

Archer, A. L., & Hughes, C. A. (2011). *Explicit instruction: Effective and efficient teaching.* Guilford Press.

Armstrong, A. W., Watson, A. J., Makredes, M., Frangos, J. E., Kimball, A. B., & Kvedar, J. C. (2009). Text-message reminders to improve sunscreen use: A randomized, controlled trial using electronic monitoring. *Archives of Dermatology, 145*(11), 1230–1236.

Arnold, K., Fleming, S., DeAnda, M., Castleman, B., & Wartman, K. L. (2009). The summer flood: The invisible gap among low-income students. *Thought and Action,* 23–34.

Association for Career and Technical Education. (2018). *Career exploration in middle school: Setting students on the path to success.* Accessed at https://files.eric.ed.gov/fulltext/ED596321.pdf on September 12, 2025.

Avery, C., Castleman, B. L., Hurwitz, M., Long, B. T., & Page, L. C. (2020). Digital messaging to improve college enrollment and success. *Economics of Education Review, 84,* Article 102170.

Avina, A., Boyle, J., Duble Moore, T., Hicks, E. A., & Wiggins, D. M. (2022). *Intensive intervention practice guide: Self-monitoring systems to improve behavior outcomes for students with comorbid academic and behavior difficulties.* U.S. Department of Education, Office of Special Education Programs, National Center for Leadership in Intensive Intervention. Accessed at https://files.eric.ed.gov/fulltext/ED628226.pdf on September 12, 2025.

Bailey, M. J., & Dynarski, S. (2011). Inequality in postsecondary education. In G. J. Duncan & R. J. Murnane (Eds.), *Whither opportunity? Rising inequality, schools, and children's life chances* (pp. 117–132). Russell Sage Foundation.

Bailey, T. R. (2020, August 10). *Is MTSS/RTI really that complicated? Let's get back to basics!* [Blog post]. Accessed at https://mtss4success.org/blog/mtssrti-really-complicated-lets-get-back-basics on September 12, 2025.

Bailey, T. R., Colpo, A., & Foley, A. (2020, December). *Assessment practices within a multi-tiered system of supports* (CEEDAR Document No. IC-18). University of Florida, Collaboration for Effective Educator, Development, Accountability, and Reform Center. Accessed at https://ceedar.education.ufl.edu/wp-content/uploads/2020/12/Assessment-Practices-Within-a-Multi-Tiered-System-of-Supports-1.pdf on September 12, 2025.

Baker, S., Lesaux, N., Jayanthi, M., Dimino, J., Proctor, C. P., Morris, J., et al. (2014, April). *Teaching academic content and literacy to English learners in elementary and middle school* (NCEE No. 2014-4012). U.S. Department of Education, Institute of Education Sciences, National Center for Education Evaluation and Regional Assistance. Accessed at https://ies.ed.gov/ncee/WWC/Docs/PracticeGuide/english_learners_pg_040114.pdf on September 12, 2025.

Balfanz, R. (2009, June). *Putting middle grades students on the graduation path: A policy and practice brief.* Everyone Graduates Center, Philadelphia Education Fund, & National Middle School Association. Accessed at www.amle.org/portals/0/pdf/articles/policy_brief_balfanz.pdf on September 12, 2025.

Balfanz, R., Bridgeland, J. M., Moore, L. A., & Hornig Fox, J. (2010, November). *Building a grad nation: Progress and challenge in ending the high school dropout epidemic.* Civic Enterprises & Everyone Graduates Center at Johns Hopkins University. Accessed at https://files.eric.ed.gov/fulltext/ED513447.pdf on September 12, 2025.

Balfanz, R., & Byrnes, V. (2019). Early warning indicators and intervention systems: State of the field. In J. A. Fredricks, A. L. Reschly, & S. L. Christenson (Eds.), *Handbook of student engagement interventions: Working with disengaged students* (pp. 45–55). Academic Press.

Balfanz, R., & Byrnes, V. (2025, June 10). *Delivering success: The GRAD Partnership year two impact results.* GRAD Partnership. Accessed at www.gradpartnership.org/wp-content/uploads/2025/06/GRAD_Year2Report_2025.pdf on September 12, 2025.

Barnett, E. (2016, February). *Building student momentum from high school into college.* Jobs for the Future. Accessed at https://files.eric.ed.gov/fulltext/ED564836.pdf on September 12, 2025.

Barnett, E., Bucceri, K., Hindo, C., & Kim, J. (2013, December). *Ten key decisions in creating early colleges: Design options based on research.* National Center for Restructuring Education, Schools and Teaching. Accessed at https://academiccommons.columbia.edu/doi/10.7916/D8BR8RKG on September 12, 2025.

Bartholomew, M., & De Jong, D. (2017). Barriers to implementing the response to intervention framework in secondary schools: Interviews with secondary principals. *NASSP Bulletin, 101*(4), 261–277. https://doi.org/10.1177/0192636517743788

Baye, A., Inns, A., Lake, C., & Slavin, R. E. (2019). A synthesis of quantitative research on reading programs for secondary students. *Reading Research Quarterly, 54*(2), 133–166. https://doi.org/10.1002/rrq.229

Beam, M. (2018). *Math 180 efficacy study: Hardin County Schools.* RMC Research Corporation.

Beam, M., & Faddis, B. (2015). *MATH 180 early implementation study: Hillsborough County Public Schools.* RMC Research Corporation.

Beattie, K. K. (2000). *The effects of intensive computer-based language intervention on language functioning and reading achievement in language-impaired adolescents* [Doctoral dissertation, George Mason University]. LearnTechLib, www.learntechlib.org/p/123642

Beckett, M., Borman, G., Capizzano, J., Parsley, D., Ross, S., Schirm, A., et al. (2009, July). *Structuring out-of-school time to improve academic achievement* (NCEE No. 2009-012). U.S. Department of Education, Institute of Education Sciences, National Center for Education Evaluation and Regional Assistance. Accessed at https://ies.ed.gov/ncee/WWC/Docs/PracticeGuide/ost_pg_072109.pdf on September 12, 2025.

Belfield, C., Bowden, A. B., Klapp, A., Levin, H., Shand, R., & Zander, S. (2015). The economic value of social and emotional learning. *Journal of Benefit-Cost Analysis, 6*(3), 508–544.

Belley, P., & Lochner, L. (2007). The changing role of family income and ability in determining educational achievement. *Journal of Human Capital, 1*(1), 37–89.

Berger, A., Turk-Bicakci, L., Garet, M., Song, M., Knudson, J., Haxton, C., et al. (2013, September). *Early college, early success: Early college high school initiative impact study.* American Institutes for Research. Accessed at www.air.org/sites/default/files/downloads/report/ECHSI_Impact_Study_Report_Final1_0.pdf on September 12, 2025.

Berkeley, S., Scanlon, D., Bailey, T. R., Sutton, J. C., & Sacco, D. M. (2020). A snapshot of RTI implementation a decade later: New picture, same story. *Journal of Learning Disabilities, 53*(5), 332–342. https://doi.org/10.1177/0022219420915867

Bethell, C., Jones, J., Gombojav, N., Linkenbach, J., & Sege, R. (2019). Positive childhood experiences and adult mental and relational health in a statewide sample. *JAMA Pediatrics, 173*(11), Article e193007.

Bhatt, M., Guryan, J., Khan, S., LaForest-Tucker, M., & Mishra, B. (2024). *Can technology facilitate scale? Evidence from a randomized evaluation of high-dosage tutoring* (Working Paper No. 24-14). Institute for Policy Research.

Blum, R. W. (2005a). A case for school connectedness. *Educational Leadership, 62*(7), 16–19.

Blum, R. W. (2005b). *School connectedness: Improving students' lives.* Johns Hopkins Bloomberg School of Public Health. Accessed at www.casciac.org/pdfs/SchoolConnectedness.pdf on September 12, 2025.

Bohanon, H., Love, L. C., & Morrissey, K. (2021). *Implementing systematic interventions: A guide for secondary school teams.* Routledge.

Bolman, L. G., & Deal, T. E. (2021). *Reframing organizations: Artistry, choice, and leadership* (7th ed.). Jossey-Bass.

Boncu, A., Costea, I., & Minulescu, M. (2017). A meta-analytic study investigating the efficiency of socio-emotional learning programs on the development of children and adolescents. *Romanian Journal of Applied Psychology, 19*(2), 35–41. https://doi.org/10.24913/rjap.19.2.02

Borman, G. D., Park, S. J., & Min, S. (2015). *The district-wide effectiveness of the Achieve3000 program: A quasi-experimental study.* Measured Decisions & University of Wisconsin–Madison. Accessed at https://eric.ed.gov/?id=ED558845 on January 13, 2026.

Bouck, E. C., & Cosby, M. D. (2019). Response to intervention in high school mathematics: One school's implementation. *Preventing School Failure: Alternative Education for Children and Youth, 63*(1), 32–42.

Bound, J., Lovenheim, M. F., & Turner, S. (2010). Why have college completion rates declined? An analysis of changing student preparation and collegiate resources. *American Economic Journal: Applied Economics, 2*(3), 129–157.

Bowman-Perrott, L., Burke, M. D., de Marin, S., Zhang, N., & Davis, H. (2015). A meta-analysis of single-case research on behavior contracts: Effects on behavioral and academic outcomes among children and youth. *Behavior Modification, 39*(2), 247–269.

Bradshaw, C. P., Mitchell, M. M., & Leaf, P. J. (2010). Examining the effects of Schoolwide Positive Behavioral Interventions and Supports on student outcomes: Results from a randomized controlled effectiveness trial in elementary schools. *Journal of Positive Behavior Interventions, 12*(3), 133–148. https://doi.org/10.1177/1098300709334798

Bresina, B. C., Baker, K., Donegan, R., & Whaley, V. M. (2018). *Intensive intervention practice guide: Applying response to intervention for secondary students who struggle with reading comprehension.* U.S. Department of Education, Office of Special Education Programs, National Center for Leadership in Intensive Intervention. Accessed at https://files.eric.ed.gov/fulltext/ED591072.pdf on September 12, 2025.

Briesch, A. M., Chafouleas, S. M., Nissen, K., & Long, S. (2020). A review of state-level procedural guidance for implementing multitiered systems of support for behavior (MTSS-B). *Journal of Positive Behavior Interventions, 22*(3), 131–144. https://doi.org/10.1177/1098300719884707

Brodersen, R. M., Gagnon, D., Liu, J., & Tedeschi, S. (2021, May). *The impact of career and technical education on postsecondary outcomes in Nebraska and South Dakota* (REL 2021–087). U.S. Department of Education, Institute of Education Sciences, National Center for Education Evaluation and Regional Assistance, Regional Educational Laboratory Central. Accessed at https://ies.ed.gov/sites/default/files/rel-central/document/2025/10/REL_2021087.pdf on January 8, 2026.

Brown, D., Reumann-Moore, R., Hugh, R., Christman, J. B., & Riffer, M. (2008). *Links to learning and sustainability: Year three report of the Pennsylvania High School Coaching Initiative*. Research for Action. Accessed at https://files.eric.ed.gov/fulltext/ED504284.pdf on September 12, 2025.

Brown, J. E., Sanford, A. K., & Sacco, D. (2024, April). *Multi-tiered system of supports for multilingual learners: Using culturally and linguistically aligned practices*. American Institutes for Research, National Center on Intensive Intervention. Accessed at https://intensiveintervention.org/sites/default/files/2024-01/mtss-culturally-responsive.pdf on September 12, 2025.

Bruhn, A., McDaniel, S., & Kreigh, C. (2015). Self-monitoring interventions for students with behavior problems: A systematic review of current research. *Behavioral Disorders, 40*(2), 102–121. https://doi.org/10.17988/bd-13-45.1

Bruns, E. J., Walker, J. S., & National Wraparound Initiative Advisory Group. (2008). Ten principles of the wraparound process. In E. J. Bruns & J. S. Walker (Eds.), *The resource guide to wraparound*. National Wraparound Initiative, Research and Training Center for Family Support and Children's Mental Health.

Bundock, K., Hawken, L. S., Kiuhara, S. A., O'Keeffe, B. V., O'Neill, R. E., & Cummings, M. B. (2019). Teaching rate of change and problem solving to high school students with high incidence disabilities at Tier 3. *Learning Disability Quarterly, 44*(1), 35–49. https://doi.org/10.1177/0731948719887341

Burchinal, M., McCartney, K., Steinberg, L., Crosnoe, R., Friedman, S. L., McLoyd, V., et al. (2011). Examining the Black–White achievement gap among low-income children using the NICHD study of early child care and youth development. *Child Development, 82*(5), 1404–1420. https://doi.org/10.1111/j.1467-8624.2011.01620.x

Burns, M. K. (2008). Response to intervention at the secondary level. *Principal Leadership, 8*(7), 12–15.

Caballero, C. J. (2023, July 7). *Building a master schedule for 180 productive days*. Edutopia. Accessed at www.edutopia.org/article/developing-school-master-plan on September 12, 2025.

Caldarella, P., Shatzer, R. H., Gray, K. M., Young, K. R., & Young, E. L. (2011). The effects of school-wide positive behavior support on middle school climate and student outcomes. *RMLE Online, 35*(4), 1–14. https://doi.org/10.1080/19404476.2011.11462087

Canter, A., Klotz, M. B., & Cowan, K. (2008). Response to intervention: The future for secondary schools. *Principal Leadership, 8*(6), 12–15.

Carbonari, M. V., DeArmond, M., Dewey, D., Dizon-Ross, E., Goldhaber, D., Kane, T. J., et al. (2024, July). *Impacts of academic recovery interventions on student achievement in 2022–23* (Working Paper No. 303-0724). CALDER. Accessed at https://caldercenter.org/sites/default/files/2024-11/CALDER%20WP%20%20303-0724.pdf on September 12, 2025.

Carr, E. G., Dunlap, G., Horner, R. H., Koegel, R. L., Turnbull, A. P., Sailor, W., et al. (2002). Positive behavior support: Evolution of an applied science. *Journal of Positive Behavior Interventions, 4*(1), 4–16.

Carr, E. G., Horner, R. H., Turnbull, A. P., Marquis, J. G., McLaughlin, D. M., McAtee, M. L., et al. (1999). *Positive behavior support for people with developmental disabilities: A research synthesis.* American Association on Mental Retardation.

Carrasco, M. (2024, July 16). *Report: The biggest barriers to higher ed enrollment are cost and lack of financial aid.* National Association of Student Financial Aid Administrators. Accessed at www.nasfaa.org/news-item/34147/Report_The_Biggest_Barriers_to_Higher_Ed_Enrollment_Are_Cost_and_Lack_of_Financial_Aid on September 12, 2025.

CAST. (2024). *Universal design for learning guidelines version 3.0.* Accessed at https://udlguidelines.cast.org on September 12, 2025.

Castleman, B. L. (2021, May 3). Why aren't text message interventions designed to boost college success working at scale? *Behavioral Scientist.* Accessed at https://behavioralscientist.org/why-arent-text-message-interventions-designed-to-boost-college-success-working-at-scale on September 12, 2025.

Castleman, B. L., Arnold, K., & Wartman, K. L. (2012). Stemming the tide of summer melt: An experimental study of the effects of post–high school summer intervention on low-income students' college enrollment. *Journal of Research on Educational Effectiveness, 5*(1), 1–17.

Castleman, B. L., & Page, L. C. (2014). A trickle or a torrent? Understanding the extent of summer "melt" among college-intending high school graduates. *Social Science Quarterly, 95*(1), 202–220.

Castleman, B. L., & Page, L. C. (2015). Summer nudging: Can personalized text messages and peer mentor outreach increase college going among low-income high school graduates? *Journal of Economic Behavior & Organization, 115*, 144–160.

Castleman, B. L., & Page, L. C. (2017). Parental influences on postsecondary decision making: Evidence from a text messaging experiment. *Educational Evaluation and Policy Analysis, 39*(2), 361–377.

Center on Multi-Tiered System of Supports. (n.d.a). *Essential components of MTSS.* American Institutes for Research. Accessed at https://mtss4success.org/essential-components on September 12, 2025.

Center on Multi-Tiered System of Supports. (n.d.b). *Progress monitoring.* American Institutes for Research. Accessed at https://mtss4success.org/essential-components/progress-monitoring on September 12, 2025.

Center on Multi-Tiered System of Supports. (2020). *Tier 2 identification procedures.* American Institutes for Research. Accessed at https://mtss4success.org/sites/default/files/2021-06/Guidance_Tier2%20_Identification_508.docx on September 12, 2025.

Center on Multi-Tiered System of Supports. (2025a). *Essential features of Tier 1 core programming* [Infographic]. American Institutes for Research. Accessed at https://mtss4success.org/sites/default/files/2023-07/tier_1_infographic.pdf on October 22, 2025.

Center on Multi-Tiered System of Supports. (2025b, February). *Multi-tiered system of supports (MTSS) fidelity of implementation rubric* (Vol. 3). American Institutes for Research. Accessed at https://mtss4success.org/sites/default/files/2025-01/mtss-fidelity-rubric-2025.pdf on September 12, 2025.

Center on Multi-Tiered System of Supports. (2025c). *School infrastructure and support mechanisms* [Fact sheet]. American Institutes for Research. Accessed at https://mtss4success.org/sites/default/files/2022-02/MTSS-Infrastructure.pdf on September 12, 2025.

Center on Multi-Tiered System of Supports. (2025d). *What is screening?* American Institutes for Research. Accessed at https://mtss4success.org/sites/default/files/2023-05/what-is-screening.pdf on September 12, 2025.

Center on Positive Behavioral Interventions and Supports. (n.d.a). *Schoolwide.* Accessed at www.pbis.org/topics/school-wide on September 12, 2025.

Center on Positive Behavioral Interventions and Supports. (n.d.b). *Tier 2.* Accessed at www.pbis.org/pbis/tier-2 on September 12, 2025.

Center on Positive Behavioral Interventions and Supports. (2022, January). *Tier 3 student-level systems guide.* University of Oregon. Accessed at https://cdn.prod.website-files.com/5d3725188825e071f1670246/61fd8575fcde71e46a028720_Tier%203%20Student%20Level%20Systems%20Guide.pdf on September 12, 2025.

Center on Positive Behavioral Interventions and Supports. (2024, May). *Supporting and responding to students' social, emotional, and behavioral needs: Evidence-based practices for educators.* University of Oregon. Accessed at https://cdn.prod.website-files.com/5d3725188825e071f1670246/664cdc2b5d9a7dc86b343a68_Supporting%20and%20Responding%20to%20Students'%20Social%2C%20Emotional%2C%20and%20Behavioral%20Needs.pdf on September 12, 2025.

Center on Positive Behavioral Interventions and Supports. (2025, July). *Tier 2 school-level systems guide.* University of Oregon. Accessed at https://cdn.prod.website-files.com/5d3725188825e071f1670246/68654794b233f564c1df554c_Tier%202%20School-Level%20Systems%20Guide.pdf on September 12, 2025.

Center on the Developing Child. (n.d.). *Toxic stress.* Harvard University. Accessed at https://developingchild.harvard.edu/science/key-concepts/toxic-stress on September 12, 2025.

Center on the Developing Child. (2014, May 6). *Activities guide: Enhancing and practicing executive function skills with children from infancy to adolescence.* Harvard University. Accessed at https://developingchild.harvard.edu/resources/handouts-tools/activities-guide-enhancing-and-practicing-executive-function-skills on September 12, 2025.

Centers for Disease Control and Prevention. (2009). *School connectedness: Strategies for increasing protective factors among youth.* U.S. Department of Health and Human Services. Accessed at https://files.eric.ed.gov/fulltext/ED511993.pdf on September 12, 2025.

Centers for Disease Control and Prevention. (2024a, October 8). *About adverse childhood experiences.* U.S. Department of Health and Human Services. Accessed at www.cdc.gov/aces/about/index.html on September 12, 2025.

Centers for Disease Control and Prevention. (2024b). *Youth Risk Behavior Survey: Data summary and trends report, 2013–2023.* U.S. Department of Health and Human Services. Accessed at www.cdc.gov/yrbs/dstr/index.html on September 12, 2025.

Cerutti, J., Burt, K. B., Moeller, R. W., & Seehuus, M. (2024). Declines in social–emotional skills in college students during the COVID-19 pandemic. *Frontiers in Psychology, 15,* Article 1392058. https://doi.org/10.3389/fpsyg.2024.1392058

Chafouleas, S. M., Kilgus, S. P., Jaffery, R., Riley-Tillman, T. C., Welsh, M., & Christ, T. J. (2013). Direct behavior rating as a school-based behavior screener for elementary and middle grades. *Journal of School Psychology, 51*(3), 367–385.

Chiefs for Change. (2019, November). *Curriculum implementation guide.* Accessed at https://chiefsforchange.org/wp-content/uploads/2020/07/Curriculum-Implementation-Guide.pdf on September 12, 2025.

Christ, T. J., & Silberglitt, B. (2007). Estimates of the standard error of measurement for curriculum-based measures of oral reading fluency. *School Psychology Review, 36*(1), 130–146.

Christenson, S. L., Thurlow, M. L., Sinclair, M. F., Lehr, C. A., Kaibel, C. M., Reschly, A. L., et al. (2012). *Check & Connect: A comprehensive student engagement intervention manual.* Institute on Community Integration.

Civil Rights Act of 1964, Pub. L. No. 88-352, 78 Stat. 241 (1964).

Civil Rights Data Collection. (n.d.). *2017–18 state and national tables.* U.S. Department of Education, Office for Civil Rights. Accessed at https://ocrdata.ed.gov/estimations/2017-2018 on September 19, 2025.

Civil Rights Data Collection. (2021, June). *An overview of exclusionary discipline practices in public schools for the 2017–18 school year.* U.S. Department of Education, Office for Civil Rights. Accessed at https://files.eric.ed.gov/fulltext/ED615866.pdf on September 19, 2025.

Clark, A. G., & Dockweiler, K. A. (2019). *Multi-tiered systems of support in secondary schools: The definitive guide to effective implementation and quality control.* Routledge.

Clear, J. (2018). *Atomic habits: An easy and proven way to build good habits and break bad ones.* Avery.

Collaborative for Academic, Social, and Emotional Learning. (n.d.). *CASEL program guide.* Accessed at https://pg.casel.org/review-programs on September 12, 2025.

College and Career Readiness and Success Center. (2013, March). *How career and technical education can help students be college and career ready: A primer.* American Institutes for Research. Accessed at www.air.org/sites/default/files/2021-06/College%20Career%20Readiness%20Primer%20Brief.pdf on September 12, 2025.

College and Career Readiness and Success Center. (2017). *Evidence-based practices to support college and career readiness in high school: Early warning indicators.* American Institutes for Research. Accessed at https://files.eric.ed.gov/fulltext/ED586415.pdf on September 12, 2025.

College and Career Readiness and Success Center, Center on Great Teachers and Leaders, & RTI International. (2016, April). *Integrating employability skills: A framework for all educators.* American Institutes for Research. Accessed at www.air.org/sites/default/files/EmployabilitySkills_Handouts.pdf on September 12, 2025.

College Board. (n.d.). *About accommodations.* Accessed at https://accommodations.collegeboard.org/how-accommodations-work/about-accommodations on January 6, 2026.

Collins, T. A., Cook, C. R., Dart, E. H., Socie, D. G., Renshaw, T. L., & Long, A. C. (2016). Improving classroom engagement among high school students with disruptive behavior: Evaluation of the Class Pass intervention. *Psychology in the Schools, 53*(2), 204–219.

ConnectEd: The California Center for College and Career. (2012, April). *College and career readiness: What do we mean? A proposed framework.* Author. Accessed at https://connectednational.org/wp-content/uploads/2018/11/CACR-Version-V1-2-Apr-12-2012_FINAL.pdf on September 12, 2025.

Conradi, L. A., Walker, V. L., McDaid, P., Johnson, H. N., & Strickland-Cohen, M. K. (2022, August). *A literature review of School-wide Positive Behavioral Interventions and Supports for students with extensive support needs* (TIES Center Report No. 106). TIES Center & Center on Positive Behavioral Interventions and Supports. Accessed at https://cdn.prod.website-files.com/5d3725188825e071f1670246/62f673c9376fced74e660e5d_TIESReport106.pdf on October 14, 2025.

Conradi Smith, K., Jang, B. G., & Ostot, T. J. (2025). It's not just about skills: Adopting a motivation-informed approach to instruction with adolescents. *Journal of Adolescent and Adult Literacy, 68*(4), 415–420. https://doi.org/10.1002/jaal.1396

Cook, C. R., Collins, T., Dart, E., Vance, M. J., McIntosh, K., Grady, E. A., et al. (2014). Evaluation of the Class Pass intervention for typically developing students with hypothesized escape-motivated disruptive classroom behavior. *Psychology in the Schools, 51*(2), 107–125. https://doi.org/10.1002/pits.21742

Cook, K. B., & Sayeski, K. L. (2022). High-school students with high-incidence disabilities' use of smartphones for self-monitoring. *Exceptionality, 30*(4), 279–295.

Cook, M. A., & Ross, S. M. (2024, November). *Evaluation of Catapult Learning Wraparound Supplemental Services in a large parochial school district.* Johns Hopkins University, Center for Research and Reform in Education.

Cook, P. J., Dodge, K., Farkas, G., Fryer, R. G., Jr., Guryan, J., Ludwig, J., et al. (2014, January). *The (surprising) efficacy of academic and behavioral intervention with disadvantaged youth from a randomized experiment in Chicago* (Working Paper No. 14-03). Institute for Policy Research. Accessed at www.ipr.northwestern.edu/documents/working-papers/2014/IPR-WP-14-03.pdf on September 12, 2025.

Corrin, W., Parise, L. M., Cerna, O., Haider, Z., & Somers, M.-A. (2015, April). *Case management for students at risk of dropping out: Implementation and interim impact findings from the Communities In Schools evaluation.* MDRC. Accessed at https://files.eric.ed.gov/fulltext/ED558497.pdf on September 12, 2025.

Corrin, W., Sepanik, S., Rosen, R., & Shane, A. (2016, June). *Addressing early warning indicators: Interim impact findings from the Investing in Innovation (i3) evaluation of Diplomas Now*. MDRC. Accessed at https://files.eric.ed.gov/fulltext/ED566904.pdf on September 12, 2025.

Council of the Great City Schools. (2017, June). *Supporting excellence: A framework for developing, implementing, and sustaining a high-quality district curriculum*. Author. Accessed at https://files.eric.ed.gov/fulltext/ED580881.pdf on September 12, 2025.

Crone, D. A., Hawken, L. S., & Horner, R. H. (2015). *Building positive behavior support systems in schools: Functional behavioral assessment* (2nd ed.). Guilford Press.

Crone, E. A. (2009). Executive functions in adolescence: Inferences from brain and behavior. *Developmental Science, 12*(6), 825–830.

Cronholm, P. F., Forke, C. M., Wade, R., Bair-Merritt, M. H., Davis, M., Harkins-Schwarz, M., et al. (2015). Adverse childhood experiences: Expanding the concept of adversity. *American Journal of Preventive Medicine, 49*(3), 354–361.

Dale, S. (2015). Heuristics and biases: The science of decision-making. *Business Information Review, 32*(2), 93–99.

Darling-Hammond, L., Alexander, M., & Hernández, L. E. (2024, March). *Redesigning high schools: 10 features for success*. Learning Policy Institute. Accessed at www.redesigninghighschool.org/sites/default/files/rk/attach/Redesigning_High_Schools_10_Features_REPORT.pdf on September 12, 2025.

Davis, D. H., Fredrick, L. D., Alberto, P. A., & Gama, R. (2012). Functional communication training without extinction using concurrent schedules of differing magnitudes of reinforcement in classrooms. *Journal of Positive Behavior Interventions, 14*(3), 162–172.

Davis, M. H. (2012). *Using data to keep all students on track to graduation: Team playbook*. Johns Hopkins University School of Education, Center for Social Organization of Schools. Accessed at https://new.every1graduates.org/wp-content/uploads/2012/01/Team_Playbook_MarciaDavis.pdf on September 17, 2025.

Daye, J. (2019). *MTSS implementation in high schools: Expert and stakeholder perspectives* [Doctoral dissertation, University of South Florida]. Digital Commons @ University of South Florida. https://digitalcommons.usf.edu/cgi/viewcontent.cgi?article=8972&context=etd

DeMatthews, D. E., & Wang, Y. (2023). How can principals lead in the school improvement planning process? Reducing biases in shared decision making. *The Clearing House: A Journal of Educational Strategies, Issues and Ideas, 96*(2), 43–51. https://doi.org/10.1080/00098655.2022.2163971

Dennis, M. S., & Gratton-Fisher, E. (2020). Use data-based individualization to improve high school students' mathematics computation and mathematics concept, and application performance. *Learning Disabilities Research and Practice, 35*(3), 126–138.

Deno, S. L. (1985). Curriculum-based measurement: The emerging alternative. *Exceptional Children, 52*(3), 219–232. https://doi.org/10.1177/001440298505200303

Deno, S. L. (2003). Developments in curriculum-based measurement. *The Journal of Special Education, 37*(3), 184–192.

Deshler, D. D., & Schumaker, J. B. (Eds.). (2006). *Teaching adolescents with disabilities: Accessing the general education curriculum*. Corwin.

Development Services Group. (2015, December). *Protective factors against delinquency*. Office of Juvenile Justice and Delinquency Prevention. Accessed at https://ojjdp.ojp.gov/model-programs-guide/literature-reviews/protective_factors_against_delinquency.pdf on September 12, 2025.

Didion, L., Toste, J. R., Benz, S. A., & Shogren, K. A. (2021). How are self-determination components taught to improve reading outcomes for elementary students with or at risk for learning disabilities? *Learning Disability Quarterly, 44*(4), 288–303. https://doi.org/10.1177/0731948721989328

Dignath, C., & Veenman, M. V. J. (2021). The role of direct strategy instruction and indirect activation of self-regulated learning: Evidence from classroom observation studies. *Educational Psychology Review, 33*(2), 489–533.

Din, F. S., Isack, L. R., & Rietveld, J. (2003, February). *Effects of contingency contracting on decreasing student tardiness* [Paper presentation]. Eastern Educational Research Association annual conference, Hilton Head Island, SC.

Djabrayan Hannigan, J., & Hannigan, J. (2024). *Behavior academies: Targeted interventions that work!* Solution Tree Press.

Dobbie, W., & Fryer, R. G., Jr. (2011). Are high-quality schools enough to increase achievement among the poor? Evidence from the Harlem Children's Zone. *American Economic Journal: Applied Economics, 3*(3), 158–187.

Domitrovich, C. E., Syvertsen, A. K., & Calin, S. S. (2017, October). *Promoting social and emotional learning in the middle and high school years.* Pennsylvania State University, Edna Bennett Pierce Prevention Research Center. Accessed at https://prevention.psu.edu/wp-content/uploads/2022/09/rwjf441241-SELMidHS.pdf on September 12, 2025.

Donini-Lenhoff, F. G., & Brotherton, S. E. (2010). Racial-ethnic diversity in allied health: The continuing challenge. *Journal of Allied Health, 39*(2), 104–109.

Drake Patrick, J., & Acosta, K. (2024). *Evidence-based reading instruction for adolescents in grades 6–12* (CEEDAR Document No. IC-13b). University of Florida, Collaboration for Effective Educator, Development, Accountability, and Reform Center. Accessed at https://ceedar.education.ufl.edu/wp-content/uploads/2024/08/Secondary-Literacy-IC.pdf on September 12, 2025.

Drummond, T. (1994). *Student Risk Screening Scale (SRSS)* [Database record]. APA PsycTests.

Duckworth, A. L., Peterson, C., Matthews, M. D., & Kelly, D. R. (2007). Grit: Perseverance and passion for long-term goals. *Journal of Personality and Social Psychology, 92*(6), 1087–1101. https://doi.org/10.1037/0022-3514.92.6.1087

Duffy, H. (2007, August). *Meeting the needs of significantly struggling learners in high school.* National High School Center. Accessed at https://air.org/sites/default/files/2021-06/NHSC_RTIBrief_08-02-07_0.pdf on September 12, 2025.

Duffy, H., & Scala, J. (2012, March). *A systemic approach to implementing response to intervention in three Colorado high schools.* American Institutes for Research, National High School Center. Accessed at https://files.eric.ed.gov/fulltext/ED532566.pdf on September 12, 2025.

DuFour, R., DuFour, R., Eaker, R., & Karhanek, G. (2010). *Raising the bar and closing the gap: Whatever it takes.* Solution Tree Press.

DuFour, R., DuFour, R., Eaker, R., Many, T. W., Mattos, M., & Muhammad, A. (2024). *Learning by doing: A handbook for Professional Learning Communities at Work* (4th ed.). Solution Tree Press.

Duncan, R., Washburn, I. J., Lewis, K. M., Bavarian, N., DuBois, D. L., Acock, A. C., et al. (2017). Can universal SEL programs benefit universally? Effects of the Positive Action Program on multiple trajectories of social-emotional and misconduct behaviors. *Prevention Science, 18*(2), 214–224.

Durlak, J. A., Weissberg, R. P., Dymnicki, A. B., Taylor, R. D., & Schellinger, K. B. (2011). The impact of enhancing students' social and emotional learning: A meta-analysis of school-based universal interventions. *Child Development, 82*(1), 405–432.

Durrance, S. (2023, January). *Implementing MTSS in secondary schools: Challenges and strategies.* SERVE at the University of North Carolina at Greensboro. Accessed at https://region6cc.uncg.edu/wp-content/uploads/2022/06/ImplementingMTSSinSecondarySchools_2022_RC6_003.pdf on September 12, 2025.

Durrance, S. (2025). *Implementing MTSS in secondary schools: Strategies from research and the field.* SERVE at the University of North Carolina at Greensboro. Accessed at https://serve.uncg.edu/wp-content/uploads/2025/03/MTSS-Strategies-and-Resources-Reference-Updates_Final_2.2025.pdf on September 12, 2025.

Durrance, S., & McColskey, W. (2024, March). *Findings on the implementation of multi-tiered systems of support (MTSS) drawn from the experiences of six high schools.* SERVE at the University of North Carolina at Greensboro. Accessed at https://region6cc.uncg.edu/wp-content/uploads/2024/04/MTSSCrossStoryAnalysis_2024_RC6_024.pdf on September 12, 2025.

Dweck, C. S. (2008). *Mindset: the new psychology of success.* Ballantine Books.

Dynarski, M., Clarke, L., Cobb, B., Finn, J., Rumberger, R., & Smink, J. (2008, September). *Dropout prevention: A practice guide* (Publication No. NCEE 2008-4025). U.S. Department of Education, Institute of Education Sciences, National Center for Education Evaluation and Regional Assistance.

Dynarski, M., Gleason, P., Rangarajan, A., & Wood, R. G. (1998). *Impacts of dropout prevention programs: Final report.* Mathematica Policy Research.

Dynarski, S., Nurshatayeva, A., Page, L. C., & Scott-Clayton, J. (2023). Addressing nonfinancial barriers to college access and success: Evidence and policy implications. In E. A. Hanushek, S. Machin, & L. Woessmann (Eds.), *Handbook of the economics of education* (Vol. 6, pp. 319–403). Elsevier.

Early, D. M., Berg, J. K., Alicea, S., Si, Y., Aber, J. L., Ryan, R. M., et al. (2016). The impact of Every Classroom, Every Day on high school student achievement: Results from a school-randomized trial. *Journal of Research on Educational Effectiveness, 9*(1), 3–29.

Early, D. M., Rogge, R. D., & Deci, E. L. (2014). Engagement, alignment, and rigor as vital signs of high-quality instruction: A classroom visit protocol for instructional improvement and research. *High School Journal, 97*(4), 219–239.

Ebbers, S., & Hougen, M. C. (2015). Academic vocabulary development: Meaningful, memorable, and morphological. In M. C. Hougen (Ed.), *Fundamentals of literacy instruction and assessment, 6–12* (pp. 41–60). Brookes.

Eberhardt, J. L. (2019). *Biased: Uncovering the hidden prejudice that shapes what we see, think, and do.* Viking.

Edmonds, M. S., Vaughn, S., Wexler, J., Reutebuch, C., Cable, A., Tackett, K. K., et al. (2009). A synthesis of reading interventions and effects on reading comprehension outcomes for older struggling readers. *Review of Educational Research, 79*(1), 262–300. https://doi.org/10.3102/0034654308325998

Edmunds, J. A., Unlu, F., Furey, J., Glennie, E., & Arshavsky, N. (2020). What happens when you combine high school and college? The impact of the early college model on postsecondary performance and completion. *Educational Evaluation and Policy Analysis, 42*(2), 257–278.

Edmunds, J. A., Unlu, F., Glennie, E., Bernstein, L., Fesler, L., Furey, J., et al. (2017). Smoothing the transition to postsecondary education: The impact of the early college model. *Journal of Research on Educational Effectiveness, 10*(2), 297–325.

Education Strategy Group, Advance CTE, & Council of Chief State School Officers. (2018, September). *Credential currency: How states can identify and promote credentials of value.* Authors. Accessed at https://edstrategy.org/wp-content/uploads/2018/10/ESG-Credential-Currency-Full-Report.pdf on September 12, 2025.

Edwards, L., Hughes, K. L., & Weisberg, A. (2011, October). *Different approaches to dual enrollment: Understanding program features and their implications.* The James Irvine Foundation.

Elliott, M. N., Hanser, L. M., & Gilroy, C. L. (2002). Career academies: Additional evidence of positive student outcomes. *Journal of Education for Students Placed at Risk, 7*(1), 71–90.

Ellis, E. S., Deshler, D. D., Lenz, B. K., Schumaker, J. B., & Clark, F. L. (1991). An instructional model for teaching learning strategies. *Focus on Exceptional Children, 23*(6), 1–24.

Ellwood, D. T., & Kane, T. J. (2000). Who is getting a college education? Family background and the growing gaps in enrollment. In S. Danziger & J. Waldfogel (Eds.), *Securing the future: Investing in children from birth to college* (pp. 283–324). Russell Sage Foundation.

Ennis, R. P. (2016). Using self-regulated strategy development to help high school students with EBD summarize informational text in social studies. *Education and Treatment of Children, 39*(4), 545–568.

Ennis, R. P., & Losinski, M. (2019). SRSD fractions: Helping students at risk for disabilities add/subtract fractions with unlike denominators. *Journal of Learning Disabilities, 52*(5), 399–412. https://doi.org/10.1177/0022219419859509

Epler, P. (2015). *Examining response to intervention (RTI) models in secondary education.* IGI Global.

Every Student Succeeds Act of 2015, Pub. L. No. 114-95, 20 U. S. C. § 1177 (2015). Accessed at www.congress.gov/114/plaws/publ95/PLAW-114publ95.pdf on September 15, 2025.

Evidence for ESSA. (n.d.a). *Evidence-based math programs.* Johns Hopkins University, Center for Research and Reform in Education. Accessed at www.evidenceforessa.org/programs/math/?grade%5B%5D=Middle+School&grade%5B%5D=High+School on January 18, 2026.

Evidence for ESSA. (n.d.b). *Evidence-based reading programs.* Johns Hopkins University, Center for Research and Reform in Education. Accessed at www.evidenceforessa.org/programs/reading/?grade%5B%5D=Middle+School&grade%5B%5D=High+School on January 17, 2026.

Fang, Z., & Drake Patrick, J. (2024). *Disciplinary literacy* (CEEDAR Document No. IC-19). University of Florida, Collaboration for Effective Educator, Development, Accountability, and Reform Center. Accessed at https://ceedar.education.ufl.edu/wp-content/uploads/2024/06/Disciplinary-Literacy-IC-1.pdf on September 15, 2025.

Faria, A.-M., Sorensen, N., Heppen, J., Bowdon, J., Taylor, S., Eisner, R., et al. (2017, April). *Getting students on track for graduation: Impacts of the Early Warning Intervention and Monitoring System after one year* (Publication No. REL 2017-272). U.S. Department of Education, Institute of Education Sciences, National Center for Education Evaluation and Regional Assistance, Regional Educational Laboratory Midwest. Accessed at https://files.eric.ed.gov/fulltext/ED573814.pdf on September 15, 2025.

Farrington, C. A., Roderick, M., Allensworth, E. M., Nagaoka, J., Keyes, T. S., Johnson, D. W., et al. (2012, June). *Teaching adolescents to become learners: The role of noncognitive factors in shaping school performance—A critical literature review.* University of Chicago Consortium on Chicago School Research.

Federal Reserve Bank of New York. (2025, August 1). *The labor market for recent college graduates: Unemployment rates for recent college graduates versus older groups* [Data set]. Accessed at www.newyorkfed.org/research/college-labor-market#--:explore:unemployment on September 15, 2025.

Felfe, C., Saurer, J., Schneider, P., Vornberger, J., Erhart, M., Kaman, A., et al. (2023). The youth mental health crisis: Quasi-experimental evidence on the role of school closures. *Science Advances, 9*(33). https://doi.org/10.1126/sciadv.adh4030

Felitti, V. J., Anda, R. F., Nordenberg, D., Williamson, D. F., Spitz, A. M., Edwards, V., et al. (1998). Relationship of childhood abuse and household dysfunction to many of the leading causes of death in adults: The Adverse Childhood Experiences (ACE) Study. *American Journal of Preventive Medicine, 14*(4), 245–258. https://doi.org/10.1016/S0749-3797(98)00017-8

Field, K. (2019, October 25). *Helping students with intellectual disabilities conquer college.* The Hechinger Report. Accessed at https://hechingerreport.org/helping-students-with-intellectual-disabilities-conquer-college on September 15, 2025.

Filderman, M. J., & Gesel, S. A. (2022). Data teams: A collaborative approach to intensifying intervention using student data. *TEACHING Exceptional Children, 56*(6), 482–491. https://doi.org/10.1177/00400599221096753

Fink, J., Griffin, S., Garcia Tulloch, A., Jenkins, D., Fay, M. P., Ramirez, C., et al. (2023, October). *DEEP insights: Redesigning dual enrollment as a purposeful pathway to college and career opportunity.* Columbia University, Teachers College, Community College Research Center. Accessed at https://ccrc.tc.columbia.edu/wp-content /uploads/2023/10/deep-insights-redesigning-dual-enrollment-1.pdf on February 23, 2026.

Fink, J., Jenkins, D., & Yanagiura, T. (2017, September). *What happens to students who take community college "dual enrollment" courses in high school?* Columbia University, Teachers College, Community College Research Center.

Fisher, D., & Frey, N. (2013). Implementing RTI in a high school: A case study. *Journal of Learning Disabilities, 46*(2), 99–114. https://doi.org/10.1177/0022219411407923

Fisher, D., & Frey, N. (2014). Scaffolded reading instruction of content-area texts. *The Reading Teacher, 67*(5), 347–351.

Fixsen, D. L., Naoom, S. F., Blase, K. A., Friedman, R. M., & Wallace, F. (2005). *Implementation research: A synthesis of the literature* (FMHI Publication No. 231). University of South Florida, Louis de la Parte Florida Mental Health Institute, National Implementation Research Network. Accessed at https://fpg.unc.edu/sites/fpg .unc.edu/files/resource-files/NIRN-MonographFull-01-2005.pdf on September 16, 2025.

Flannery, K. B., Fenning, P., Kato, M. M., & McIntosh, K. (2014). Effects of School-wide Positive Behavioral Interventions and Supports and fidelity of implementation on problem behavior in high schools. *School Psychology Quarterly, 29*(2), 111–124. https://doi.org/10.1037/spq0000039

Flannery, K. B., Hershfeldt, P., & Freeman, J. (Eds.). (2018). *Lessons learned on implementation of PBIS in high schools: Current trends and future directions.* University of Oregon Press. Accessed at https://pbismissouri.org /wp-content/uploads/2018/09/Monograph-PBIS-in-High-Schools.pdf on September 16, 2025.

Flannery, K. B., & Kato, M. M. (2017). Implementation of SWPBIS in high school: Why is it different? *Preventing School Failure: Alternative Education for Children and Youth, 61*(1), 69–79. https://doi.org/10.1080/10459 88X.2016.1196644

Flannery, K. B., & Sugai, G. (Eds.). (2009). *Monograph on SWPBS implementation in high schools: Current practice and future directions.* University of Oregon, Center on Positive Behavioral Interventions and Supports.

Fletcher, E. C., Jr. (2023). Reengaging high school students through career academies. *State Education Standard, 23*(3), 33–35.

Fletcher, E. C., Jr., Dumford, A. D., Hernandez-Gantes, V. M., & Minar, N. (2020). Examining the engagement of career academy and comprehensive high school students in the United States. *The Journal of Educational Research, 113*(4), 247–261. https://doi.org/10.1080/00220671.2020.1787314

Fletcher, E. C., Jr., & Tan, T. X. (2024). Implementation matters: A comparison study of career academy and comprehensive high school students' engagement in college and career readiness activities. *Educational Studies, 50*(6), 1336–1352. https://doi.org/10.1080/03055698.2022.2079374

Fletcher, J. M., & Vaughn, S. (2009). Response to intervention: Preventing and remediating academic difficulties. *Child Development Perspectives, 3*(1), 30–37.

Flores, M. M., & Milton, J. H. (2020). Teaching the partial products algorithm using the concrete-representational-abstract sequence. *Exceptionality, 28*(2), 142–160.

Franks, A., & Fraser, J. (2020). *2020–21 support for instructional content prioritization in high school mathematics.* Student Achievement Partners. Accessed at https://achievethecore.org/content/upload/2020-21%20Support%20 for%20Instructional%20Content%20Prioritization%20in%20HS%20Mathematics_August%202020.pdf on September 16, 2025.

Frederick, M. L., Courtney, S., & Caniglia, J. (2014). With a little help from my friends: Scaffolding techniques in problem solving. *Investigations in Mathematics Learning, 7*(2), 21–32.

Freeman, J., Simonsen, B., McCoach, D. B., Sugai, G., Lombardi, A., & Horner, R. H. (2015). An analysis of the relationship between implementation of school-wide positive behavior interventions and supports and high school dropout rates. *High School Journal, 98*(4), 290–315.

Freeman, J., Simonsen, B., McCoach, D. B., Sugai, G., Lombardi, A., & Horner, R. H. (2016). Relationship between school-wide positive behavior interventions and supports and academic, attendance, and behavior outcomes in high schools. *Journal of Positive Behavior Interventions, 18*(1), 41–51.

Friedman, K. (2019, June 27). *Three ways to build college knowledge in high school* [Blog post]. Accessed at https://ies.ed.gov/learn/blog/three-ways-build-college-knowledge-high-school on September 16, 2025.

Fryer, R. G., Jr. (2016, March). *The production of human capital in developed countries: Evidence from 196 randomized field experiments* (Working Paper No. 22130). National Bureau of Economic Research. Accessed at www.nber.org/system/files/working_papers/w22130/w22130.pdf on January 27, 2026.

Fuchs, D., & Fuchs, L. S. (2006). Introduction to response to intervention: What, why, and how valid is it? *Reading Research Quarterly, 41*(1), 93–99.

Fuchs, D., & Fuchs, L. S. (2017). Critique of the national evaluation of response to intervention: A case for simpler frameworks. *Exceptional Children, 83*(3), 255–268.

Fuchs, L. S., Deno, S. L., & Mirkin, P. K. (1984). The effects of frequent curriculum-based measurement and evaluation on pedagogy, student achievement, and student awareness of learning. *American Educational Research Journal, 21*(2), 449–460.

Fuchs, L. S., & Fuchs, D. (2009). On the importance of a unified model of responsiveness to intervention. *Child Development Perspectives, 3*(1), 41–43. https://doi.org/10.1111/j.1750-8606.2008.00074.x

Fuchs, L. S., Fuchs, D., & Compton, D. L. (2010). Rethinking response to intervention at middle school and high school. *School Psychology Review, 39*(1), 22–28.

Fuchs, L. S., Fuchs, D., & Malone, A. S. (2017). The Taxonomy of Intervention Intensity. *TEACHING Exceptional Children, 50*(1), 35–43.

Gaddie, R., & Bryce. C. (2021, July 8). *Differentiated instruction* [Presentation]. LaRue County Public Schools.

Gage, N. A., Katsiyannis, A., Carrero, K. M., Miller, R., & Pico, D. (2020). Exploring disproportionate discipline for Latinx students with and without disabilities: A national analysis. *Behavioral Disorders, 47*(1), 3–13. https://doi.org/10.1177/0198742920961356

Gage, N. A., Lee, A., Grasley-Boy, N., & Peshak George, H. (2018). The impact of school-wide positive behavior interventions and supports on school suspensions: A statewide quasi-experimental analysis. *Journal of Positive Behavior Interventions, 20*(4), 217–226. https://doi.org/10.1177/1098300718768204

Gage, N. A., Leite, W., Childs, K., & Kincaid, D. (2017). Average treatment effect of School-wide Positive Behavioral Interventions and Supports on school-level academic achievement in Florida. *Journal of Positive Behavior Interventions, 19*(3), 158–167. https://doi.org/10.1177/1098300717693556

Gambrell, L., & Marinak, B. (n.d.). *Reading motivation: What the research says*. Reading Rockets. Accessed at www.readingrockets.org/topics/motivation/articles/reading-motivation-what-research-says on September 16, 2025.

García, E. (2014, December 2). *The need to address noncognitive skills in the education policy agenda* (Briefing Paper No. 386). Economic Policy Institute. Accessed at www.epi.org/publication/the-need-to-address-noncognitive-skills-in-the-education-policy-agenda on September 16, 2025.

Gebhard, M., & Graham, H. (2018). Bats and grammar: Developing critical language awareness in the context of school reform. *English Teaching: Practice and Critique, 17*(4), 281–297.

Gee, K. A., Beno, C., Lindstrom, L., Lind, J., Post, C., & Hirano, K. (2020). Enhancing college and career readiness programs for underserved adolescents. *Journal of Youth Development, 15*(6), 222–251. https://doi.org/10.5195/jyd.2020.832

Gersten, R., Beckmann, S., Clarke, B., Foegen, A., Marsh, L., Star, J. R., et al. (2009, April). *Assisting students struggling with mathematics: Response to intervention (RTI) for elementary and middle schools* (Publication No. NCEE 2009-4060). U.S. Department of Education, Institute of Education Sciences, National Center for Education Evaluation and Regional Assistance.

Giani, M., Alexander, C., & Reyes, P. (2014). Exploring variation in the impact of dual-credit coursework on postsecondary outcomes: A quasi-experimental analysis of Texas students. *High School Journal, 97*(4), 200–218.

Goldstein, D. (2025, March 6). Why some schools are rethinking "college for all." *The New York Times.*

Graham, S., Bruch, J., Fitzgerald, J., Friedrich, L., Furgeson, J., Greene, K., et al. (2016, November). *Teaching secondary students to write effectively* (Publication No. NCEE 2017-4002). U.S. Department of Education, Institute of Education Sciences, National Center for Education Evaluation and Regional Assistance. Accessed at https://ies.ed.gov/ncee/wwc/Docs/PracticeGuide/508_WWCPG_SecondaryWriting_122719.pdf on September 16, 2025.

Graham, S., & Harris, K. R. (2005). Improving the writing performance of young struggling writers: Theoretical and programmatic research from the Center on Accelerating Student Learning. *The Journal of Special Education, 39*(1), 19–33.

Graham-Day, K. J., Gardner, R., III, & Hsin, Y.-W. (2010). Increasing on-task behaviors of high school students with attention deficit hyperactivity disorder: Is it enough? *Education and Treatment of Children, 33*(3), 205–221.

Graves, M. F., Flynn, K., & Ringstaff, C. (2021). Reflections on seven years of strategy instruction. *Journal of Education, 201*(3), 271–279.

Guha, R., Caspary, K., Stites, R., Padilla, C., Arshan, N., Park, C., et al. (2014, December). *Taking stock of the California Linked Learning District Initiative: Fifth-year evaluation report.* SRI International.

Guryan, J., Ludwig, J., Bhatt, M. P., Cook, P. J., Davis, J. M. V., Dodge, K., et al. (2023). Not too late: Improving academic outcomes among adolescents. *American Economic Review, 113*(3), 738–765. https://doi.org/10.1257/aer.20210434

Hamedani, M. G., & Darling-Hammond, L. (2015). *Social emotional learning in high school: How three urban high schools engage, educate, and empower youth.* Stanford Center for Opportunity Policy in Education.

Hamilton, L., & Gross, B. (2021, August). *How has the pandemic affected students' social-emotional well-being? A review of the evidence to date.* Center on Reinventing Public Education.

Hamilton, L., Halverson, R., Jackson, S., Mandinach, E., Supovitz, J., & Wayman, J. (2009, September). *Using student achievement data to support instructional decision making* (Publication No. NCEE 2009-4067). U.S. Department of Education, Institute of Education Sciences, National Center for Education Evaluation and Regional Assistance.

Hammond, Z. (2015). *Culturally responsive teaching and the brain: Promoting authentic engagement and rigor among culturally and linguistically diverse students.* Corwin.

Hannigan, J., Djabrayan Hannigan, J., Mattos, M., & Buffum, A. (2021). *Behavior solutions: Teaching academic and social skills through RTI at Work.* Solution Tree Press.

Hanover Research. (2014, February). *Optimal scheduling for secondary school students.* Author. Accessed at www.mansfieldisd.org/uploaded/main/departments/CIA/assets/MasterScheduleStudy/Research-OptimalScheduling_Secondary.pdf on September 16, 2025.

Harris, M. L., Schumaker, J. B., & Deshler, D. D. (2011). The effects of strategic morphological analysis instruction on the vocabulary performance of secondary students with and without disabilities. *Learning Disability Quarterly, 34*(1), 17–33.

Hart, E. J., Doyle, L., Cantero, C., & Garrington, F. O. (2022). *Intensive intervention practice guide: Teaching self-regulation skills to students with disabilities (K–12).* U.S. Department of Education, Office of Special Education Programs.

Hawken, L. S., Adolphson, S. L., Macleod, K. S., & Schumann, J. (2009). Secondary-tier interventions and supports. In W. Sailor, G. Dunlap, G. Sugai, & R. Horner (Eds.), *Handbook of positive behavior support* (pp. 395–420). Springer. https://doi.org/10.1007/978-0-387-09632-2_17

Haxton, C., Song, M., Zeiser, K., Berger, A., Turk-Bicakci, L., Garet, M. S., et al. (2016). Longitudinal findings from the Early College High School Initiative impact study. *Educational Evaluation and Policy Analysis, 38*(2), 410–430. https://doi.org/10.3102/0162373716642861

Hays-Grudo, J., & Morris, A. S. (2020). *Adverse and protective childhood experiences: A developmental perspective.* American Psychological Association.

Heath, C., & Heath, D. (2010). *Switch: How to change things when change is hard.* Broadway Books.

Hemelt, S. W., Lenard, M. A., & Paeplow, C. G. (2017, January). *Building better bridges to life after high school: Experimental evidence on contemporary career academies* (Working Paper No. 176). CALDER. Accessed at https://files.eric.ed.gov/fulltext/ED572934.pdf on September 16, 2025.

Heppen, J. B., & Therriault, S. B. (2008, July). *Developing early warning systems to identify potential high school dropouts.* American Institutes for Research, National High School Center.

Hernández, L. E., & Darling-Hammond, L. (2024a, November). *Cultivating relationships in secondary classrooms: Practices that matter.* Learning Policy Institute. Accessed at https://learningpolicyinstitute.org/product/cultivating-relationships-secondary-classrooms-brief on September 16, 2025.

Hernández, L. E., & Darling-Hammond, L. (2024b, November). *Cultivating relationships in secondary schools: Structures that matter.* Learning Policy Institute. Accessed at https://learningpolicyinstitute.org/product/cultivating-relationships-secondary-schools-brief on September 16, 2025.

Hoffman, N., Vargas, J., & Santos, J. (2008, May). *On ramp to college: A state policymaker's guide to dual enrollment.* Jobs for the Future. Accessed at www.jff.org/wp-content/uploads/2023/09/OnRamp.pdf on September 16, 2025.

Hosp, J. L., Hosp, M. K., Howell, K. W., & Allison, R. (2014). *The ABCs of curriculum-based evaluation: A practical guide to effective decision making.* Guilford Press.

Hougen, M. (2015, May). *Evidence-based reading instruction for adolescents, grades 6–12* (CEEDAR Document No. IC-13). University of Florida, Collaboration for Effective Educator, Development, Accountability, and Reform Center. Accessed at https://ceedar.education.ufl.edu/wp-content/uploads/2015/05/IC-13_FINAL_05-26-15.pdf on September 17, 2025.

Hoxby, C., & Turner, S. (2013, March). *Expanding college opportunities for high-achieving, low-income students* (SIEPR Discussion Paper No. 12-014). Stanford University, Stanford Institute for Economic Policy Research. Accessed at https://siepr.stanford.edu/publications/working-paper/expanding-college-opportunities-high-achieving-low-income-students on January 26, 2026.

Hughes, J., & Petscher, Y. (2016, January). *A guide to developing and evaluating a college readiness screener* (Publication No. REL 2016-169). U.S. Department of Education, Institute of Education Sciences, National Center for Education Evaluation and Regional Assistance, Regional Educational Laboratory Southeast. Accessed at https://ies.ed.gov/use-work/resource-library/resource/other-resource/guide-developing-and-evaluating-college-readiness-screener on September 17, 2025.

Hughes, K. L., & Karp, M. M. (2004, February). *School-based career development: A synthesis of the literature.* Columbia University, Institute on Education and the Economy. Accessed at https://files.eric.ed.gov/fulltext/ED498580.pdf on September 17, 2025.

ideas42, Nudge4, & Heckscher Foundation for Children. (2016). *Nudges, norms, and new solutions: Evidence-based strategies to get students to and through college.* Authors. Accessed at www.ideas42.org/wp-content/uploads/2018/05/NudgesNormsNewSolutions.pdf on September 16, 2025.

Individuals With Disabilities Education Act Amendments of 1997, Pub. L. No. 105-17 (1997).

Individuals With Disabilities Education Act of 2004, Pub. L. No. 108-446 § 1400 (2004). Accessed at https://sites.ed.gov/idea/statute-chapter-33/subchapter-ii/1414 on January 10, 2026.

Ingram, K., Lewis-Palmer, T., & Sugai, G. (2005). Function-based intervention planning: Comparing the effectiveness of FBA function-based and non-function-based intervention plans. *Journal of Positive Behavior Interventions, 7*(4), 224–236.

Institute on Community Integration. (n.d.). *Check & Connect.* University of Minnesota. Accessed at https://checkandconnect.umn.edu on January 26, 2026.

IRIS Center. (n.d.). *Progress monitoring: Reading.* Vanderbilt University. Accessed at https://iris.peabody.vanderbilt.edu/module/pmr on January 26, 2026.

IRIS Center. (2022a). *Executive functions (part 1): Understanding why some students struggle.* Vanderbilt University. Accessed at https://iris.peabody.vanderbilt.edu/module/ef1 on September 17, 2025.

IRIS Center. (2022b). *Providing instructional supports: Facilitating mastery of new skills.* Vanderbilt University. Accessed at https://iris.peabody.vanderbilt.edu/module/sca on September 17, 2025.

IRIS Center. (2022c). *RTI (part 3): Reading instruction.* Vanderbilt University. Accessed at https://iris.peabody.vanderbilt.edu/module/rti03-reading on September 17, 2025.

IRIS Center. (2025a). *Evidence-based practice summaries.* Vanderbilt University. Accessed at https://iris.peabody.vanderbilt.edu/resources/ebp_summaries on September 17, 2025.

IRIS Center. (2025b). *Functional behavioral assessment (elementary): Identifying the reasons for student behavior.* Vanderbilt University. Accessed at https://iris.peabody.vanderbilt.edu/module/fba/#content on September 17, 2025.

IRIS Center. (2026). *Intensive intervention (part 1): Using data-based individualization to intensify instruction.* Vanderbilt University. Accessed at https://iris.peabody.vanderbilt.edu/module/dbi1/cresource/q1/p01/#content on December 27, 2025.

Isbell, L. J., & Szabo, S. (2014). Understanding secondary teachers' concerns about RTI: Purposeful professional communication. *Delta Kappa Gamma Bulletin, 80*(3), 11–23.

Jeong, Y., & Copeland, S. R. (2020). Comparing functional behavior assessment-based interventions and non-functional behavior assessment-based interventions: A systematic review of outcomes and methodological quality of studies. *Journal of Behavioral Education, 29*(1), 1–41. https://doi.org/10.1007/s10864-019-09355-4

Jerald, C. D. (2006, June). *Identifying potential dropouts: Key lessons for building an early warning data system.* Achieve.

Jimerson, S. R., Burns, M. K., & VanDerHeyden, A. M. (Eds.). (2016). *Handbook of response to intervention: The science and practice of multi-tiered systems of support* (2nd ed.). Springer.

Johnson, E. S., Galow, P. A., & Allenger, R. (2012). Application of algebra curriculum-based measurements for decision making in middle and high school. *Assessment for Effective Intervention, 39*(1), 3–11. https://doi.org/10.1177/1534508412461435

Johnson, E. S., & Smith, L. (2016). Implementation of response to intervention at middle school: Challenges and potential benefits. *TEACHING Exceptional Children, 40*(3), 46–52. https://doi.org/10.1177/004005990804000305 (Original work published 2008)

Johnson, E. S., Smith, L., & Harris, M. L. (2009). *How RTI works in secondary schools.* Corwin.

Johnson, L., White, R., Charner, I., Cole, J., & Promboin, G. (2018). *Work-based learning manual: A how-to guide for work-based learning.* Accessed at https://wbl.fhi360.org on September 17, 2025.

Johnson, L. E., Wang, E. W., Gilinsky, N., He, Z., Carpenter, C., Nelson, C. M., et al. (2013). Youth outcomes following implementation of universal SW-PBIS strategies in a Texas secure juvenile facility. *Education and Treatment of Children, 36*(3), 135–145.

Jones, S. M., Brush, K. E., Wettje, S., Ramirez, T., Poddar, A., Kannarr, A., et al. (2022, November). *Navigating SEL from the inside out: Looking inside and across leading SEL programs—A practical resource for schools and OST providers, middle and high school focus.* Harvard Graduate School of Education, the Easel Lab. Accessed at https://wallacefoundation.org/sites/default/files/2023-09/navigating-social-and-emotional-learning-from-the-inside-out-middle-high-school.pdf on September 17, 2025.

Joy, L., & O'Hara, R. E. (2022, May 9). *Nudging students toward holistic supports and postsecondary success* [Blog post]. Accessed at www.jff.org/nudging-students-toward-holistic-supports-and-postsecondary-success on September 17, 2025.

Joyner, R. E., & Wagner, R. K. (2020). Co-occurrence of reading disabilities and math disabilities: A meta-analysis. *Scientific Studies of Reading, 24*(1), 14–22. https://doi.org/10.1080/10888438.2019.1593420

Kamil, M. L., Borman, G. D., Dole, J., Kral, C. C., Salinger, T., & Torgesen, J. (2008, August). *Improving adolescent literacy: Effective classroom and intervention practices* (NCEE No. 2008-4027). U.S. Department of Education, Institute of Education Sciences, National Center for Education Evaluation and Regional Assistance. Accessed at https://ies.ed.gov/ncee/wwc/docs/practiceguide/adlit_pg_082608.pdf on September 17, 2025.

Kantrov, I. (2017). *Achieving educational equity and justice in career academies: Challenges and promising strategies.* Ford Next Generation Learning.

Karp, M. M., Calcagno, J. C., Hughes, K. L., Jeong, D. W., & Bailey, T. R. (2007, October). *The postsecondary achievement of participants in dual enrollment: An analysis of student outcomes in two states.* National Research Center for Career and Technical Education.

Keller, C. L., Bucholz, J., & Brady, M. P. (2007). Yes, I can! Empowering paraprofessionals to teach learning strategies. *TEACHING Exceptional Children, 39*(3), 18–23.

Kemple, J. J. (2004). *Career academies: Impacts on labor market outcomes and educational attainment.* MDRC.

Kemple, J. J., & Snipes, J. C. (2000). *Career academies: Impacts on students' engagement and performance in high school.* MDRC.

Kemple, J. J., & Willner, C. (2008). *Career academies: Long-term impacts on labor market outcomes, educational attainment, and transitions to adulthood.* MDRC.

Kennedy, C. H., Long, T., Jolivette, K., Cox, J., Tang, J.-C., & Thompson, T. (2001). Facilitating general education participation for students with behavior problems by linking positive behavior supports and person-centered planning. *Journal of Emotional and Behavioral Disorders, 9*(3), 161–171.

Kennelly, L., & Monrad, M. (2007, October). *Approaches to dropout prevention: Heeding early warning signs with appropriate interventions.* American Institutes for Research, National High School Center. Accessed at www.air.org/sites/default/files/2021-06/NHSC_ApproachestoDropoutPrevention_0.pdf on September 17, 2025.

Kern, L., Starosta, K. M., Cook, C. R., Bambara, L. M., & Gresham, F. R. (2007). Functional assessment-based intervention for selective mutism. *Behavioral Disorders, 32*(2), 94–108.

Kim, H., Montague, M. L., & Castillo, L. G. (2025). The effects of gaining early awareness and readiness for undergraduate programs on educational outcomes: A meta-analysis. *Journal of Diversity in Higher Education, 18*(Suppl. 1), S473–S481. https://doi.org/10.1037/dhe0000586

Kim, J., & Bragg, D. (2008). The impact of dual and articulated credit on college readiness and retention in four community colleges. *Career and Technical Education Research, 33*(2), 133–158. https://doi.org/10.5328/CTER33.2.133

Kim, J. S., Hemphill, L., Troyer, M., Thomson, J. M., Jones, S. M., LaRusso, M. D., et al. (2017). Engaging struggling adolescent readers to improve reading skills. *Reading Research Quarterly, 52*(3), 357–382. https://doi.org/10.1002/rrq.171

King, S. A., Lemons, C. J., & Hill, D. R. (2012). Response to intervention in secondary schools: Considerations for administrators. *NASSP Bulletin, 96*(1), 5–22.

Kistler, H. C., Childs, J., & Dougherty, S. M. (2024). Can career academies work as a school turnaround strategy? *Educational Evaluation and Policy Analysis, 47*(4), 1202–1218. https://doi.org/10.3102/01623737241289152

Klee, I. C., Brasch, S. M., Neyman, J., McLaughlin, T. F., & Stookey, S. (2015). The effect using the REWARDS® Reading Program on vowel sounds, word part, and prefix and suffix identification in multi-syllabic words: A case report. *Educational Research Quarterly, 38*(4), 31–50.

Klingner, J. K., & Vaughn, S. (1999). Promoting reading comprehension, content learning, and English acquisition through Collaborative Strategic Reading (CSR). *The Reading Teacher, 52*(7), 738–747.

Koomar, S. (2024). *What is "nudging" and how does it change behaviour in education?* (Learning Brief No. 4). EdTech Hub. https://doi.org/10.53832/edtechhub.1011

Koselak, J. (2011). *Transforming high schools through response to intervention: Lessons learned and a pathway forward.* Eye on Education.

Kraft, M. A. (2015). How to make additional time matter: Integrating individualized tutorials into an extended day. *Education Finance and Policy, 10*(1), 81–116.

Kraft, M. A., & Rogers, T. (2015). The underutilized potential of teacher-to-parent communication: Evidence from a field experiment. *Economics of Education Review, 47*, 49–63.

Kreamer, K. (2025, June 16). *Protect the "and": Why college* and *career readiness matters* [Blog post]. Advance CTE. Accessed at https://careertech.org/blog/protect-the-and-why-college-and-career-readiness-matters on January 8, 2026.

Kurtz, H., Lloyd, S., Harwin, A., Daniels, A. B., & Guo, B. (2023). *Student motivation: Student and educator perceptions.* Editorial Projects in Education & EdWeek Research Center. Accessed at https://epe.brightspotcdn.com/4f/67/b04470cb45e19be401bc43bef0c6/3-21-23-studentmotivationspotlight-sponsored.pdf on September 17, 2025.

La Charite, J., Khan, M., Dudovitz, R., Nuckols, T., Sastry, N., Huang, C., et al. (2023). Specific domains of positive childhood experiences (PCEs) associated with improved adult health: A nationally representative study. *SSM—Population Health, 24*, Article 101558. https://doi.org/10.1016/j.ssmph.2023.101558

Lammers, J., & Mathers, K. (2024, July 25). *The state of career exploration in middle school* [Blog post]. Accessed at www.ecs.org/state-of-middle-school-career-exploration on September 17, 2025.

Lane, K. L., Harris, K., Graham, S., Driscoll, S., Sandmel, K., Morphy, P., et al. (2011). Self-Regulated Strategy Development at Tier 2 for second-grade students with writing and behavioral difficulties: A randomized controlled trial. *Journal of Research on Educational Effectiveness, 4*(4), 322–353.

Lane, K. L., Rogers, L. A., Parks, R. J., Weisenbach, J. L., Mau, A. C., Merwin, M. T., et al. (2007). Function-based interventions for students who are nonresponsive to primary and secondary prevention efforts: Illustrations at the elementary and middle school levels. *Journal of Emotional and Behavioral Disorders, 15*(3), 169–183.

Lane, K. L., Weisenbach, J. L., Phillips, A., & Wehby, J. H. (2007). Designing, implementing, and evaluating function-based interventions using a systematic, feasible approach. *Behavioral Disorders, 32*(2), 122–139.

Lanford, M., & Maruco, T. (2019). Six conditions for successful career academies. *Phi Delta Kappan, 100*(5), 50–52.

Lang, L., Torgesen, J., Vogel, W., Chanter, C., Lefsky, E., & Petscher, Y. (2009). Exploring the relative effectiveness of reading interventions for high school students. *Journal of Research on Educational Effectiveness, 2*(2), 149–175.

Lariviere, D. O., Agrawal, V., & Wang, J. J. (2022). *Intensive intervention practice guide: Mathematics-language instruction for emergent bilingual students with mathematics difficulty.* U.S. Department of Education, Office of Special Education Programs, National Center for Leadership in Intensive Intervention. Accessed at https://files.eric.ed.gov/fulltext/ED628227.pdf on September 17, 2025.

Larson, K. A., & Rumberger, R. W. (1995). ALAS: Achievement for Latinos through academic success. In H. Thorton (Ed.), *Staying in school: A technical report of three dropout prevention projects for middle high school students with learning and emotional disabilities* (pp. A-1–A-71). University of Minnesota, Institute on Community Integration.

Lavecchia, A. M., Liu, H., & Oreopoulos, P. (2014, October). *Behavioral economics of education: Progress and possibilities* (Working Paper No. 20609). National Bureau of Economic Research. Accessed at www.nber.org/system/files/working_papers/w20609/w20609.pdf on September 17, 2025.

Lee, A., Gage, N. A., McLeskey, J., & Huggins-Manley, A. C. (2021). The impacts of school-wide positive behavior interventions and supports on school discipline outcomes for diverse students. *The Elementary School Journal, 121*(3), 410–429. https://doi.org/10.1086/712625

Lenz, B. K., & Hughes, C. A. (1990). A word identification strategy for adolescents with learning disabilities. *Journal of Learning Disabilities, 23*(3), 149–158, 163.

Lenz, B. K., Schumaker, J. B., Deshler, D. D., & Beals, V. L. (1984). *The word identification strategy*. University of Kansas.

Leverson, M., Smith, K., McIntosh, K., Rose, J., & Pinkelman, S. (2021, March). *PBIS cultural responsiveness field guide: Resources for trainers and coaches*. University of Oregon, Center on Positive Behavioral Interventions and Supports. Accessed at https://assets-global.website-files.com/5d3725188825e071f1670246/6062383b3f8932b212e9c98b_PBIS%20Cultural%20Responsiveness%20Field%20Guide%20v2.pdf on September 17, 2025.

Lewis, T. J., & Sugai, G. (1999). Effective behavior support: A systems approach to proactive schoolwide management. *Focus on Exceptional Children, 31*(6), 1–24.

Linkow, T., Miller, H., Parsad, A., Price, C., & Martinez, A. (2021, February). *Study of college transition messaging in GEAR UP: Impacts on enrolling and staying in college* (Publication No. NCEE 2021-005). U.S. Department of Education, Institute of Education Sciences, National Center for Education Evaluation and Regional Assistance. Accessed at https://ies.ed.gov/use-work/resource-library/report/evaluation-report/study-college-transition-messaging-gear-impacts-enrolling-and-staying-college on September 17, 2025.

Lloyd, B. P., Barton, E. E., Pokorski, E. A., Ledbetter-Cho, K., & Pennington, B. (2019). Function-based interventions in K–8 general education settings: A focus on teacher implementation. *The Elementary School Journal, 119*(4), 601–628. https://doi.org/10.1086/703114

Lochner, L., & Moretti, E. (2004). The effect of education on crime: Evidence from prison inmates, arrests, and self-reports. *The American Economic Review, 94*(1), 155–189.

Losinski, M., Ennis, R. P., Sanders, S., & Wiseman, N. (2019). An investigation of SRSD to teach fractions to students with disabilities. *Exceptional Children, 85*(3), 291–308. https://doi.org/10.1177/0014402918813980

Losinski, M., Maag, J. W., Katsiyannis, A., & Ryan, J. B. (2015). The use of structural behavioral assessment to develop interventions for secondary students exhibiting challenging behaviors. *Education and Treatment of Children, 38*(2), 149–174.

Lushen, K., Kim, O., & Reid, R. (2012). Paraeducator-led strategy instruction for struggling writers. *Exceptionality, 20*(4), 250–265. https://doi.org/10.1080/09362835.2012.724626

Lyon, J., & Palmer, T. (2021). *Self-assessment guide for college and career academies* (Rev. ed.). College and Career Alliance and Support Network. Accessed at https://casn.berkeley.edu/wp-content/uploads/2022/02/UCB-CCASN-Self-Assessment-Guide-Updated-FILLABLE.pdf on September 17, 2025.

Maccini, P., Mulcahy, C. A., & Wilson, M. G. (2007). A follow-up of mathematics interventions for secondary students with learning disabilities. *Learning Disabilities Research and Practice, 22*(1), 58–74.

Mac Iver, M. A., Stein, M. L., Davis, M. H., Balfanz, R., & Fox, J. H. (2019). An efficacy study of a ninth-grade early warning indicator intervention. *Journal of Research on Educational Effectiveness, 12*(3), 363–390. https://doi.org/10.1080/19345747.2019.1615156

Mager, U., & Nowak, P. (2012). Effects of student participation in decision making at school: A systematic review and synthesis of empirical research. *Educational Research Review, 7*(1), 38–61.

Mahoney, M. (2020). Implementing evidence-based practices within multi-tiered systems of support to promote inclusive secondary classroom settings. *The Journal of Special Education Apprenticeship, 9*(1).

Makori, A., Burch, P., & Loeb, S. (2024, March). *Scaling high-impact tutoring: School level perspectives on implementation challenges and strategies* (Working Paper No. 24-923). Annenberg Institute at Brown University. https://doi.org/10.26300/h8z5-t461

Malloy, J. M., Bohanon, H., & Francoeur, K. (2018). Positive Behavioral Interventions and Supports in high schools: A case study from New Hampshire. *Journal of Educational and Psychological Consultation, 28*(2), 219–247. https://doi.org/10.1080/10474412.2017.1385398

Mann, A., Denis, V., & Percy, C. (2020, December). *Career ready? How schools can better prepare young people for working life in the era of COVID-19* (OECD Education Working Paper No. 241). Organisation for Economic Co-operation and Development. https://doi.org/10.1787/e1503534-en

Marken, A., Scala, J., Husby-Slater, M., & Davis, G. (2020, June). *Early Warning Intervention and Monitoring System implementation guide.* American Institutes for Research. Accessed at https://pathwaystoadultsuccess.org/wp-content/uploads/2021/04/EWIMS_Implementation-Guide_FINAL_July_2020.pdf on September 18, 2025.

Marlowe, A. (2021). *Multi-tiered system of supports: A case study examining effective MTSS implementation at the middle school level* [Doctoral dissertation, Gardner-Webb University]. Digital Commons @ Gardner-Webb University. https://digitalcommons.gardner-webb.edu/cgi/viewcontent.cgi?article=1049&context=education-dissertations

Martin, B., Sargent, K., Van Camp, A., & Wright, J. (2018). *Intensive intervention practice guide: Increasing opportunities to respond as an intensive intervention.* U.S. Department of Education, Office of Special Education Programs, National Center for Leadership in Intensive Intervention. Accessed at https://files.eric.ed.gov/fulltext/ED591076.pdf on September 18, 2025.

Martinez, S., Kern, L., Hershfeldt, P., George, H. P., White, A., Flannery, B., et al. (2019, September). *High school PBIS implementation: Student voice.* University of Oregon, OSEP Technical Assistance Center on Positive Behavioral Interventions and Supports. Accessed at www.pbis.org/resource/high-school-pbis-implementation-student-voice on September 18, 2025.

Marzano, R. J. (2003). *What works in schools: Translating research into action.* ASCD.

Marzano, R. J. (2004). *Building background knowledge for academic achievement: Research on what works in schools.* ASCD.

Marzano, R. J., & Pickering, D. J. (2005). *Building academic vocabulary: Teacher's manual.* ASCD.

Massachusetts Department of Elementary and Secondary Education, Rodriguez Educational Consulting Agency, & Novak Educational Consulting. (2020). *Scheduling guidance for MTSS.* Authors. Accessed at www.doe.mass.edu/sfss/mtss/mobilization/scheduling-guidance.docx on September 18, 2025.

Masten, A. S. (2001). Ordinary magic: Resilience processes in development. *American Psychologist, 56*(3), 227–238.

Masten, A. S., & Reed, M.-G. J. (2002). Resilience in development. In C. R. Snyder & S. J. Lopez (Eds.), *Handbook of positive psychology* (pp. 74–88). Oxford University Press.

Matta, M., Volpe, R. J., Briesch, A. M., & Owens, J. S. (2020). Five direct behavior rating multi-item scales: Sensitivity to the effects of classroom interventions. *Journal of School Psychology, 81*, 28–46.

Mattos, M., Buffum, A., Malone, J., Cruz, L. F., Dimich, N., & Schuhl, S. (2025). *Taking action: A handbook for RTI at Work* (2nd ed.). Solution Tree Press.

Maynard, B. R., Kjellstrand, E. K., & Thompson, A. M. (2014). Effects of Check & Connect on attendance, behavior, and academics: A randomized effectiveness trial. *Research on Social Work Practice*, *24*(3), 296–309. https://doi.org/10.1177/1049731513497804

McDaniel, S. C., & Bloomfield, B. S. (2020). School-wide positive behavior support telecoaching in a rural district. *Journal of Educational Technology Systems*, *48*(3), 335–355. https://doi.org/10.1177/0047239519886283

McIntosh, K., & Goodman, S. (2016). *Integrated multi-tiered systems of support: Blending RTI and PBIS.* Guilford Press.

McPartland, J., Balfanz, R., Jordan, W., & Legters, N. (1998). Improving climate and achievement in a troubled urban high school through the Talent Development Model. *Journal of Education for Students Placed at Risk*, *3*(4), 337–361.

McQuillin, S., Smith, B., & Strait, G. (2011). Randomized evaluation of a single semester transitional mentoring program for first year middle school students: A cautionary result for brief, school-based mentoring programs. *Journal of Community Psychology*, *39*(7), 844–859.

Mehl, G., Wyner, J., Barnett, E., Fink, J., & Jenkins, D. (2020). *The dual enrollment playbook: A guide to equitable acceleration for students.* The Aspen Institute. Accessed at https://ccrc.tc.columbia.edu/publications/dual-enrollment-playbook-equitable-acceleration.html on September 18, 2025.

Metz, A., Burke, K., Albers, B., Louison, L., & Bartley, L. (2020, December). *A practice guide to supporting implementation: What competencies do we need?* University of North Carolina, Frank Porter Graham Child Development Institute, National Implementation Research Network. Accessed at https://implementation.fpg.unc.edu/wp-content/uploads/ISP-Practice-Guide.pdf on September 18, 2025.

Midwest Comprehensive Center (2018, May). *Student goal setting: An evidence-based practice.* American Institutes for Research. Accessed at https://files.eric.ed.gov/fulltext/ED589978.pdf on January 12, 2026.

Midwest PBIS Network. (2021, December 15). *Classroom practices.* Accessed at www.midwestpbis2.org/training-content/tier-1-and-classroom/classroom-practices on September 18, 2025.

Miller, F. G., Crovello, N., & Swenson, N. (2017). Bridging the gap: Direct behavior rating—Single item scales. *Assessment for Effective Intervention*, *43*(1), 60–63.

Miller, F. G., Patwa, S. S., & Chafouleas, S. M. (2014). Using direct behavior rating–single item scales to assess student behavior within multi-tiered systems of support. *Journal of Special Education Leadership*, *27*(2), 76–85.

Miller, S. P., & Hudson, P. J. (2007). Using evidence-based practices to build mathematics competence related to conceptual, procedural, and declarative knowledge. *Learning Disabilities Research and Practice*, *22*(1), 47–57.

Minahan, J., & Rappaport, N. (2012). *The behavior code: A practical guide to understanding and teaching the most challenging students.* Harvard Education Press.

Mitra, D. (2018). Student voice in secondary schools: The possibility for deeper change. *Journal of Educational Administration*, *56*(5), 473–487. https://doi.org/10.1108/JEA-01-2018-0007

Moats, L. (2014, April 3). *When older kids can't read* [Presentation slides]. Voyager Sopris Learning. Accessed at www.voyagersopris.com/docs/default-source/webinar-series/webinar_slides_lmoats_040314.pdf?sfvrsn=b1b4557_2 on September 18, 2025.

Morris, A. S., & Hays-Grudo, J. (2023). Protective and compensatory childhood experiences and their impact on adult mental health. *World Psychiatry*, *22*(1),150–151. https://doi.org/10.1002/wps.21042

Morrison, J. R., Wolf, B., Ross, S. M., Risman, K. L., & McLemore, C. C. (2019, April). *Efficacy study of Zearn Math in a large urban school district.* Johns Hopkins University, Center for Research and Reform in Education.

Morrissey, K. L., Bohanon, H., & Fenning, P. (2010). Positive behavior support: Teaching and acknowledging expected behaviors in an urban high school. *TEACHING Exceptional Children, 42*(5), 26–35. https://doi.org/10.1177/004005991004200503

MTSS Center American Institutes for Research. (2016, February 4). *The High School Tiered Interventions Initiative: Progress monitoring* [Video file]. YouTube. Accessed at www.youtube.com/watch?v=9V-LulyDIKw on September 18, 2025.

Mundschenk, N. A., & Fuchs, W. W. (2016). Professional learning communities: An effective mechanism for the successful implementation and sustainability of response to intervention. *SRATE Journal, 25*(2), 55–64.

Muoneke, A., & Shankland, L. (2009). Uncharted territory: Using tiered intervention to improve high school performance. *SEDL Letter, 21*(1).

Murray, D. W., & Rosanbalm, K. (2017, May). *Promoting self-regulation in adolescents and young adults: A practice brief* (OPRE Report No. 2015-82). U.S. Department of Health and Human Services, Administration for Children and Families, Office of Planning, Research, and Evaluation.

National Academies of Sciences, Engineering, and Medicine. (2017). *Supporting students' college success: The role of assessing intrapersonal and interpersonal competencies.* National Academies Press. https://doi.org/10.17226/24697

National Academies of Sciences, Engineering, and Medicine. (2019). *The promise of adolescence: Realizing opportunity for all youth.* National Academies Press.

National Assessment of Educational Progress. (n.d.a). *NAEP data explorer.* U.S. Department of Education, Institute of Education Sciences, National Center for Education Statistics. Accessed at www.nationsreportcard.gov/ndecore/landing on September 18, 2025.

National Assessment of Educational Progress. (n.d.b). *NAEP report card: 2019 NAEP reading assessment—Highlighted results at grade 12 for the nation.* U.S. Department of Education, Institute of Education Sciences, National Center for Education Statistics. Accessed at www.nationsreportcard.gov/highlights/reading/2019/g12 on March 2, 2024.

National Assessment of Educational Progress. (n.d.c). *NAEP report card: Mathematics.* U.S. Department of Education, Institute of Education Sciences, National Center for Education Statistics. Accessed at www.nationsreportcard.gov/reports/mathematics/2024/g4_8/?grade=8 on January 1, 2026.

National Assessment of Educational Progress. (n.d.d). *NAEP report card: Reading.* U.S. Department of Education, Institute of Education Sciences, National Center for Education Statistics. Accessed at www.nationsreportcard.gov/reports/reading/2024/g4_8 on March 2, 2024.

National Association of School Psychologists. (2016). *NASP position statement: Integrated model of academic and behavior supports.* Author.

National Career Academy Coalition. (n.d.). *The academy model.* Accessed at www.ncacinc.com/about/the-academy-model on February 3, 2025.

National Center for Chronic Disease Prevention and Health Promotion, Division of Adolescent and School Health. (2023, December). *Promoting mental health and well-being in schools: An action guide for school and district leaders.* Centers for Disease Control and Prevention. Accessed at https://stacks.cdc.gov/view/cdc/136371 on September 18, 2025.

National Center for Education Statistics. (2020, December). *Dual or concurrent enrollment in public schools in the United States* (Publication No. NCES 2020-125). U.S. Department of Education, Institute of Education Sciences. Accessed at https://nces.ed.gov/pubs2020/2020125.pdf on September 17, 2025.

National Center for Education Statistics. (2024a, May). *College enrollment rates.* U.S. Department of Education, Institute of Education Sciences. Accessed at https://nces.ed.gov/programs/coe/indicator/cpb on September 18, 2025.

National Center for Education Statistics. (2024b, May). *High school graduation rates*. U.S. Department of Education, Institute of Education Sciences. Accessed at https://nces.ed.gov/programs/coe/indicator/coi/high-school-graduation-rates on September 18, 2025.

National Center for Education Statistics. (2025). *Fast facts: Students with disabilities*. U.S. Department of Education, Institute of Education Sciences. Accessed at https://nces.ed.gov/fastfacts/display.asp?id=64 on September 20, 2025.

National Center for Innovation in Career and Technical Education. (n.d.). *Work-based learning tool kit*. U.S. Department of Education. Accessed at https://cte.ed.gov/wbltoolkit/index.html on September 18, 2025.

National Center on Intensive Intervention. (n.d.a). *Direct behavior rating overview*. American Institutes for Research. Accessed at https://intensiveintervention.org/resource/direct-behavior-rating-overview on September 18, 2025.

National Center on Intensive Intervention. (n.d.b). *Example diagnostic tools*. American Institutes for Research. Accessed at https://intensiveintervention.org/tools-charts/example-diagnostic-tools on September 18, 2025.

National Center on Intensive Intervention. (n.d.c). *Intensive intervention and MTSS*. American Institutes for Research. Accessed at https://intensiveintervention.org/special-topics/mtss on September 18, 2025.

National Center on Intensive Intervention. (n.d.d). *What is the Taxonomy of Intervention Intensity?* American Institutes for Research. Accessed at https://intensiveintervention.org/implementation-intervention/taxonomy-intervention-intensity on September 16, 2025.

National Center on Intensive Intervention. (2013, March). *Data-based individualization: A framework for intensive intervention*. U.S. Department of Education, Office of Special Education Programs. Accessed at https://intensiveintervention.org/sites/default/files/DBI_Framework.pdf on January 26, 2026.

National Center on Intensive Intervention. (2014, February). *Designing and delivering intensive intervention in behavior*. U.S. Department of Education, Office of Special Education Programs. Accessed at https://intensiveintervention.org/sites/default/files/PPT_Designing_Delivering_Behavior_Intervention.pdf on September 18, 2025.

National Center on Intensive Intervention. (2015, February). *Behavior contracts*. U.S. Department of Education, Office of Special Education Programs. Accessed at https://intensiveintervention.org/sites/default/files/Behavior_Contracts_508.pdf on January 26, 2026.

National Center on Intensive Intervention. (2016a). *Principles for designing intervention in mathematics*. U.S. Department of Education, Office of Special Education Programs. Accessed at https://intensiveintervention.org/sites/default/files/Princip_Effect_Math_508.pdf on September 18, 2025.

National Center on Intensive Intervention. (2016b, January). *Self-management*. U.S. Department of Education, Office of Special Education Programs. Accessed at https://intensiveintervention.org/sites/default/files/Self_Management_508.pdf on January 26, 2026.

National Center on Intensive Intervention. (2019, September). *Intensification strategy checklist*. Accessed at https://intensiveintervention.org/resource/intensification-strategy-checklist on September 12, 2025.

National Center on Intensive Intervention. (2021, September). *Academic intervention tools chart*. American Institutes for Research. Accessed at https://charts.intensiveintervention.org/aintervention?_gl=1*1hmbw0c*_ga*NDc3Mjg3MzI1LjE3MjcxMTk1MDM.*_ga_8HTR3VBRFZ*MTcyNzcyNTMyMy4zLjAuMTcyNzcyNTMyMy4wLjAuMA.. on September 18, 2025.

National Center on Response to Intervention. (2011, July). *RTI scheduling processes for middle schools*. U.S. Department of Education, Office of Special Education Programs. Accessed at https://mtss4success.org/sites/default/files/2020-07/0681MS_RTI_Rescheduling_Brief_d2.pdf on September 19, 2025.

National Center on Response to Intervention. (2019). *Contextual factors of implementation planning template: Middle school settings*. American Institutes for Research. Accessed at https://mtss4success.org/sites/default/files/2020-08/MS%20ContextualFactors_CRTI.pdf on September 12, 2025.

National Child Traumatic Stress Network. (2008, October). *Child trauma toolkit for educators*. National Center for Child Traumatic Stress. Accessed at www.nctsn.org/sites/default/files/resources/child_trauma_toolkit_educators.pdf on September 18, 2025.

National Child Traumatic Stress Network. (2017). *Creating, supporting, and sustaining trauma-informed schools: A system framework*. National Center for Child Traumatic Stress. Accessed at www.nctsn.org/sites/default/files/resources/creating_supporting_sustaining_trauma_informed_schools_a_systems_framework.pdf on September 18, 2025.

National Council of Teachers of Mathematics. (2000). *Principles and standards for school mathematics*. Author.

National Gang Center. (2021, April 7). *Career academies*. U.S. Department of Justice, Office of Justice Programs. Accessed at https://nationalgangcenter.ojp.gov/spt/Programs/4397 on February 11, 2025.

National Governors Association Center for Best Practices & Council of Chief State School Officers. (2010a). *Key shifts in English language arts*. Accessed at www.thecorestandards.org/other-resources/key-shifts-in-english-language-arts on September 12, 2025.

National Governors Association Center for Best Practices & Council of Chief State School Officers. (2010b). *Standards for mathematical practices*. Accessed at www.thecorestandards.org/Math/Practice on September 12, 2025.

National High School Center, National Center on Response to Intervention, & Center on Instruction. (2010, May). *Tiered interventions in high schools: Using preliminary "lessons learned" to guide ongoing discussion*. American Institutes for Research.

National Implementation Research Network (2025, June). *Tool: Initiative inventory*. University of North Carolina, Frank Porter Graham Child Development Institute. Accessed at https://implementation.fpg.unc.edu/resource/initiative-inventory on September 18, 2025.

National Mathematics Advisory Panel. (2008). *Foundations for success: The final report of the National Mathematics Advisory Panel*. U.S. Department of Education. Accessed at https://files.eric.ed.gov/fulltext/ED500486.pdf on January 26, 2026.

National Research Council. (1998). *Preventing reading difficulties in young children*. National Academies Press.

National Research Council. (2001). *Adding it up: Helping children learn mathematics*. National Academies Press.

National Student Support Accelerator. (2023, September). *Integrating high-impact tutoring with multi-tiered systems of support (MTSS)*. Author. Accessed at https://nssa.stanford.edu/sites/default/files/Integrating%20High-Impact%20Tutoring%20with%20MTSS.pdf on September 18, 2025.

National Wraparound Initiative. (2019, January). *Wraparound basics: Frequently asked questions*. Author.

Nelson, J. R., Martella, R. M., & Marchand-Martella, N. (2002). Maximizing student learning: The effects of a comprehensive school-based program for preventing problem behaviors. *Journal of Emotional and Behavioral Disorders, 10*(3), 136–148. https://doi.org/10.1177/10634266020100030201

Nese, R. N. T., Nese, J. F. T., McCroskey, C., Meng, P., Triplett, D., & Bastable, E. (2021). Moving away from disproportionate exclusionary discipline: Developing and utilizing a continuum of preventative and instructional supports. *Preventing School Failure: Alternative Education for Children and Youth, 65*(4), 301–311. https://doi.org/10.1080/1045988X.2021.1937019

Nickow, A., Oreopoulos, P., & Quan, V. (2024). The promise of tutoring for preK–12 learning: A systematic review and meta-analysis of the experimental evidence. *American Educational Research Journal, 61*(1), 74–107.

No Child Left Behind (NCLB) Act of 2001, Pub. L. No 107-110, 115 Stat. 1425 (2001).

Novosel, L. C. (2015). Social and emotional consequences of reading disabilities. In M. C. Hougen (Ed.), *Fundamentals of literacy instruction and assessment, 6–12* (pp. 15–26). Brookes.

Nurshatayeva, A., Page, L. C., White, C. C., & Gehlbach, H. (2021). Are artificially intelligent conversational chatbots uniformly effective in reducing summer melt? Evidence from a randomized controlled trial. *Research in Higher Education, 62*(3), 392–402. https://doi.org/10.1007/s11162-021-09633-z

Oakes, J. (2005). *Keeping track: How schools structure inequality* (2nd ed.). Yale University Press.

O'Connor, R. E. (2007). *Teaching word recognition: Effective strategies for students with learning difficulties.* Guilford Press.

O'Hara, R. E., Sparrow, B., & Joy, L. (2022). Values-based interventions increase reenrollment and equity among community college pre-allied health students. *Journal of Postsecondary Student Success, 1*(3), 75–102.

O'Neill, R. E., Albin, R. W., Storey, K., Horner, R. H., & Sprague, J. R. (2015). *Functional assessment and program development for problem behavior: A practical handbook* (3rd ed.). Cengage Learning.

Oreopoulos, P., & Dunn, R. (2012, November). *Information and college access: Evidence from a randomized field experiment* (Working Paper No. 18551). National Bureau of Economic Research.

Oreopoulos, P., & Petronijevic, U. (2019, July). *The remarkable unresponsiveness of college students to nudging and what we can learn from it* (Working Paper No. 26059). National Bureau of Economic Research.

Organisation for Economic Co-operation and Development. (2018). *Social and emotional skills: Well-being, connectedness and success.* Author. Accessed at www.cfchildren.org/wp-content/uploads/research/oecd-social-and-emotional-skills-well-being-connectedness-and-success_compressed.pdf on January 26, 2026.

OSEP Technical Assistance Center on Positive Behavioral Interventions and Supports. (2015, October). *Positive Behavioral Interventions and Supports (PBIS) implementation blueprint: Part 1—Foundations and supporting information.* University of Oregon.

Oswald, K., Safran, S., & Johanson, G. (2005). Preventing trouble: Making schools safer places using positive behavior supports. *Education and Treatment of Children, 28*(3), 265–278.

Page, L. C., Castleman, B. L., & Meyer, K. (2020). Customized nudging to improve FAFSA completion and income verification. *Educational Evaluation and Policy Analysis, 42*(1), 3–21.

Page, L. C., & Gehlbach, H. (2017). How an artificially intelligent virtual assistant helps students navigate the road to college. *AERA Open, 3*(4). https://doi.org/10.1177/2332858417749220

Page, L. C., Meyer, K., Lee, J., & Gehlbach, H. (2023, August). *Conditions under which college students can be responsive to nudging* (Working Paper No. 20-242). Annenberg Institute at Brown University. https://doi.org/10.26300/vjfs-kv29

Page, L. C., & Scott-Clayton, J. (2016). Improving college access in the United States: Barriers and policy responses. *Economics of Education Review, 51*, 4–22. https://doi.org/10.1016/j.econedurev.2016.02.009

Palinscar, A. S., & Brown, A. L. (1984). Reciprocal teaching of comprehension-fostering and comprehension-monitoring activities. *Cognition and Instruction, 1*(2), 117–175. https://doi.org/10.1207/s1532690xci0102_1

Pane, J. F., Doss, C., Todd, I., & Seaman, D. (2025, June). *Efficacy of Zearn Math over two years in grades 3 to 5: An experiment in Texas* (Working Paper No. 25-1211). Annenberg Institute at Brown University.

Pas, E. T., Ryoo, J. H., Musci, R. J., & Bradshaw, C. P. (2019). A state-wide quasi-experimental effectiveness study of the scale-up of School-wide Positive Behavioral Interventions and Supports. *Journal of School Psychology, 73*, 41–55. https://doi.org/10.1016/j.jsp.2019.03.001

Paschall, K. W., Gershoff, E. T., & Kuhfeld, M. (2018). A two decade examination of historical race/ethnicity disparities in academic achievement by poverty status. *Journal of Youth Adolescence, 47*(6), 1164–1177. https://doi.org/10.1007/s10964-017-0800-7

Perkins Collaborative Resource Network. (n.d.a). *About legislation and regulations*. U.S. Department of Education, Office of Career, Technical, and Adult Education. Accessed at https://cte.ed.gov/legislation/about-legislation on September 20, 2025.

Perkins Collaborative Resource Network. (n.d.b). *Employability skills*. U.S. Department of Education, Office of Career, Technical, and Adult Education. Accessed at https://cte.ed.gov/initiatives/employability-skills-framework on March 4, 2025.

Pfeffer, J., & Sutton, R. I. (2000). *The knowing-doing gap: How smart companies turn knowledge into action*. Harvard Business School Press.

Plasman, J. S. (2018). Career/education plans and student engagement in secondary school. *American Journal of Education, 124*(2), 217–246. https://doi.org/10.1086/695608

Porter, S. C., Jackson, C. K., Kiguel, S., & Easton, J. Q. (2023, April). *Investing in adolescents: High school climate and organizational context shape student development and educational attainment*. University of Chicago Consortium on School Research. Accessed at https://consortium.uchicago.edu/sites/default/files/2023-04/Investing%20in%20Adolescents-Apr%202023-Consortium.pdf on September 19, 2025.

Powell, S. R., Lembke, E. S., Ketterlin-Geller, L. R., Petscher, Y., Hwang, J., Bos, S. E., et al. (2021). Data-based individualization in mathematics to support middleschool teachers and their students with mathematics learning difficulty. *Studies in Educational Evaluation, 69*, Article 100897. https://doi.org/10.1016/j.stueduc.2020.100897

Prewett, S., Mellard, D. F., Deshler, D. D., Allen, J., Alexander, R., & Stern, A. (2012). Response to intervention in middle schools: Practices and outcomes. *Learning Disabilities Research and Practice, 27*(3), 136–147.

Prothero, A. (2020, May 4). Schools struggle to meet students' mounting mental-health needs. *Education Week*. Accessed at www.edweek.org/leadership/schools-struggle-to-meet-students-mounting-mental-health-needs/2020/05 on August 7, 2025.

Pyle, N., & Vaughn, S. (2012). Remediating reading difficulties in a response to intervention model with secondary students. *Psychology in the Schools, 49*(3), 273–284.

The Reading League. (2024). *Adolescent reading intervention evaluation guidelines (grades 4–12)*. Author. Accessed at www.thereadingleague.org/wp-content/uploads/2024/10/the-reading-league-adolescent-reading-intervention-evaluation-guidelines.pdf?utm_campaign=Conference%20-%202024&utm_content=312844939&utm_medium=social&utm_source=twitter&hss_channel=tw-4808423728 on September 19, 2025.

Reading Plus. (2008). *Reading improvement report: Miami-Dade regions II and III*. Taylor Associates/Communications.

Regional Educational Laboratory Appalachia at SRI International. (2020, September). *Paving the pathway to college and careers: Resource compilation*. U.S. Department of Education, Institute of Education Sciences, National Center for Education Evaluation and Regional Assistance. Accessed at https://ies.ed.gov/ncee/rel/regions/appalachia/events/materials/03-16-21_paving-pathway-to-college-careers-resource-compilation_acc.pdf on September 19, 2025.

Regional Educational Laboratory Southeast at Florida State University. (n.d.a). *Evidence-based teaching practices* [Infographic]. U.S. Department of Education, Institute of Education Sciences, National Center for Education Evaluation and Regional Assistance. Accessed at https://ies.ed.gov/sites/default/files/migrated/rel/infographics/pdf/REL_SE_Evidence-based_teaching_practices.pdf on September 19, 2025.

Regional Educational Laboratory Southeast at Florida State University. (n.d.b). *Preparing a career-ready student* [Infographic]. U.S. Department of Education, Institute of Education Sciences, National Center for Education Evaluation and Regional Assistance. Accessed at https://ies.ed.gov/sites/default/files/migrated/rel/infographics/pdf/REL_SE_Preparing_A_Career_Ready_Student.pdf on September 19, 2025.

Reutzel, D. R., Petscher, Y., & Spichtig, A. N. (2012). Exploring the value added of a guided, silent reading intervention: Effects on struggling third-grade readers' achievement. *The Journal of Educational Research, 105*(6), 404–415.

Robinson, C. D., Kraft, M. A., Loeb, S., & Schueler, B. (2024, June). *Design principles for accelerating student learning with high-impact tutoring* (Brief No. 30). EdResearch for Action. Accessed at https://edresearchforaction.org/wp-content/uploads/EdResearch-Accelerating-Student-Learning-With-High-Impact-Tutoring.pdf on September 19, 2025.

Roderick, M., Nagaoka, J., Coca, V. M., Moeller, E., Roddie, K., Gilliam, J., et al. (2008, March). *From high school to the future: Potholes on the road to college.* University of Chicago Consortium on School Research.

Rodríguez-Planas, N. (2012). Longer-term impacts of mentoring, educational services, and learning incentives: Evidence from a randomized trial in the United States. *American Economic Journal: Applied Economics, 4*(4), 121–139.

Rosenshine, B. (2012). Principles of instruction: Research-based strategies that all teachers should know. *American Educator, 36*(1), 12–19, 39.

Ross, K. M., Kim, H., Tolan, P. H., & Jennings, P. A. (2019). An exploration of normative social and emotional skill growth trajectories during adolescence. *Journal of Applied Developmental Psychology, 62*, 102–115. https://doi.org/10.1016/j.appdev.2019.02.006

Rumberger, R., Addis, H., Allensworth, E. M., Balfanz, R., Bruch, J., Dillon, E., et al. (2017, September). *Preventing dropout in secondary schools* (Publication No. NCEE 2017-4028). U.S. Department of Education, Institute of Education Sciences, National Center for Education Evaluation and Regional Assistance. Accessed at https://ies.ed.gov/ncee/WWC/Docs/PracticeGuide/wwc_dropout_092617.pdf on September 19, 2025.

Safran, S. P., & Oswald, K. (2003). Positive behavior supports: Can schools reshape disciplinary practices? *Exceptional Children, 69*(3), 361–373.

Sailor, W., Doolittle, J., Bradley, R., & Danielson, L. (2009). Response to intervention and positive behavior support. In W. Sailor, G. Dunlap, G. Sugai, & R. Horner (Eds.), *Handbook of positive behavior support* (pp. 729–753). Springer. https://doi.org/10.1007/978-0-387-09632-2_29

Sailor, W., Skrtic, T. M., Cohn, M., & Olmstead, C. (2021). Preparing teacher educators for statewide scale-up of multi-tiered system of support (MTSS). *Teacher Education and Special Education, 44*(1), 24–41.

Samuels, C. A. (2009). High schools try out RTI. *Education Week, 28*(19), 20–22.

Sansosti, F. J., Noltemeyer, A., & Goss, S. (2010). Principals' perceptions of the importance and availability of response to intervention practices within high school settings. *School Psychology Review, 39*(2), 286–295.

Sansosti, F. J., Telzrow, C., & Noltemeyer, A. (2010). Barriers and facilitators to implementing response to intervention in secondary schools: Qualitative perspectives of school psychologists. *School Psychology Forum: Research in Practice, 4*(1), 1–21.

Santiago-Rosario, M. R., McIntosh, K., Izzard, S., Cohen Lissman, D., & Calhoun, E. (2023, September). *Is Positive Behavioral Interventions and Supports (PBIS) an evidence-based practice?* University of Oregon, Center on Positive Behavioral Interventions and Supports. Accessed at https://assets-global.website-files.com/5d3725188825e071f1670246/651c4d7d5174726ec6da1d86_Is%20Positive%20Behavioral%20Interventions%20and%20Supports%20(PBIS)%20an%20Evidence-Based%20Practice.pdf on September 19, 2025.

Sayeski, K. L., & Brown, M. R. (2014). Developing a classroom management plan using a tiered approach. *TEACHING Exceptional Children, 47*(2), 119–127. (Original work published 2011)

Scala, J., Husby-Slater, M., Chamberlain, R., & McPhee, K. (2023a, November). *High school Early Warning Intervention and Monitoring System implementation guide*. American Institutes for Research. Accessed at https://mtss4success.org/sites/default/files/2024-06/23-22124-High-School-EWIMS-Guide_FINAL.pdf on September 19, 2025.

Scala, J., Husby-Slater, M., Chamberlain, R., & McPhee, K. (2023b, November). *Middle grades Early Warning Intervention and Monitoring System implementation guide*. American Institutes for Research. Accessed at https://mtss4success.org/sites/default/files/2024-06/23-22124_Middle-Grades-EWIMS-Guide_FINAL.pdf on September 19, 2025.

Scales, P. C., Roehlkepartain, E. C., & Houltberg, B. J. (2022). *The elements of developmental relationships: A review of selected research underlying the framework*. Search Institute. Accessed at www.search-institute.org/wp-content/uploads/2022/09/ElementsofDevelopmentalRelationships-FINAL.pdf on September 19, 2025.

Scammacca, N., Roberts, G., Vaughn, S., Edmonds, M., Wexler, J., Reutebuch, C. K., et al. (2007). *Interventions for adolescent struggling readers: A meta-analysis with implications for practice*. RMC Research Corporation, Center on Instruction. Accessed at https://files.eric.ed.gov/fulltext/ED521837.pdf on September 19, 2025.

Schaffer, G. E. (2023). *Multi-tiered systems of support: A practical guide to preventative practice*. SAGE.

Schreiber, A., Miller, B. A., & Dressler, K. (2022, August). *An introduction to restorative practices*. University of Michigan, School of Public Health, National Center for School Safety. Accessed at www.nc2s.org/wp-content/uploads/2022/07/An-Introduction-to-Restorative-Practices.pdf on September 19, 2025.

Schrieber, S. R., Ware, M. E., & Dart, E. H. (2023). Student interview-informed behavior contracts for high school students identified as at risk. *Behavioral Disorders*, *49*(1), 31–45.

Schueler, B. E. (2020). Making the most of school vacation: A field experiment of small-group math instruction. *Education Finance and Policy*, *15*(2), 310–331.

Schumaker, J. B., & Deshler, D. D. (2009). Adolescents with learning disabilities as writers: Are we selling them short? *Learning Disabilities Research and Practice*, *24*(2), 81–92.

Schumaker, J. B., Fisher, J. B., & Walsh, L. D. (2019). Effects of computerized instruction on the use of punctuation strategies by students with LD. *Learning Disabilities Research and Practice*, *34*(3), 158–170.

Schwartz, B. (2009). Incentives, choice, education and well-being. *Oxford Review of Education*, *35*(3), 391–403.

Scott, C., Nelsestuen, K., Autio, E., Deussen, T., & Hanita, M. (2010, June). *Evaluation of Read Right in Omaha middle and high schools, 2009–2010*. Education Northwest.

Scott, T. M. (2017). *Teaching behavior: Managing classrooms through effective instruction*. Corwin.

Scott, T. M., & Barrett, S. B. (2004). Using staff and student time engaged in disciplinary procedures to evaluate the impact of School-wide PBS. *Journal of Positive Behavior Interventions*, *6*(1), 21–27. https://doi.org/10.1177/10983007040060010401

Scruggs, T. E., Mastropieri, M. A., Berkeley, S., & Graetz, J. E. (2010). Do special education interventions improve learning of secondary content? A meta-analysis. *Remedial and Special Education*, *31*(6), 437–449. https://doi.org/10.1177/0741932508327465

Section 504 of the Rehabilitation Act of 1973, 29 U.S.C. § 794. Accessed at www.hhs.gov/sites/default/files/sec-504-ria-final-rule-2024.pdf on January 2, 2026.

Seeskin, A., Massion, T., & Usher, A. (2022, October). *Elementary on-track: Elementary school students' grades, attendance, and future outcomes*. University of Chicago Consortium on School Research. Accessed at https://consortium.uchicago.edu/sites/default/files/2023-04/Elementary%20On-Track-Oct2022-ConsortiumAndTT.pdf on September 19, 2025.

Seftor, N. (2022, May). *Project 4.2.1: Ask an expert 1—College- and career-readiness interventions.* U.S. Department of Education, Institute of Education Sciences, Regional Educational Laboratory Appalachia. Accessed at https://ies.ed.gov/rel-appalachia/2025/01/main-resource-file-8 on September 19, 2025.

Serido, J., & Wilhelm, M. S. (2006). *The effects of My Reading Coach on reading achievement of elementary education students.* University of Arizona.

Shanahan, T. (2014, May 10–12). *Text complexity and learning to read* [Conference presentation]. International Reading Association 59th annual conference, New Orleans, LA.

Shanahan, T., Callison, K., Carriere, C., Duke, N. K., Pearson, P. D., Schatschneider, C., et al. (2010, September). *Improving reading comprehension in kindergarten through 3rd grade—A practice guide* (Publication No. NCEE 2010|-4038). U.S. Department of Education, Institute of Education Sciences, National Center for Education Evaluation and Regional Assistance.

Shanahan, T., & Shanahan, C. (2012). What is disciplinary literacy and why does it matter? *Topics in Language Disorders, 32*(1), 7–18.

Shechtman, N., Yarnall, L., Stites, R., & Cheng, B. (2016). *Empowering adults to thrive at work: Personal success skills for 21st century jobs—A report on promising research and practice.* Joyce Foundation.

Sheffield, K., & Waller, R. J. (2010). A review of single-case studies utilizing self-monitoring interventions to reduce problem classroom behaviors. *Beyond Behavior, 19*(2), 7–13.

Shinn, M. R., Windram, H. S., & Bollman, K. A. (2016). Implementing response to intervention in secondary schools. In S. R. Jimerson, M. K. Burns, & A. M. VanDerHeyden (Eds.), *Handbook of response to intervention: The science and practice of multi-tiered systems of support* (2nd ed., pp. 563–586). Springer.

Shippen, M. E., Houchins, D. E., Steventon, C., & Sartor, D. (2005). A comparison of two direct instruction reading programs for urban middle school students. *Remedial and Special Education, 26*(3), 175–182. https://doi.org/10.1177/07419325050260030501

Shores, K., Kim, H., & Still, M. (2020). Categorical inequality in Black and White: Linking disproportionality across multiple educational outcomes. *American Educational Research Journal, 57*(5), 2089–2131. https://doi.org/10.3102/0002831219900128

Simonsen, B., Fairbanks, S., Briesch, A., Myers, D., & Sugai, G. (2008). Evidence-based practices in classroom management: Considerations for research to practice. *Education and Treatment of Children, 31*(3), 351–380.

Simonsen, B., Goodman, S., Robbie, K., Power, M., Rodriguez, C., & Burns, D. (2021, January). *Effective instruction as a protective factor.* University of Oregon, Center on Positive Behavioral Interventions and Supports. Accessed at www.pbis.org/resource/effective-instruction-as-a-protective-factor on September 19, 2025.

Simonsen, B., Robbie, K., Meyer, K., Freeman, J., Everett, S., & Feinberg A. (2021, November). *Multi-tiered system of supports (MTSS) in the classroom.* University of Oregon, Center on Positive Behavioral Interventions and Supports. Accessed at https://cdn.prod.website-files.com/5d3725188825e071f1670246/61dc7e332fd7990f774d1ab0_Multi-Tiered%20System%20of%20Supports%20(MTSS)%20in%20the%20Classroom.pdf on September 19, 2025.

Sims, W. A., Yu, R., King, K. R., Zahn, D., Mandracchia, N., Monteiro, E., et al. (2023). Measuring classroom management in secondary settings: Ongoing validation of the Direct Behavior Rating–Classroom Management. *Assessment for Effective Intervention, 48*(3), 149–158. https://doi.org/10.1177/15345084221118316

Sinclair, M. F., Christenson, S. L., Evelo, D. L., & Hurley, C. M. (1998). Dropout prevention for youth with disabilities: Efficacy of a sustained school engagement procedure. *Exceptional Children, 65*(1), 7–21.

Sinclair, M. F., Christenson, S. L., & Thurlow, M. L. (2005). Promoting school completion of urban secondary youth with emotional or behavioral disabilities. *Exceptional Children, 71*(4), 465–482.

Skiba, R. J., Arredondo, M. I., & Williams, N. T. (2014). More than a metaphor: The contribution of exclusionary discipline to a school-to-prison pipeline. *Equity and Excellence in Education, 47*(4), 546–564. https://doi.org/10.1080/10665684.2014.958965

Skiba, R. J., Horner, R. H., Chung, C.-G., Rausch, M. K., May, S. L., & Tobin, T. (2011). Race is not neutral: A national investigation of African American and Latino disproportionality in school discipline. *School Psychology Review, 40*(1), 85–107.

Skiba, R. J., & Rausch, M. K. (2006). School disciplinary systems: Alternatives to suspension and expulsion. In G. G. Bear & K. M. Minke (Eds.), *Children's needs III: Development, prevention, and intervention* (pp. 87–102). National Association of School Psychologists.

Slater, W. H., & Horstman, F. R. (2002). Teaching reading and writing to struggling middle school and high school students: The case for reciprocal teaching. *Preventing School Failure: Alternative Education for Children and Youth, 46*(4), 163–166. https://doi.org/10.1080/10459880209604416

Slavin, R. E., Lake, C., & Groff, C. (2009). Effective programs in middle and high school mathematics: A best-evidence synthesis. *Review of Educational Research, 79*(2), 839–911.

Smith, K. G., Dombek, J. L., Foorman, B. R., Hook, K. S., Lee, L., Cote, A.-M., et al. (2016, August). *Self-study guide for implementing high school academic interventions* (Publication No. REL 2016-218). U.S. Department of Education, Institute of Education Sciences, National Center for Education Evaluation and Regional Assistance, Regional Educational Laboratory Southeast. Accessed at https://ies.ed.gov/sites/default/files/migrated/rel/regions/southeast/pdf/REL_2016218.pdf on September 19, 2025.

Smith, K. G., Lee, L., Carr, M., Weatherill, A., & Lancashire, H. (2020, August). *Self-study guide for career readiness in secondary schools* (Publication No. REL 2020-035). U.S. Department of Education, Institute of Education Sciences, National Center for Education Evaluation and Regional Assistance, Regional Educational Laboratory Southeast. Accessed at https://ies.ed.gov/sites/default/files/migrated/rel/regions/southeast/pdf/REL_2020035.pdf on September 19, 2025.

Smolkowski, K., Strycker, L., & Ward, B. (2016). Scale-up of safe and civil schools' model for School-wide Positive Behavioral Interventions and Supports. *Psychology in the Schools, 53*(4), 339–358. https://doi.org/10.1002/pits.21908

Smylie, M. A., Murphy, J. F., & Louis, K. S. (2020). *Caring school leadership*. Corwin.

Solberg, V. S. (2019). *Making school relevant with individualized learning plans: Helping students create their own career and life goals*. Harvard Education Press.

Solberg, V. S., Donnelly, H. K., Kroyer-Kubicek, R., Basha, R., Curtis, G., Jaques, E., et al. (2022). *Condition of career readiness in the United States*. Coalition for Career Development Center & Boston University Center for Future Readiness. Accessed at https://careertech.org/wp-content/uploads/2023/01/CCDC-Report-V9_0.pdf on September 19, 2025.

Solberg, V. S., Wills, J., Redmon, K., & Skaff, L. (2014). *Use of individualized learning plans: A promising practice for driving college and career efforts—Findings and recommendations from a multi-method, multi-study effort*. Institute for Educational Leadership, National Collaborative on Workforce and Disability for Youth. Accessed at https://files.eric.ed.gov/fulltext/ED588651.pdf on September 19, 2025.

Solomon, B. G., Klein, S. A., Hintze, J. M., Cressey, J. M., & Peller, S. L. (2012). A meta-analysis of school-wide positive behavior support: An exploratory study using single-case synthesis. *Psychology in the Schools, 49*(2), 105–121. https://doi.org/10.1002/pits.20625

Song, M., & Zeiser, K. L. (2019, September). *Early college, continued success: Longer-term impact of early college high schools*. American Institutes for Research.

Southern Regional Education Board. (2020, November). *Making schools work: Key practices for high schools*. Author. Accessed at www.sreb.org/sites/main/files/file-attachments/msw_highschool_key_practices_r_nov_2020.pdf?1659976311 on September 19, 2025.

Sprague, J. R., Walker, H., Golly, A., White, K., Myers, D. R., & Shannon, T. (2001). Translating research into effective practice: The effects of a universal staff and student intervention on indicators of discipline and school safety. *Education and Treatment of Children, 24*(4), 495–511. www.jstor.org/stable/42900505

Sprague, K., Zaller, C., Kite, A., & Hussar, K. (2012, March). *Springfield-Chicopee school districts Striving Readers (SR) program: Final report years 1–5—Evaluation of implementation and impact*. Brown University, Education Alliance. Accessed at https://files.eric.ed.gov/fulltext/ED600926.pdf on January 11, 2026.

Star, J. R., Caronongan, P., Foegen, A., Furgeson, J., Keating, B., Larson, M. R., et al. (2015, April). *Teaching strategies for improving algebra knowledge in middle and high school students* (Publication No. NCEE 2014-4333). U.S. Department of Education, Institute of Education Sciences, National Center for Education Evaluation and Regional Assistance. Accessed at https://ies.ed.gov/ncee/wwc/docs/practiceguide/wwc_algebra_040715.pdf on September 19, 2025.

State Education Resource Center. (2012). *Secondary assessments: Universal screening, diagnostic, and progress monitoring*. Accessed at https://portal.ct.gov/-/media/sde/srbi/secondary_assessments_4-9-12.pdf on September 19, 2025.

Stecker, P. M., Fuchs, L. S., & Fuchs, D. (2005). Using curriculum-based measurement to improve student achievement: Review of research. *Psychology in the Schools, 42*(8), 795–819.

Steinberg, L. (2014). *Age of opportunity: Lessons from the new science of adolescence*. Dolan.

Steiner, R. J., Sheremenko, G., Lesesne, C., Dittus, P. J., Sieving, R. E., & Ethier, K. A. (2019). Adolescent connectedness and adult health outcomes. *Pediatrics, 144*(1), Article e20183766. https://doi.org/10.1542/peds.2018-3766

Stern, D., Dayton, C., & Raby, M. (2010). *Career academies: A proven strategy to prepare high school students for college and careers*. University of California at Berkeley, Career Academy Support Network.

St. Martin, K., Vaughn, S., Troia, G., Fien, H., & Coyne, M. (2020). *Intensifying literacy instruction: Essential practices*. Michigan Department of Education, Michigan's Multi-Tiered System of Supports Technical Assistance Center. Accessed at https://intensiveintervention.org/sites/default/files/Intensifying_Literacy_Instruction_Essential_Practices.pdf on September 19, 2025.

Stockslager, K., Castillo, J., Brundage, A., Childs, K., & Romer, N. (2022, April 18). *Self-assessment of MTSS (SAM)*. University of South Florida, Florida's Problem Solving/Response to Intervention Project & Florida's Positive Behavior Intervention and Support Project. Accessed at https://web01.browardschools.com/ospa/ospa-central2/_sip_all_plans/2025/2971_09192024_Self-Assessment-of-MTSS-Implementation-SAM_SLMS_2971.pdf on September 19, 2025.

Stoiber, K. C., & Gettinger, M. (2016). Multi-tiered systems of support and evidence-based practices. In S. R. Jimerson, M. K. Burns, & A. M. VanDerHeyden (Eds.), *Handbook of response to intervention: The science and practice of multi-tiered systems of support* (2nd ed., pp. 121–141). Springer.

Storey, N. S., & Neitzel, A. J. (2025, April). *Evaluation of Zearn Supplemental with dedicated implementation support*. Johns Hopkins University, Center for Research and Reform in Education.

Strickland-Cohen, M. K., & Simonsen, B. (2022, January). *Function-based support: An overview*. University of Oregon, Center on Positive Behavioral Interventions and Supports. Accessed at https://assets-global.website-files.com/5d3725188825e071f1670246/61d891b56231a2a5edf60ba0_Function_Based_Support_Overview_1.4.22.pdf on September 19, 2025.

Struhl, B., & Vargas, J. (2012, October). *Taking college courses in high school: A strategy for college readiness—The college outcomes of dual enrollment in Texas.* Jobs for the Future. Accessed at https://files.eric.ed.gov/fulltext/ED537253.pdf on September 19, 2025.

Student Achievement Partners. (2021, August 9). *Priority Instructional Content in ELA/literacy and mathematics.* Author. Accessed at https://achievethecore.org/page/3267/priority-instructional-content-in-english-language-arts-literacy-and-mathematics on September 19, 2025.

Sugai, G., & Horner, R. H. (2002). The evolution of discipline practices: School-wide positive behavior supports. *Child and Family Behavior Therapy, 24*(1–2), 23–50.

Swain-Bradway, J., Pinkney, C., & Flannery, K. B. (2015). Implementing schoolwide positive behavior interventions and supports in high schools: Contextual factors and stages of implementation. *TEACHING Exceptional Children, 47*(5), 245–255.

Swanson, H. L., & Deshler, D. (2003). Instructing adolescents with learning disabilities: Converting a meta-analysis to practice. *Journal of Learning Disabilities, 36*(2), 124–135. https://doi.org/10.1177/002221940303600205

Taylor, J. J., Buckley, K., Hamilton, L. S., Stecher, B. M., Read, L., & Schweig, J. (2018). *Choosing and using SEL competency assessments: What schools and districts need to know.* Rand Corporation. Accessed at https://csaa.wested.org/resource/choosing-and-using-sel-competency-assessments-what-schools-and-districts-need-to-know on September 19, 2025.

Thapa, A., Cohen, J., Guffey, S., & Higgins-D'Alessandro, A. (2013). A review of school climate research. *Review of Educational Research, 83*(3), 357–385. https://doi.org/10.3102/0034654313483907

Therriault, S. B., O'Cummings, M., Heppen, J., Yerhot, L., & Scala, J. (2023). *Early Warning Intervention and Monitoring System (EWIMS) implementation guide.* Michigan Department of Education. (Original work published 2017). Accessed at www.michigan.gov/-/media/Project/Websites/mde/EWIMS/Michigan_EWIMS_Implementation_Guide.pdf?rev=20ccbedd8b144927b7eb925d210f194c on September 19, 2025.

Therriault, S. B., O'Cummings, M., Heppen, J., Yerhot, L., Scala, J., & Perry, M. (2013, February). *Middle grades early warning intervention monitoring system implementation guide.* American Institutes for Research, National High School Center. Accessed at www.air.org/sites/default/files/Middle-Grades-Early-Warning-Intervention-Implementation-Guide-February-2013.pdf on January 11, 2026.

Therrien, W. J., Hughes, C., Kapelski, C., & Mokhtari, K. (2009). Effectiveness of a test-taking strategy on achievement in essay tests for students with learning disabilities. *Journal of Learning Disabilities, 42*(1), 14–23.

Tierney, W. G., Bailey, T. R., Constantine, J., Finkelstein, N., & Hurd, N. F. (2009, September). *Helping students navigate the path to college: What high schools can do—A practice guide* (Publication No. NCEE 2009-4066). U.S. Department of Education, Institute of Education Sciences, National Center for Education Evaluation and Regional Assistance. Accessed at https://ies.ed.gov/ncee/wwc/Docs/PracticeGuide/higher_ed_pg_091509.pdf on September 19, 2025.

Tillery, C., Cech, T., & Mania, J. (2022). *Examining relationships: Service activities and FAFSA completion, high school graduation, and postsecondary enrollment.* Accessed at https://static1.squarespace.com/static/5ac285c04eddecf58e185097/t/64343ef0d6768d471bb4aa70/1681145591895/CCREC_1.0_Evaluation_Report.pdf on January 11, 2026.

TNTP. (2018). *The opportunity myth: What students can show us about how school is letting them down—and how to fix it.* Author. Accessed at https://tntp.org/wp-content/uploads/2023/02/TNTP_The-Opportunity-Myth_Web.pdf on September 19, 2025.

TNTP. (2021). *Disrupting barriers to strong instructional scaffolding: A toolkit for advancing mindsets, principles, practices and conditions.* Author. Accessed at https://tntp.org/wp-content/uploads/Tools/disrupting-barriers-to-strong-instructional-scaffolding.pdf on September 19, 2025.

TNTP. (2024a). *The opportunity makers: How a diverse group of public schools helps students catch up—and how far more can.* Author. Accessed at https://tntp.org/wp-content/uploads/2024/09/The-Opportunity-Makers-TNTP.pdf on September 19, 2025.

TNTP. (2024b). *Paths of opportunity: What it will take for all young people to thrive.* Author. Accessed at https://tntp.org/wp-content/uploads/2024/08/Paths-of-Opportunity-Report-TNTP.pdf on September 19, 2025.

Torgesen, J. K., Houston, D. D., Rissman, L. M., Decker, S. M., Roberts, G., Vaughn, S., et al. (2007). *Academic literacy instruction for adolescents: A guidance document from the Center on Instruction.* RMC Research Corporation, Center on Instruction.

Torre Gibney, T., & Rauner, M. (2021, November). *Education and career planning in high school: A national study of school and student characteristics and college-going behaviors* (Publication No. REL 2022-127). U.S. Department of Education, Institute of Education Sciences, National Center for Education Evaluation and Regional Assistance, Regional Educational Laboratory West. Accessed at https://files.eric.ed.gov/fulltext/ED615855.pdf on September 19, 2025.

Troia, G. (2014, September). *Evidence-based practices for writing instruction* (CEEDAR Document No. IC-5). University of Florida, Collaboration for Effective Educator, Development, Accountability, and Reform Center. Accessed at https://ceedar.education.ufl.edu/wp-content/uploads/2014/09/IC-5_FINAL_08-31-14.pdf on September 19, 2025.

Truckenmiller, A. J., McKindles, J. V., Petscher, Y., Eckert, T. L., & Tock, J. (2020). Expanding curriculum-based measurement in written expression for middle school. *The Journal of Special Education, 54*(3), 133–145. https://doi.org/10.1177/0022466919887150

Tucker, C. (2024, February 19). *Using the station rotation model in math* [Blog post]. Accessed at https://catlin tucker.com/2024/02/station-rotation-model-math on September 19, 2025.

Umbreit, J., Ferro, J. B., Liaupsin, C., & Lane, K. (2007). *Functional behavioral assessment and function-based intervention: An effective practical approach.* Pearson.

U.S. Census Bureau. (2025, August 8). *PINC-03. Educational attainment-people eighteen years old and over, by total money earnings, work experience, age, race, Hispanic origin, and sex.* U.S. Department of Commerce. Accessed at www.census.gov/data/tables/time-series/demo/income-poverty/cps-pinc/pinc-03.html on October 26, 2023.

U.S. Public Health Service. (2023). *Social media and youth mental health: The U.S. Surgeon General's advisory.* U.S. Department of Health and Human Services. Accessed at www.hhs.gov/sites/default/files/sg-youth-mental -health-social-media-advisory.pdf on September 20, 2025.

Van Camp, A. M., Wehby, J. H., Copeland, B. A., & Bruhn, A. L. (2021). Building from the bottom up: The importance of Tier 1 supports in the context of Tier 2 interventions. *Journal of Positive Behavior Interventions, 23*(1), 53–64. https://doi.org/10.1177/1098300720916716

VanDerHeyden, A. M., & Allsopp, D. (2014, September). *Innovation configuration for mathematics* (CEEDAR Document No. IC-6). University of Florida, Collaboration for Effective Educator, Development, Accountability, and Reform Center. Accessed at https://ceedar.education.ufl.edu/wp-content/uploads/2014/09/IC-6_FINAL_09 -25-14.pdf on September 20, 2025.

VanDerHeyden, A. M., & Witt, J. C. (2008). Best practices in can't do/won't do assessment. In A. Thomas & J. P. Grimes (Eds.), *Best practices in school psychology* (5th ed., pp. 131–140). National Association of School Psychologists.

Vaughn, S., Cirino, P. T., Wanzek, J., Wexler, J., Fletcher, J. M., Denton, C. D., et al. (2010). Response to intervention for middle school students with reading difficulties: Effects of a primary and secondary intervention. *School Psychology Review, 39*(1), 3–21.

Vaughn, S., & Fletcher, J. M. (2010). Thoughts on rethinking response to intervention with secondary students. *School Psychology Review, 39*(2), 296–299. https://doi.org/10.1080/02796015.2010.12087780

Vaughn, S., Gersten, R., Dimino, J., Taylor, M. J., Newman-Gonchar, R., Krowka, S., et al. (2022, March). *Providing reading interventions for students in grades 4–9* (Publication No. WWC 2022007). U.S. Department of Education, Institute of Education Sciences, National Center for Education Evaluation and Regional Assistance. Accessed at https://ies.ed.gov/ncee/wwc/Docs/PracticeGuide/WWC-practice-guide-reading-intervention-full-text.pdf on September 20, 2025.

Vaughn, S., Klingner, J. K., Swanson, E. A., Boardman, A. G., Roberts, G., Mohammed, S. S., et al. (2011). Efficacy of collaborative strategic reading with middle school students. *American Educational Research Journal, 48*(4), 938–964. https://doi.org/10.3102/0002831211410305

Vaughn, S., & Wanzek, J. (2024). Promoting adolescents' comprehension of text: Efficacy and effectiveness. *Remedial and Special Education, 45*(1), 58–67. https://doi.org/10.1177/07419325231190805

Visher, M. G., & Stern, D. (2015, August). *New pathways to careers and college: Examples, evidence, and prospects.* MDRC. Accessed at https://files.eric.ed.gov/fulltext/ED558505.pdf on September 20, 2025.

Walker, V. L., Chung, Y.-C., & Bonnet, L. K. (2018). Function-based intervention in inclusive school settings: A meta-analysis. *Journal of Positive Behavior Interventions, 20*(4), 203–216. https://doi.org/10.1177/1098300717718350

Walter, H. J., Kaye, A. J., Dennery, K. M., & DeMaso, D. R. (2019). Three-year outcomes of a school-hospital partnership providing multitiered mental health services in urban schools. *Journal of School Health, 89*(8), 643–652.

Walton, G. M., & Cohen, G. L. (2011). A brief social-belonging intervention improves academic and health outcomes of minority students. *Science, 331*(6023), 1447–1451.

Wanzek, J., Vaughn, S., Scammacca, N. K., Metz, K., Murray, C. S., Roberts, G., et al. (2013). Extensive reading interventions for students with reading difficulties after grade 3. *Review of Educational Research, 83*(2), 163–195.

Warner, M., Harris, J., Yarnall, L., Ball, A., & Jonas, D. (2019, July). *Measuring career readiness in high school literature scan.* U.S. Department of Education, Institute of Education Sciences, Regional Educational Laboratory Appalachia. Accessed at https://ies.ed.gov/rel-appalachia/2025/01/handout-literature-scan on September 20, 2025.

Warner, M., Yarnall, L., Ball, A., & Jonas, D. (2020). *Supporting and measuring career readiness: Hot topics, common challenges, and practical resources.* U.S. Department of Education, Institute of Education Sciences, Regional Educational Laboratory Appalachia at SRI International. Accessed at https://ies.ed.gov/rel-appalachia/2025/01/resource-1 on September 20, 2025.

Weingarten, Z., Bailey, T. R., & Peterson, A. (2019). *Strategies for scheduling: How to find time to intensify and individualize intervention.* U.S. Department of Education, Office of Special Education Programs, National Center on Intensive Intervention. Accessed at https://intensiveintervention.org/sites/default/files/NCII-Scheduling-508.pdf on September 20, 2025.

What Works Clearinghouse. (n.d.). *Using the WWC to find ESSA tiers of evidence.* U.S. Department of Education, Institute of Education Sciences. Accessed at https://ies.ed.gov/ncee/wwc/essa on January 10, 2026.

What Works Clearinghouse. (2015, September). *Career academies.* U.S. Department of Education, Institute of Education Sciences. Accessed at https://ies.ed.gov/ncee/WWC/Docs/InterventionReports/wwc_careeracademies_092215.pdf on September 20, 2025.

What Works Clearinghouse. (2017a, February). *Dual enrollment programs.* U.S. Department of Education, Institute of Education Sciences. Accessed at https://ies.ed.gov/ncee/WWC/Docs/InterventionReports/wwc_dual_enrollment_022817.pdf on September 20, 2025.

What Works Clearinghouse. (2017b, November). *Self-Regulated Strategy Development.* U.S. Department of Education, Institute of Education Sciences. Accessed at https://ies.ed.gov/ncee/wwc/Docs/InterventionReports/wwc_srsd_111417.pdf on September 20, 2025.

What Works Clearinghouse. (2025a). *Literacy practices, intervention reports, and study reviews for grades 9–12* [Search results]. U.S. Department of Education, Institute of Education Sciences. Accessed at https://ies.ed.gov/ncee/WWC/Search/Products?searchTerm=&Topic=3&gradeLevel=9&gradeLevel=10&gradeLevel=11&gradeLevel=12 on September 20, 2025.

What Works Clearinghouse. (2025b). *Math practices, intervention reports, and study reviews for grades for 9–12* [Search results]. U.S. Department of Education, Institute of Education Sciences. Accessed at https://ies.ed.gov/ncee/WWC/Search/Products?searchTerm=math&gradeLevel=9&gradeLevel=10&gradeLevel=11&gradeLevel=12 on September 20, 2025.

Whitlock, J. L. (2006). Youth perceptions of life at school: Contextual correlates of school connectedness in adolescence. *Applied Developmental Science, 10*(1), 13–29.

Wiener, R., & Pimentel, S. (2017, April). *Practice what you teach: Connecting curriculum and professional learning in schools.* The Aspen Institute Education & Society Program. Accessed at www.aspeninstitute.org/wp-content/uploads/2025/05/Practice-What-You-Teach.pdf on September 20, 2025.

Wills, H. P., & Mason, B. A. (2014). Implementation of a self-monitoring application to improve on-task behavior: A high-school pilot study. *Journal of Behavioral Education, 23*(4), 421–434.

Wisconsin Department of Public Instruction. (n.d.). *Guidelines for using the emotional regulation action plans.* Author. Accessed at https://dpi.wi.gov/sites/default/files/imce/sspw/pdf/mhsecondaryeregplan.pdf on September 20, 2025.

Witzel, B. S., Mercer, C. D., & Miller, M. D. (2003). Teaching algebra to students with learning difficulties: An investigation of an explicit instruction model. *Learning Disabilities Research and Practice, 18*(2), 121–131.

Woodward, J., Beckmann, S., Driscoll, M., Franke, M., Herzig, P., Jitendra, A., et al. (2018, October). *Improving mathematical problem solving in grades 4 through 8—A practice guide* (Publication No. NCEE 2012-4055). U.S. Department of Education, Institute of Education Sciences, National Center for Education Evaluation and Regional Assistance. (Original work published 2012). Accessed at https://ies.ed.gov/ncee/WWC/Docs/PracticeGuide/MPS_PG_043012.pdf on September 20, 2025.

Xu, D., Fink, J., & Solanki, S. (2019, October). *College acceleration for all? Mapping racial/ethnic gaps in Advanced Placement and dual enrollment participation* (Working Paper No. 113). Columbia University, Teachers College, Community College Research Center.

Yeager, D. S. (2017). Social and emotional learning programs for adolescents. *The Future of Children, 27*(1), 73–94. https://doi.org/10.1353/foc.2017.0004

York, B. N., & Loeb, S. (2018, March). *One step at a time: The effects of an early literacy text messaging program for parents of preschoolers* (Working Paper No. 20659). National Bureau of Economic Research.

Young, E. L., Caldarella, P., Richardson, M. J., & Young, K. R. (2012). *Positive behavior support in secondary schools: A practical guide.* Guilford Press.

Zagata, E., Payne, B., & Arsenault, T. (2021). *Intensive intervention practice guide: Literacy supports for math content instruction for students with reading and language difficulty.* U.S. Department of Education, Office of Special Education Programs, National Center for Leadership in Intensive Intervention. Accessed at https://files.eric.ed.gov/fulltext/ED619745.pdf on September 20, 2025.

Zeng, S., Corr, C. P., O'Grady, C., & Guan, Y. (2019). Adverse childhood experiences and preschool suspension expulsion: A population study. *Child Abuse and Neglect, 97,* Article 104149. https://doi.org/10.1016/j.chiabu.2019.104149

Zimmerman, B. J. (2002). Becoming a self-regulated learner: An overview. *Theory Into Practice, 41*(2), 64–70.

Zinth, J., & Barnett, E. (2018, May). *Promising practices: Rethinking dual enrollment to reach more students.* Education Commission of the States. Accessed at https://files.eric.ed.gov/fulltext/ED582909.pdf on September 20, 2025.

Index

C

D

E

F

G

H

I

L

M

T

U

V

W

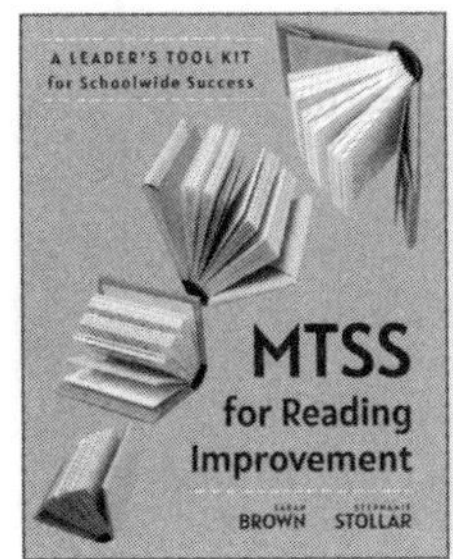

MTSS for Reading Improvement
Sarah Brown and Stephanie Stollar
Transform schoolwide reading achievement through systematic implementation of the science of reading within an MTSS framework. Brown and Stollar provide over fifty practical tools that help leaders engineer robust support systems and create lasting, system-level improvements for all students.
BKG251

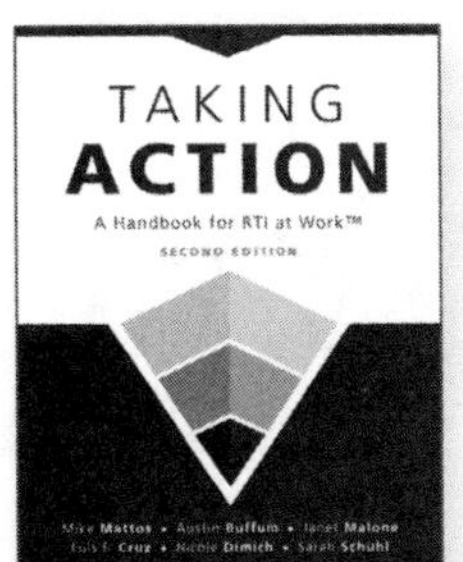

Taking Action (Second Edition)
Mike Mattos, Austin Buffum, Janet Malone, Luis F. Cruz, Nicole Dimich, and Sarah Schuhl
The second edition of the bestseller *Taking Action* delves deeper into the essential actions needed to create a highly effective multitiered system of supports. New recommendations and tools are included to better target assessments, engage students, and proactively address resistance.
BKG136

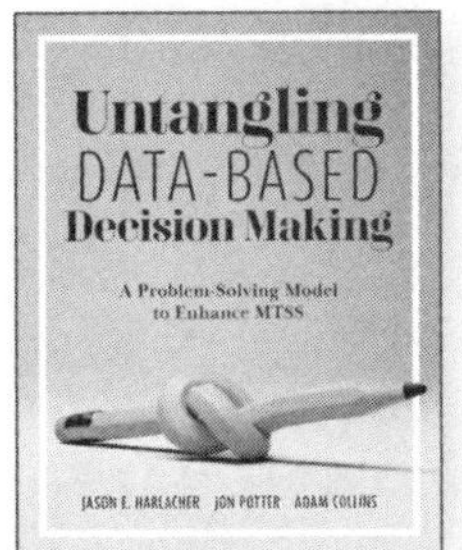

Untangling Data-Based Decision Making
Jason E. Harlacher, Jon Potter, and Adam Collins
Applicable to any content area, the four steps in this book's problem-solving model include specific questions that will guide your use of data to identify and solve problems by making changes to instruction, curriculum, and environment.
BKL072

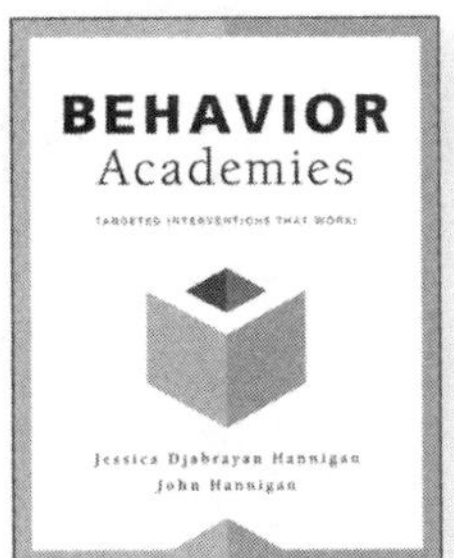

Behavior Academies
Jessica Djabrayan Hannigan and John Hannigan
With its practical behavior intervention method, this book replaces problematic behaviors with essential life skills for school and beyond. Educators can implement effective targeted interventions in twenty-five minutes or less using eight predefined behavior academies and a process to create their own.
BKG114

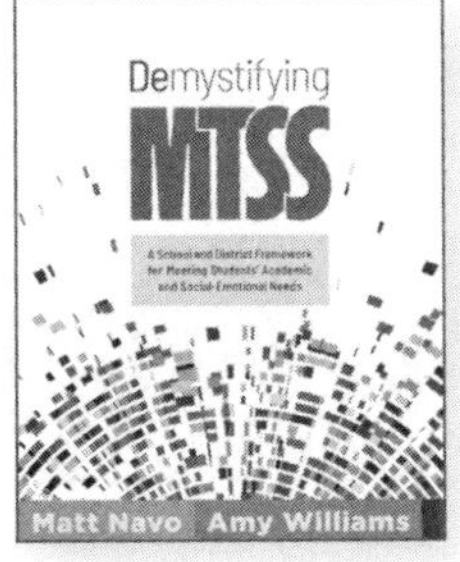

Demystifying MTSS
Matt Navo and Amy Williams
Demystifying MTSS distills a complex system into a customizable framework built around four fundamental components. Drawing from research and their experience in building and sustaining effective MTSS, the authors share high-leverage, practical actions school improvement teams can take to ensure all students' diverse needs are met.
BKF984

Solution Tree | Press 

Visit SolutionTree.com or call 800.733.6786 to order.